FREE Test Taking Tips Video/DVD Offer

To better serve you, we created videos covering test taking tips that we want to give you for FREE. **These videos cover world-class tips that will help you succeed on your test.**

We just ask that you send us feedback about this product. Please let us know what you thought about it—whether good, bad, or indifferent.

To get your **FREE videos**, you can use the QR code below or email freevideos@studyguideteam.com with "Free Videos" in the subject line and the following information in the body of the email:

   a. The title of your product

   b. Your product rating on a scale of 1-5, with 5 being the highest

   c. Your feedback about the product

If you have any questions or concerns, please don't hesitate to contact us at info@studyguideteam.com.

Thank you!

ASTB Test Prep
3 Practice Exams and ASTB-E Study Guide
[7th Edition]

Joshua Rueda

Interested in buying more than 10 copies of our product? Contact us about bulk discounts: bulkorders@studyguideteam.com

ISBN 13: 9781637756089
ISBN 10: 1637756089

Table of Contents

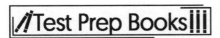

Welcome

Dear Reader,

Welcome to your new Test Prep Books study guide! We are pleased that you chose us to help you prepare for your exam. There are many study options to choose from, and we appreciate you choosing us. Studying can be a daunting task, but we have designed a smart, effective study guide to help prepare you for what lies ahead.

Whether you're a parent helping your child learn and grow, a high school student working hard to get into your dream college, or a nursing student studying for a complex exam, we want to help give you the tools you need to succeed. We hope this study guide gives you the skills and the confidence to thrive, and we can't thank you enough for allowing us to be part of your journey.

In an effort to continue to improve our products, we welcome feedback from our customers. We look forward to hearing from you. Suggestions, success stories, and criticisms can all be communicated by emailing us at info@studyguideteam.com.

Sincerely,
Test Prep Books Team

FREE Videos/DVD OFFER

Doing well on your exam requires both knowing the test content and understanding how to use that knowledge to do well on the test. We offer completely FREE test taking tip videos. **These videos cover world-class tips that you can use to succeed on your test.**

To get your **FREE videos**, you can use the QR code below or email freevideos@studyguideteam.com with "Free Videos" in the subject line and the following information in the body of the email:

    a. The title of your product
    b. Your product rating on a scale of 1-5, with 5 being the highest
    c. Your feedback about the product

If you have any questions or concerns, please don't hesitate to contact us at info@studyguideteam.com.

SCAN HERE

Quick Overview

As you draw closer to taking your exam, effective preparation becomes more and more important. Thankfully, you have this study guide to help you get ready. Use this guide to help keep your studying on track and refer to it often.

This study guide contains several key sections that will help you be successful on your exam. The guide contains tips for what you should do the night before and the day of the test. Also included are test-taking tips. Knowing the right information is not always enough. Many well-prepared test takers struggle with exams. These tips will help equip you to accurately read, assess, and answer test questions.

A large part of the guide is devoted to showing you what content to expect on the exam and to helping you better understand that content. In this guide are practice test questions so that you can see how well you have grasped the content. Then, answer explanations are provided so that you can understand why you missed certain questions.

Don't try to cram the night before you take your exam. This is not a wise strategy for a few reasons. First, your retention of the information will be low. Your time would be better used by reviewing information you already know rather than trying to learn a lot of new information. Second, you will likely become stressed as you try to gain a large amount of knowledge in a short amount of time. Third, you will be depriving yourself of sleep. So be sure to go to bed at a reasonable time the night before. Being well-rested helps you focus and remain calm.

Be sure to eat a substantial breakfast the morning of the exam. If you are taking the exam in the afternoon, be sure to have a good lunch as well. Being hungry is distracting and can make it difficult to focus. You have hopefully spent lots of time preparing for the exam. Don't let an empty stomach get in the way of success!

When travelling to the testing center, leave earlier than needed. That way, you have a buffer in case you experience any delays. This will help you remain calm and will keep you from missing your appointment time at the testing center.

Be sure to pace yourself during the exam. Don't try to rush through the exam. There is no need to risk performing poorly on the exam just so you can leave the testing center early. Allow yourself to use all of the allotted time if needed.

Remain positive while taking the exam even if you feel like you are performing poorly. Thinking about the content you should have mastered will not help you perform better on the exam.

Once the exam is complete, take some time to relax. Even if you feel that you need to take the exam again, you will be well served by some down time before you begin studying again. It's often easier to convince yourself to study if you know that it will come with a reward!

Test-Taking Strategies

1. Predicting the Answer

When you feel confident in your preparation for a multiple-choice test, try predicting the answer before reading the answer choices. This is especially useful on questions that test objective factual knowledge. By predicting the answer before reading the available choices, you eliminate the possibility that you will be distracted or led astray by an incorrect answer choice. You will feel more confident in your selection if you read the question, predict the answer, and then find your prediction among the answer choices. After using this strategy, be sure to still read all of the answer choices carefully and completely. If you feel unprepared, you should not attempt to predict the answers. This would be a waste of time and an opportunity for your mind to wander in the wrong direction.

2. Reading the Whole Question

Too often, test takers scan a multiple-choice question, recognize a few familiar words, and immediately jump to the answer choices. Test authors are aware of this common impatience, and they will sometimes prey upon it. For instance, a test author might subtly turn the question into a negative, or he or she might redirect the focus of the question right at the end. The only way to avoid falling into these traps is to read the entirety of the question carefully before reading the answer choices.

3. Looking for Wrong Answers

Long and complicated multiple-choice questions can be intimidating. One way to simplify a difficult multiple-choice question is to eliminate all of the answer choices that are clearly wrong. In most sets of answers, there will be at least one selection that can be dismissed right away. If the test is administered on paper, the test taker could draw a line through it to indicate that it may be ignored; otherwise, the test taker will have to perform this operation mentally or on scratch paper. In either case, once the obviously incorrect answers have been eliminated, the remaining choices may be considered. Sometimes identifying the clearly wrong answers will give the test taker some information about the correct answer. For instance, if one of the remaining answer choices is a direct opposite of one of the eliminated answer choices, it may well be the correct answer. The opposite of obviously wrong is obviously right! Of course, this is not always the case. Some answers are obviously incorrect simply because they are irrelevant to the question being asked. Still, identifying and eliminating some incorrect answer choices is a good way to simplify a multiple-choice question.

4. Don't Overanalyze

Anxious test takers often overanalyze questions. When you are nervous, your brain will often run wild, causing you to make associations and discover clues that don't actually exist. If you feel that this may be a problem for you, do whatever you can to slow down during the test. Try taking a deep breath or counting to ten. As you read and consider the question, restrict yourself to the particular words used by the author. Avoid thought tangents about what the author *really* meant, or what he or she was *trying* to say. The only things that matter on a multiple-choice test are the words that are actually in the question. You must avoid reading too much into a multiple-choice question, or supposing that the writer meant something other than what he or she wrote.

5. No Need for Panic

It is wise to learn as many strategies as possible before taking a multiple-choice test, but it is likely that you will come across a few questions for which you simply don't know the answer. In this situation, avoid panicking. Because most multiple-choice tests include dozens of questions, the relative value of a single wrong answer is small. As much as possible, you should compartmentalize each question on a multiple-choice test. In other words, you should not allow your feelings about one question to affect your success on the others. When you find a question that you either don't understand or don't know how to answer, just take a deep breath and do your best. Read the entire question slowly and carefully. Try rephrasing the question a couple of different ways. Then, read all of the answer choices carefully. After eliminating obviously wrong answers, make a selection and move on to the next question.

6. Confusing Answer Choices

When working on a difficult multiple-choice question, there may be a tendency to focus on the answer choices that are the easiest to understand. Many people, whether consciously or not, gravitate to the answer choices that require the least concentration, knowledge, and memory. This is a mistake. When you come across an answer choice that is confusing, you should give it extra attention. A question might be confusing because you do not know the subject matter to which it refers. If this is the case, don't eliminate the answer before you have affirmatively settled on another. When you come across an answer choice of this type, set it aside as you look at the remaining choices. If you can confidently assert that one of the other choices is correct, you can leave the confusing answer aside. Otherwise, you will need to take a moment to try to better understand the confusing answer choice. Rephrasing is one way to tease out the sense of a confusing answer choice.

7. Your First Instinct

Many people struggle with multiple-choice tests because they overthink the questions. If you have studied sufficiently for the test, you should be prepared to trust your first instinct once you have carefully and completely read the question and all of the answer choices. There is a great deal of research suggesting that the mind can come to the correct conclusion very quickly once it has obtained all of the relevant information. At times, it may seem to you as if your intuition is working faster even than your reasoning mind. This may in fact be true. The knowledge you obtain while studying may be retrieved from your subconscious before you have a chance to work out the associations that support it. Verify your instinct by working out the reasons that it should be trusted.

8. Key Words

Many test takers struggle with multiple-choice questions because they have poor reading comprehension skills. Quickly reading and understanding a multiple-choice question requires a mixture of skill and experience. To help with this, try jotting down a few key words and phrases on a piece of scrap paper. Doing this concentrates the process of reading and forces the mind to weigh the relative importance of the question's parts. In selecting words and phrases to write down, the test taker thinks about the question more deeply and carefully. This is especially true for multiple-choice questions that are preceded by a long prompt.

9. Subtle Negatives

One of the oldest tricks in the multiple-choice test writer's book is to subtly reverse the meaning of a question with a word like *not* or *except*. If you are not paying attention to each word in the question, you can easily be led astray by this trick. For instance, a common question format is, "Which of the following is...?" Obviously, if the question instead is, "Which of the following is not...?," then the answer will be quite different. Even worse, the test makers are aware of the potential for this mistake and will include one answer choice that would be correct if the question were not negated or reversed. A test taker who misses the reversal will find what he or she believes to be a correct answer and will be so confident that he or she will fail to reread the question and discover the original error. The only way to avoid this is to practice a wide variety of multiple-choice questions and to pay close attention to each and every word.

10. Reading Every Answer Choice

It may seem obvious, but you should always read every one of the answer choices! Too many test takers fall into the habit of scanning the question and assuming that they understand the question because they recognize a few key words. From there, they pick the first answer choice that answers the question they believe they have read. Test takers who read all of the answer choices might discover that one of the latter answer choices is actually *more* correct. Moreover, reading all of the answer choices can remind you of facts related to the question that can help you arrive at the correct answer. Sometimes, a misstatement or incorrect detail in one of the latter answer choices will trigger your memory of the subject and will enable you to find the right answer. Failing to read all of the answer choices is like not reading all of the items on a restaurant menu: you might miss out on the perfect choice.

11. Spot the Hedges

One of the keys to success on multiple-choice tests is paying close attention to every word. This is never truer than with words like almost, most, some, and sometimes. These words are called "hedges" because they indicate that a statement is not totally true or not true in every place and time. An absolute statement will contain no hedges, but in many subjects, the answers are not always straightforward or absolute. There are always exceptions to the rules in these subjects. For this reason, you should favor those multiple-choice questions that contain hedging language. The presence of qualifying words indicates that the author is taking special care with their words, which is certainly important when composing the right answer. After all, there are many ways to be wrong, but there is only one way to be right! For this reason, it is wise to avoid answers that are absolute when taking a multiple-choice test. An absolute answer is one that says things are either all one way or all another. They often include words like *every, always, best,* and *never.* If you are taking a multiple-choice test in a subject that doesn't lend itself to absolute answers, be on your guard if you see any of these words.

12. Long Answers

In many subject areas, the answers are not simple. As already mentioned, the right answer often requires hedges. Another common feature of the answers to a complex or subjective question are qualifying clauses, which are groups of words that subtly modify the meaning of the sentence. If the question or answer choice describes a rule to which there are exceptions or the subject matter is complicated, ambiguous, or confusing, the correct answer will require many words in order to be expressed clearly and accurately. In essence, you should not be deterred by answer choices that seem

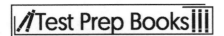

excessively long. Oftentimes, the author of the text will not be able to write the correct answer without offering some qualifications and modifications. Your job is to read the answer choices thoroughly and completely and to select the one that most accurately and precisely answers the question.

13. Restating to Understand

Sometimes, a question on a multiple-choice test is difficult not because of what it asks but because of how it is written. If this is the case, restate the question or answer choice in different words. This process serves a couple of important purposes. First, it forces you to concentrate on the core of the question. In order to rephrase the question accurately, you have to understand it well. Rephrasing the question will concentrate your mind on the key words and ideas. Second, it will present the information to your mind in a fresh way. This process may trigger your memory and render some useful scrap of information picked up while studying.

14. True Statements

Sometimes an answer choice will be true in itself, but it does not answer the question. This is one of the main reasons why it is essential to read the question carefully and completely before proceeding to the answer choices. Too often, test takers skip ahead to the answer choices and look for true statements. Having found one of these, they are content to select it without reference to the question above. Obviously, this provides an easy way for test makers to play tricks. The savvy test taker will always read the entire question before turning to the answer choices. Then, having settled on a correct answer choice, he or she will refer to the original question and ensure that the selected answer is relevant. The mistake of choosing a correct-but-irrelevant answer choice is especially common on questions related to specific pieces of objective knowledge. A prepared test taker will have a wealth of factual knowledge at their disposal, and should not be careless in its application.

15. No Patterns

One of the more dangerous ideas that circulates about multiple-choice tests is that the correct answers tend to fall into patterns. These erroneous ideas range from a belief that B and C are the most common right answers, to the idea that an unprepared test-taker should answer "A-B-A-C-A-D-A-B-A." It cannot be emphasized enough that pattern-seeking of this type is exactly the WRONG way to approach a multiple-choice test. To begin with, it is highly unlikely that the test maker will plot the correct answers according to some predetermined pattern. The questions are scrambled and delivered in a random order. Furthermore, even if the test maker was following a pattern in the assignation of correct answers, there is no reason why the test taker would know which pattern he or she was using. Any attempt to discern a pattern in the answer choices is a waste of time and a distraction from the real work of taking the test. A test taker would be much better served by extra preparation before the test than by reliance on a pattern in the answers.

Bonus Content

We host multiple bonus items online, including all three practice tests in digital format. Scan the QR code or go to this link to access this content:

testprepbooks.com/bonus/astb

The first time you access the page, you will need to register as a "new user" and verify your email address.

If you have any issues, please email support@testprepbooks.com.

Introduction to the ASTB-E

Function of the Test

The Aviation Standard Test Battery is used by the United States Navy to select individuals for flight and pilot officer training programs offered by the U.S. Coast Guard, the U.S. Marine Corps, and the U.S. Navy. Any persons interested in becoming an officer are required to take the ASTB-E so that it can be determined whether or not they meet the standards for officer training or other military occupations.

Test Administration

Candidates can take the ASTB-E test at over 250 registered locations all over the world. These locations include naval officer recruiting stations, military institutes, and NROTC units at major universities. Officer recruiters schedule test dates for exam candidates once examinees prove that they meet the qualifications. The exam is offered as a computer adaptive (online) exam.

Test takers who wish to retake the ASTB-E test must wait thirty days after the first test in order to do so, and ninety days before their third retake. They can only take the ASTB-E test a total of three times over the course of their lifetime. It is important to note that a test taker's most recent test score replaces any score on record, even if he or she received a higher score on a previous test. Test scores are valid for life.

Test Format

The Math Skills Test (MST) utilizes both word problems and equations to test examinees on high school math concepts dealing with algebra and geometry. The Reading Comprehension Test (RCT) incorporates text passages to test examinees on their ability to extract information and make conclusions from what they have read. Finally, the Mechanical Comprehension Test (MCT) is comprised of questions involving high school physics concepts, as well as simple machine mechanics.

The Aviation and Nautical Information Test (ANIT) tests one's knowledge over aviation history, aviation-related concepts, and nautical terminology and procedures. The Naval Aviation Trait Facet Inventory (NATFI) consists of 44 statement pairs that ask how you think, feel, and act regarding different situations. This subsection measures personality traits. The Performance Based Measures Battery (PBM) is a subtest that measures manual dexterity, processing speed, spatial orientation, and divided-attention-driven assessments. Finally, the Biographical Inventory with Response Verification (BI-RV) asks you to identify your experience and background related to aviation.

The following table contains a breakdown of the number of questions and the corresponding time limits for the sections on the ASTB-E.

Sections of the ASTB-E Test – CAT version		
Subject Areas	Number of Questions (Multiple-Choice)	Time Limit
Math Skills Test	30	40 minutes
Reading Comprehension Test	20	30 minutes
Mechanical Comprehension Test	30	15 minutes
Aviation and Nautical Information Test	20 to 30	Unspecified
Naval Aviation Trait Facet Inventory	88	Unspecified
Performance Based Measures Battery	20 to 30	Unspecified
Biographical Inventory with Response Validation	20 to 30	Unspecified
Total	228 to 258	2 to 3 ¼ hours

Note that individuals can take the Biographical Inventory with Response Validation (BI-RV) portion of the exam on any web-based computer outside of the testing area.

Scoring

The first three sections of the exam use a 1-point increment rating scored between a 20 and 80. For the rest of the categories (besides the BI-RV), the Standard Nine (or stanine) system is used. The Academic Qualifications Rating (AQR), the Pilot Flight Aptitude Rating (PFAR), and the Flight Officer Aptitude Rating (FOFAR) are all scores based on the ASTB subtests using the stanine system. Scores will be shown immediately once all 7 subtests are finished. Blind guessing on the ASTB-E is discouraged, as these points will count against you.

Recent/Future Developments

At the end of 2013, a new version of the larger Aviation Selection Test Battery (ASTB) was released, which is known as the ASTB-E. Three of the seven subtests still make up the OAR test. The overall exam is now better able to gauge how test takers think in different dimensions (hand-eye coordination, physical dexterity, and dividing attention between tasks) through what is known as the Performance Based Measures Battery.

Study Prep Plan for the ASTB-E

1 **Schedule** - Use one of our study schedules below or come up with one of your own.

2 **Relax** - Test anxiety can hurt even the best students. There are many ways to reduce stress. Find the one that works best for you.

3 **Execute** - Once you have a good plan in place, be sure to stick to it.

One Week Study Schedule		
Day 1	Math Skills
Day 2	Reading Comprehension
Day 3	Mechanical Comprehension
Day 4	Aviation and Nautical Information Test (ANIT)
Day 5	Practice Tests #1 & #2
Day 6	Practice Test #3
Day 7	Take Your Exam!

Two Week Study Schedule			
Day 1	Math Skills	Day 8	Helicopters
Day 2	Algebra	Day 9	Practice Test #1
Day 3	Geometry	Day 10	Answer Explanations
Day 4	Reading Comprehension	Day 11	Practice Test #2
Day 5	Mechanical Comprehension	Day 12	Answer Explanations
Day 6	Aviation and Nautical Information Test (ANIT)	Day 13	Practice Test #3
Day 7	Aviation Concepts	Day 14	Take Your Exam!

One Month Study Schedule								
Day 1	Math Skills		Day 11	Practice Quiz		Day 21	Helicopters
Day 2	Classification of Angles		Day 12	Mechanical Comprehension		Day 22	Airport Information
Day 3	Algebra		Day 13	Potential and Kinetic Energy		Day 23	Practice Quiz
Day 4	Factoring		Day 14	Machines		Day 24	Practice Test #1
Day 5	Geometry		Day 15	Practice Quiz		Day 25	Answer Explanations
Day 6	Symmetry		Day 16	Aviation and Nautical Information Test (ANIT)		Day 26	Practice Test #2
Day 7	Practice Quiz		Day 17	Types of Vessels		Day 27	Answer Explanations
Day 8	Reading Comprehension		Day 18	Aviation Concepts		Day 28	Practice Test #3
Day 9	Paragraph Comprehension		Day 19	Helicopter Maneuvers		Day 29	Answer Explanations
Day 10	Author's Use of Language		Day 20	Fixed-Wing Maneuvers		Day 30	Take Your Exam!

Build your prep plan online by visiting:

testprepbooks.com/prep

Math Skills

Arithmetic

How to Prepare

These problems involve basic arithmetic skills as well as the ability to break down a word problem to see where to apply these skills in order to get the correct answer. The basics of arithmetic and the approach to solving word problems are discussed here.

Note that math requires practice in order to become proficient. In this guide, make sure to read through the material, try out the practice questions, and check the answers provided. Just reading through examples does not necessarily mean that a student can do the problems themselves. Note that sometimes there can be multiple approaches to getting a solution when doing the problems. What matters is getting the correct answer, so it is okay if the approach to a problem is different than the solution method provided.

Basic Operations of Arithmetic

There are four basic operations used with numbers: addition, subtraction, multiplication, and division.

- Addition takes two numbers and combines them into a total called the sum. The sum is the total when combining two collections into one. If there are 5 things in one collection and 3 in another, then after combining them, there is a total of $5 + 3 = 8$. Note the order does not matter when adding numbers. For example,

$$3 + 5 = 8$$

- Subtraction is the opposite (or "inverse") operation to addition. Whereas addition combines two quantities together, subtraction takes one quantity away from another. For example, if there are 20 gallons of fuel and 5 are removed, that gives $20 - 5 = 15$ gallons remaining. Note that for subtraction, the order does matter because it makes a difference which quantity is being removed from which.

- Multiplication is repeated addition. 3×4 can be thought of as putting together 3 sets of items, each set containing 4 items. The total is 12 items. An example would be to think of each number as the length of one side of a rectangle. If a rectangle is covered in tiles with 3 columns of 4 tiles each, then there are 12 tiles in total. From this, one can see that the answer is the same if the rectangle has 4 rows of 3 tiles each: $4 \times 3 = 12$. By expanding this reasoning, the order of the numbers multiplied does not matter.

- Division is the opposite of multiplication. It means taking one quantity and dividing it into sets the size of the second quantity. If there are 16 sandwiches to be distributed to 4 people, then each person gets $16 \div 4 = 4$ sandwiches. As with subtraction, the order in which the numbers appear does matter for division.

Addition

Addition is the combination of two numbers so their quantities are added together cumulatively. The sign for an addition operation is the + symbol. For example, 9 + 6 = 15. The 9 and 6 combine to achieve a cumulative value, called a sum.

Addition holds the commutative property, which means that the order of the numbers in an addition equation can be switched without altering the result. The formula for the commutative property is $a + b = b + a$. Let's look at a few examples to see how the commutative property works:

$$7 = 3 + 4 = 4 + 3 = 7$$

$$20 = 12 + 8 = 8 + 12 = 20$$

Addition also holds the associative property, which means that the grouping of numbers doesn't matter in an addition problem. In other words, the presence or absence of parentheses is irrelevant. The formula for the associative property is $(a + b) + c = a + (b + c)$. Here are some examples of the associative property at work:

$$30 = (6 + 14) + 10 = 6 + (14 + 10) = 30$$

$$35 = 8 + (2 + 25) = (8 + 2) + 25 = 35$$

Subtraction

Subtraction is taking away one number from another, so their quantities are reduced. The sign designating a subtraction operation is the − symbol, and the result is called the difference. For example,

$$9 - 6 = 3$$

The number *6* detracts from the number *9* to reach the difference *3*.

Unlike addition, subtraction follows neither the commutative nor associative properties. The order and grouping in subtraction impact the result.

$$15 = 22 - 7 \neq 7 - 22 = -15$$

$$3 = (10 - 5) - 2 \neq 10 - (5 - 2) = 7$$

When working through subtraction problems involving larger numbers, it's necessary to regroup the numbers. Let's work through a practice problem using regrouping:

$$\begin{array}{r} 3\ 2\ 5 \\ -\ 7\ 7 \\ \hline \end{array}$$

Here, it is clear that the ones and tens columns for 77 are greater than the ones and tens columns for 325. To subtract this number, borrow from the tens and hundreds columns. When borrowing from a column, subtracting 1 from the lender column will add 10 to the borrower column:

$$\begin{array}{ccc} 3\text{-}1 & 10\text{+}2\text{-}1 & 10\text{+}5 \\ - & 7 & 7 \end{array} = \begin{array}{ccc} 2 & 11 & 15 \\ - & 7 & 7 \\ \hline 2 & 4 & 8 \end{array}$$

After ensuring that each digit in the top row is greater than the digit in the corresponding bottom row, subtraction can proceed as normal, and the answer is found to be 248.

Multiplication

Multiplication involves adding together multiple copies of a number. It is indicated by an $\times$ symbol or a number immediately outside of a parenthesis. For example:

$$5(8 - 2)$$

The two numbers being multiplied together are called factors, and their result is called a product. For example,

$$9 \times 6 = 54$$

This can be shown alternatively by expansion of either the 9 or the 6:

$$9 \times 6 = 9 + 9 + 9 + 9 + 9 + 9 = 54$$

$$9 \times 6 = 6 + 6 + 6 + 6 + 6 + 6 + 6 + 6 + 6 = 54$$

Like addition, multiplication holds the commutative and associative properties:

$$115 = 23 \times 5 = 5 \times 23 = 115$$

$$84 = 3 \times (7 \times 4) = (3 \times 7) \times 4 = 84$$

Multiplication also follows the distributive property, which allows the multiplication to be distributed through parentheses. The formula for distribution is $a \times (b + c) = ab + ac$. This is clear after the examples:

$$45 = 5 \times 9 = 5(3 + 6) = (5 \times 3) + (5 \times 6) = 15 + 30 = 45$$

$$20 = 4 \times 5 = 4(10 - 5) = (4 \times 10) - (4 \times 5) = 40 - 20 = 20$$

Multiplication becomes slightly more complicated when multiplying numbers with decimals. The easiest way to answer these problems is to ignore the decimals and multiply as if they were whole numbers. After multiplying the factors, place a decimal in the product. The placement of the decimal is determined by taking the cumulative number of decimal places in the factors.

For example:

$$
\begin{array}{ccc}
0.7 & 2.6 & 1.5 \\
\underline{\times 3} & \underline{\times\ 4.2} & \underline{\times 6.4} \\
2.1 & 10.92 & 9.60
\end{array}
$$

Let's tackle the first example. First, ignore the decimal and multiply the numbers as though they were whole numbers to arrive at a product: 21. Second, count the number of digits that follow a decimal (one). Finally, move the decimal place that many positions to the left, as the factors have only one decimal place. The second example works the same way, except that there are two total decimal places in the factors, so the product's decimal is moved two places over. In the third example, the decimal should be moved over two digits, but the digit zero is no longer needed, so it is erased, and the final answer is 9.6.

Division

Division and multiplication are inverses of each other in the same way that addition and subtraction are opposites. The signs designating a division operation are the ÷ and / symbols. In division, the second number divides into the first.

The number before the division sign is called the dividend or, if expressed as a fraction, the numerator. For example, in $a \div b$, a is the dividend, while in $\frac{a}{b}$, a is the numerator.

The number after the division sign is called the divisor or, if expressed as a fraction, the denominator. For example, in $a \div b$, b is the divisor, while in $\frac{a}{b}$, b is the denominator.

Like subtraction, division doesn't follow the commutative property, as it matters which number comes before the division sign, and division doesn't follow the associative or distributive properties for the same reason. For example:

$$\frac{3}{2} = 9 \div 6 \neq 6 \div 9 = \frac{2}{3}$$

$$2 = 10 \div 5 = (30 \div 3) \div 5 \neq 30 \div (3 \div 5) = 30 \div \frac{3}{5} = 50$$

$$25 = 20 + 5 = (40 \div 2) + (40 \div 8) \neq 40 \div (2 + 8) = 40 \div 10 = 4$$

If a divisor doesn't divide into a dividend evenly, whatever is left over is termed the remainder. The remainder can be further divided out into decimal form by using long division; however, this doesn't always give a quotient with a finite number of decimal places, so the remainder can also be expressed as a fraction over the original divisor.

Division with decimals is similar to multiplication with decimals in that when dividing a decimal by a whole number, ignore the decimal and divide as if it were a whole number.

Upon finding the answer, or quotient, place the decimal at the decimal place equal to that in the dividend.

$$15.75 \div 3 = 5.25$$

When the divisor is a decimal number, multiply both the divisor and dividend by 10. Repeat this until the divisor is a whole number, then complete the division operation as described above.

$$17.5 \div 2.5 = 175 \div 25 = 7$$

Fractions

A **fraction** is a number used to express a ratio. It is written as a number x over a line with another number y underneath: $\frac{x}{y}$, and can be thought of as x out of y equal parts. The number on top (x) is called the **numerator**, and the number on the bottom is called the **denominator** (y). It is important to remember the only restriction is that the denominator is not allowed to be 0.

Imagine that an apple pie has been baked for a holiday party, and the full pie has eight slices. After the party, there are five slices left. How could the amount of the pie that remains be expressed as a fraction? The numerator is 5 since there are 5 pieces left, and the denominator is 8 since there were eight total slices in the whole pie. Thus, expressed as a fraction, the leftover pie totals $\frac{5}{8}$ of the original amount.

Another way of thinking about fractions is like this:

$$\frac{x}{y} = x \div y$$

Two fractions can sometimes equal the same number even when they look different. The value of a fraction will remain equal when multiplying both the numerator and the denominator by the same number. The value of the fraction does not change when dividing both the numerator and the denominator by the same number. For example,

$$\frac{4}{8} = \frac{2}{4} = \frac{1}{2}$$

If two fractions look different, but are actually the same number, these are **equivalent fractions**.

A number that can divide evenly into a second number is called a **divisor** or **factor** of that second number; 3 is a divisor of 6, for example. If the numerator and denominator in a fraction have no common factors other than 1, the fraction is said to be **simplified**. $\frac{2}{4}$ is not simplified (since the numerator and denominator have a factor of 2 in common), but $\frac{1}{2}$ is simplified. Often, when solving a problem, the final answer generally requires us to simplify the fraction.

It is often useful when working with fractions to rewrite them so they have the same denominator. This process is called finding a **common denominator**. The common denominator of two fractions needs to be a number that is a multiple of both denominators. For example, given $\frac{1}{6}$ and $\frac{5}{8}$, a common denominator is:

$$6 \times 8 = 48$$

However, there are often smaller choices for the common denominator. The smallest number that is a multiple of two numbers is called the **least common multiple** of those numbers. For this example, use the numbers 6 and 8. The multiples of 6 are 6, 12, 18, 24... and the multiples of 8 are 8, 16, 24..., so the least common multiple is 24. The two fractions are rewritten as $\frac{4}{24}, \frac{15}{24}$.

If two fractions have a common denominator, then the numerators can be added or subtracted. For example:

$$\frac{4}{5} - \frac{3}{5} = \frac{4-3}{5} = \frac{1}{5}$$

If the fractions are not given with the same denominator, a common denominator needs to be found before adding or subtracting them.

It is always possible to find a common denominator by multiplying the denominators by each other. However, when the denominators are large numbers, this method is unwieldy, especially if the answer must be provided in its simplest form. Thus, it's beneficial to find the least common denominator of the fractions—the least common denominator is incidentally also the least common multiple.

Once equivalent fractions have been found with common denominators, simply add or subtract the numerators to arrive at the answer:

1) $\frac{1}{2} + \frac{3}{4} = \frac{2}{4} + \frac{3}{4} = \frac{5}{4}$

2) $\frac{3}{12} + \frac{11}{20} = \frac{15}{60} + \frac{33}{60} = \frac{48}{60} = \frac{4}{5}$

3) $\frac{7}{9} - \frac{4}{15} = \frac{35}{45} - \frac{12}{45} = \frac{23}{45}$

4) $\frac{5}{6} - \frac{7}{18} = \frac{15}{18} - \frac{7}{18} = \frac{8}{18} = \frac{4}{9}$

One of the most fundamental concepts of fractions is their ability to be manipulated by multiplication or division. This is possible since $\frac{n}{n} = 1$ for any non-zero integer. As a result, multiplying or dividing by $\frac{n}{n}$ will not alter the original fraction since any number multiplied or divided by 1 doesn't change the value of that number. Fractions of the same value are known as equivalent fractions. For example, $\frac{2}{4}, \frac{4}{8}, \frac{50}{100}$, and $\frac{75}{150}$ are equivalent, as they all equal $\frac{1}{2}$.

To multiply two fractions, multiply the numerators to get the new numerator as well as multiply the denominators to get the new denominator. For example:

$$\frac{3}{5} \times \frac{2}{7} = \frac{3 \times 2}{5 \times 7} = \frac{6}{35}$$

Switching the numerator and denominator is called taking the **reciprocal** of a fraction. So the reciprocal of $\frac{4}{5}$ is $\frac{5}{4}$.

To divide one fraction by another, multiply the first fraction by the reciprocal of the second. So:

$$\frac{3}{4} \div \frac{2}{5} = \frac{3}{4} \times \frac{5}{2} = \frac{15}{8}$$

If the numerator is smaller than the denominator, the fraction is a **proper fraction**. Otherwise, the fraction is said to be **improper**.

A **mixed number** is a number that is an integer plus some proper fraction, and is written with the integer first and the proper fraction to the right of it. Any mixed number can be written as an improper fraction by multiplying the integer by the denominator, adding the product to the value of the numerator, and dividing the sum by the original denominator. For example:

$$3\frac{1}{2} = \frac{3 \times 2 + 1}{2} = \frac{7}{2}$$

Whole numbers can also be converted into fractions by placing the whole number as the numerator and making the denominator 1. For example, $3 = \frac{3}{1}$.

Percentages

Think of percentages as fractions with a denominator of 100. In fact, percentage means "per hundred." Problems often require converting numbers from percentages, fractions, and decimals. The following explains how to work through those conversions.

Converting Fractions to Percentages: Convert the fraction by using an equivalent fraction with a denominator of 100. For example:

$$\frac{3}{4} = \frac{3}{4} \times \frac{25}{25} = \frac{75}{100} = 75\%$$

Converting Percentages to Fractions: Percentages can be converted to fractions by turning the percentage into a fraction with a denominator of 100. Be wary of questions asking the converted fraction to be written in the simplest form. For example, $35\% = \frac{35}{100}$ which, although correctly written, has a numerator and denominator with a greatest common factor of 5 and can be simplified to $\frac{7}{20}$.

Converting Percentages to Decimals: As a percentage is based on "per hundred," decimals and percentages can be converted by multiplying or dividing by 100. Practically speaking, this always amounts to moving the decimal point two places to the right or left, depending on the conversion. To convert a percentage to a decimal, move the decimal point two places to the left and remove the % sign. To convert a decimal to a percentage, move the decimal point two places to the right and add a % sign. Here are some examples:

65% = 0.65
0.33 = 33%
0.215 = 21.5%
99.99% = 0.9999
500% = 5.00
7.55 = 755%

Questions dealing with percentages can be difficult when they are phrased as word problems. These word problems almost always come in three varieties. The first type will ask to find what percentage of some number will equal another number. The second asks to determine what number is some percentage of another given number. The third will ask what number another number is a given percentage of.

One of the most important parts of correctly answering percentage word problems is to identify the numerator and the denominator. This fraction can then be converted into a percentage, as described above.

The following word problem shows how to make this conversion:

A department store carries several different types of footwear. The store is currently selling 8 athletic shoes, 7 dress shoes, and 5 sandals. What percentage of the store's footwear are sandals?

First, calculate what serves as the "whole," as this will be the denominator. How many total pieces of footwear does the store sell? The store sells 20 different types (8 athletic + 7 dress + 5 sandals).

Second, what footwear type is the question specifically asking about? Sandals. Thus, 5 is the numerator.

Third, the resultant fraction must be expressed as a percentage. The first two steps indicate that $\frac{5}{20}$ of the footwear pieces are sandals. This fraction must now be converted into a percentage:

$$\frac{5}{20} \times \frac{5}{5} = \frac{25}{100} = 25\%$$

Ratios and Proportions

Ratios are used to show the relationship between two quantities. The ratio of oranges to apples in the grocery store may be 3 to 2. That means that for every 3 oranges, there are 2 apples. This comparison can be expanded to represent the actual number of oranges and apples. Another example may be the number of boys to girls in a math class. If the ratio of boys to girls is given as 2 to 5, that means there are 2 boys to every 5 girls in the class. Ratios can also be compared if the units in each ratio are the same. The ratio of boys to girls in the math class can be compared to the ratio of boys to girls in a science class by stating which ratio is higher and which is lower.

Rates are used to compare two quantities with different units. **Unit rates** are the simplest form of rate. With unit rates, the denominator in the comparison of two units is one. For example, if someone can type at a rate of 1000 words in 5 minutes, then their unit rate for typing is $\frac{1000}{5} = 200$ words in one minute or 200 words per minute. Any rate can be converted into a unit rate by dividing to make the denominator one. 1000 words in 5 minutes has been converted into the unit rate of 200 words per minute.

Ratios and rates can be used together to convert rates into different units. For example, if someone is driving 50 kilometers per hour, that rate can be converted into miles per hour by using a ratio known as the **conversion factor**. Since the given value contains kilometers and the final answer needs to be in miles, the ratio relating miles to kilometers needs to be used. There are 0.62 miles in 1 kilometer. This, written as a ratio and in fraction form, is:

$$\frac{0.62 \text{ miles}}{1 \text{ km}}$$

To convert 50km/hour into miles per hour, the following conversion needs to be set up:

$$\frac{50 \text{ km}}{\text{hour}} \times \frac{0.62 \text{ miles}}{1 \text{ km}} = 31 \text{ miles per hour}$$

The ratio between two similar geometric figures is called the *scale factor*. For example, a problem may depict two similar triangles, A and B. The scale factor from the smaller triangle A to the larger triangle B is given as 2 because the length of the corresponding side of the larger triangle, 16, is twice the corresponding side on the smaller triangle, 8. This scale factor can also be used to find the value of a missing side, x, in triangle A. Since the scale factor from the smaller triangle (A) to the larger one (B) is 2, the larger corresponding side in triangle B (given as 25) can be divided by 2 to find the missing side in A (x = 12.5). The scale factor can also be represented in the equation $2A = B$ because two times the lengths of A gives the corresponding lengths of B. This is the idea behind similar triangles.

Much like a scale factor can be written using an equation like $2A = B$, a **relationship** is represented by the equation $Y = kX$. X and Y are proportional because as values of X increase, the values of Y also increase. A relationship that is inversely proportional can be represented by the equation $Y = \frac{k}{x}$, where the value of Y decreases as the value of x increases and vice versa.

Proportional reasoning can be used to solve problems involving ratios, percentages, and averages. Ratios can be used in setting up proportions and solving them to find unknowns. For example, if a student completes an average of 10 pages of math homework in 3 nights, how long would it take the student to complete 22 pages? Both ratios can be written as fractions. The second ratio would contain the unknown.

The following proportion represents this problem, where x is the unknown number of nights:

$$\frac{10 \text{ pages}}{3 \text{ nights}} = \frac{22 \text{ pages}}{x \text{ nights}}$$

Solving this proportion entails cross-multiplying and results in the following equation:

$$10x = 22 \times 3$$

Simplifying and solving for x results in the exact solution: $x = 6.6 \; nights$. The result would be rounded up to 7 because the homework would actually be completed on the 7th night.

The following problem uses ratios involving percentages:

If 20% of the class is girls and 30 students are in the class, how many girls are in the class?

To set up this problem, it is helpful to use the common proportion:

$$\frac{\%}{100} = \frac{is}{of}$$

Within the proportion, % is the percentage of girls, 100 is the total percentage of the class, *is* is the number of girls, and *of* is the total number of students in the class. Most percentage problems can be written using this language. To solve this problem, the proportion should be set up as $\frac{20}{100} = \frac{x}{30}$, and then solved for x. Cross-multiplying results in the equation $20 \times 30 = 100x$, which results in the solution $x = 6$. There are 6 girls in the class.

Ratios can be used to solve problems that concern length, volume, and other units. A problem may ask for the volume of a cone that has a radius, $r = 7m$ and a height, $h = 16m$. Referring to the formulas provided on the test, the volume of a cone is given as:

$$V = \pi r^2 \frac{h}{3}$$

r is the radius, and h is the height. Plugging $r = 7$ and $h = 16$ into the formula, the following is obtained:

$$V = \pi(7^2)\frac{16}{3}$$

Therefore, the volume of the cone is found to be approximately 821m³. Sometimes, answers in different units are sought. If this problem wanted the answer in liters, 821m³ would need to be converted.

Using the equivalence statement 1m³ = 1000L, the following ratio would be used to solve for liters:

$$821\text{m}^3 \times \frac{1000L}{1m^3}$$

Cubic meters in the numerator and denominator cancel each other out, and the answer is converted to 821,000 liters, or 8.21×10^5 L.

Other conversions can also be made between different given and final units. If the temperature in a pool is 30°C, what is the temperature of the pool in degrees Fahrenheit? To convert these units, an equation is used relating Celsius to Fahrenheit. The following equation is used:

$$T_{°F} = 1.8T_{°C} + 32$$

Plugging in the given temperature and solving the equation for T yields the result:

$$T_{°F} = 1.8(30) + 32 = 86°F$$

Units in both the metric system and U.S. customary system are widely used.

Basic Geometry Relationships

The basic unit of geometry is a point. A point represents an exact location on a plane, or flat surface. The position of a point is indicated with a dot and usually named with a single uppercase letter, such as point *A* or point *T*. A point is a place, not a thing, and therefore has no dimensions or size. A set of points that lies on the same line is called collinear. A set of points that lies on the same plane is called coplanar.

The image above displays point *A*, point *B*, and point *C*.

A line is a series of points that extends in both directions without ending. It consists of an infinite number of points and is drawn with arrows on both ends to indicate it extends infinitely. Lines can be named by two points on the line or with a single, cursive, lower case letter. The two lines below could be named line *AB* or line *BA* or $\overleftrightarrow{AB}$ or $\overleftrightarrow{BA}$; and line *m*.

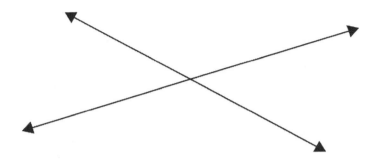

Two lines are considered parallel to each other if, while extending infinitely, they will never intersect (or meet). Parallel lines point in the same direction and are always the same distance apart. Two lines are considered perpendicular if they intersect to form right angles. Right angles are 90°. Typically, a small box is drawn at the intersection point to indicate the right angle.

Parallel Lines   Perpendicular Lines

Line 1 is parallel to line 2 in the left image and is written as line 1 || line 2. Line 1 is perpendicular to line 2 in the right image and is written as line 1 ⊥ line 2.

A ray has a specific starting point and extends in one direction without ending. The endpoint of a ray is its starting point. Rays are named using the endpoint first, and any other point on the ray. The following ray can be named ray *AB* and written $\overrightarrow{AB}$.

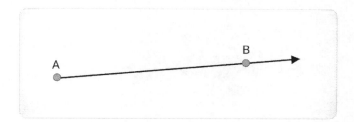

A line segment has specific starting and ending points. A line segment consists of two endpoints and all the points in between. Line segments are named by the two endpoints. The example below is named segment *KL* or segment *LK*, written $\overline{KL}$ or $\overline{LK}$.

Classification of Angles

An angle consists of two rays that have a common endpoint. This common endpoint is called the vertex of the angle. The two rays can be called sides of the angle. The angle below has a vertex at point *B* and the sides consist of ray *BA* and ray *BC*. An angle can be named in three ways:

- Using the vertex and a point from each side, with the vertex letter in the middle.
- Using only the vertex. This can only be used if it is the only angle with that vertex.
- Using a number that is written inside the angle.

The angle below can be written ∠*ABC* (read angle *ABC*), ∠*CBA*, ∠*B*, or ∠1.

An angle divides a plane, or flat surface, into three parts: the angle itself, the interior (inside) of the angle, and the exterior (outside) of the angle. The figure below shows point *M* on the interior of the angle and point *N* on the exterior of the angle.

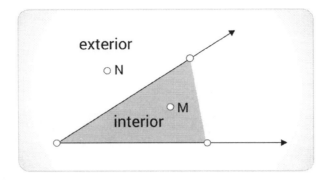

Angles can be measured in units called degrees, with the symbol °. The degree measure of an angle is between 0° and 180° and can be obtained by using a protractor.

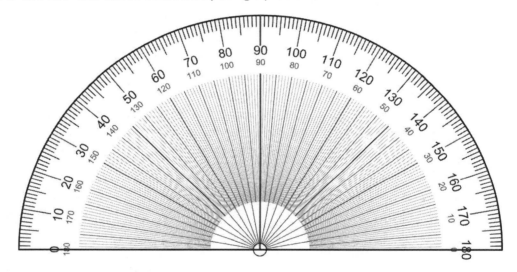

A straight angle (or simply a line) measures exactly 180°. A right angle's sides meet at the vertex to create a square corner. A right angle measures exactly 90° and is typically indicated by a box drawn in the interior of the angle. An acute angle has an interior that is narrower than a right angle. The measure of an acute angle is any value less than 90° and greater than 0°. For example, 89.9°, 47°, 12°, and 1°. An obtuse angle has an interior that is wider than a right angle. The measure of an obtuse angle is any value greater than 90° but less than 180°. For example, 90.1°, 110°, 150°, and 179.9°.

- Acute angles: Less than 90°
- Obtuse angles: Greater than 90°
- Right angles: 90°
- Straight angles: 180°

If two angles add together to give 90°, the angles are **complementary**.

If two angles add together to give 180°, the angles are **supplementary**.

24

When two lines intersect, the pairs of angles they form are always supplementary. The two angles marked here are supplementary:

When two supplementary angles are next to one another or "adjacent" in this way, they always give rise to a straight line.

A polygon is a closed geometric figure in a plane (flat surface) consisting of at least 3 sides formed by line segments. These are often defined as two-dimensional shapes. Common two-dimensional shapes include circles, triangles, squares, rectangles, pentagons, and hexagons. Note that a circle is a two-dimensional shape without sides.

Two dimensional shapes

Circle   Triangle   Square

Pentagon   Hexagon   Rectangle

Polygons can be classified by the number of sides (also equal to the number of angles) they have. The following are the names of polygons with a given number of sides or angles:

# of Sides	Name of Polygon
3	Triangle
4	Quadrilateral
5	Pentagon
6	Hexagon
7	Septagon (or heptagon)
8	Octagon
9	Nonagon
10	Decagon

Triangles can be further classified by their sides and angles. A triangle with its largest angle measuring 90° is a right triangle. A triangle with the largest angle less than 90° is an acute triangle. A triangle with the largest angle greater than 90° is an obtuse triangle. Below is an example of a right triangle.

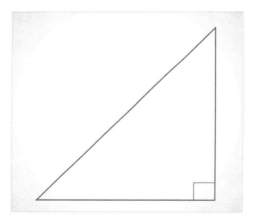

A triangle consisting of two equal sides and two equal angles is an isosceles triangle. A triangle with three equal sides and three equal angles is an equilateral triangle. A triangle with no equal sides or angles is a scalene triangle.

The three angles inside the triangle are called **interior angles** and add up to 180°.

For any triangle, the **Triangle Inequality Theorem** says that the following holds true:

$$A + B > C, A + C > B, B + C > A$$

In addition, the sum of two angles must be less than 180°.

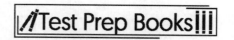

If two triangles have angles that agree with one another, that is, the angles of the first triangle are equal to the angles of the second triangle, then the triangles are called **similar**. Similar triangles look the same, but one can be a "magnification" of the other.

Two triangles with sides that are the same length must also be similar triangles. In this case, such triangles are called **congruent**. Congruent triangles have the same angles and lengths, even if they are rotated from one another.

Quadrilaterals can be further classified according to their sides and angles. A quadrilateral with exactly one pair of parallel sides is called a trapezoid. A quadrilateral that shows both pairs of opposite sides parallel is a parallelogram. Parallelograms include rhombuses, rectangles, and squares. A rhombus has four equal sides. A rectangle has four equal angles (90° each). A square has four 90° angles and four equal sides. Therefore, a square is both a rhombus and a rectangle.

A solid figure, or simple solid, is a figure that encloses a part of space. Some solids consist of flat surfaces only while others include curved surfaces. Solid figures are often defined as three-dimensional shapes. Common three-dimensional shapes include spheres, prisms, cubes, pyramids, cylinders, and cones.

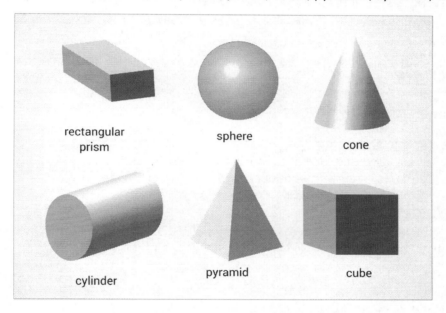

Perimeter is the measurement of a distance around something. It can be thought of as the length of the boundary, like a fence. It is found by adding together the lengths of all of the sides of a figure. Since a square has four equal sides, its perimeter can be calculated by multiplying the length of one side by 4. Thus, the formula is $P = 4 \times s$, where s equals one side. Like a square, a rectangle's perimeter is measured by adding together all of the sides. But as the sides are unequal, the formula is different. A rectangle has equal values for its lengths (long sides) and equal values for its widths (short sides), so the perimeter formula for a rectangle is $P = l + l + w + w = 2l + 2w$, where l is length and w is width. Perimeter is measured in simple units such as inches, feet, yards, centimeters, meters, miles, etc.

In contrast to perimeter, area is the space occupied by a defined enclosure, like a field enclosed by a fence. It is measured in square units such as square feet or square miles. Here are some formulas for the areas of basic planar shapes:

- The area of a rectangle is $l \times w$, where w is the width and l is the length
- The area of a square is s^2, where s is the length of one side (this follows from the formula for rectangles)
- The area of a triangle with base b and height h is $\frac{1}{2}bh$
- The area of a circle with radius r is πr^2

Volume is the measurement of how much space an object occupies, like how much space is in the cube. Volume questions will typically ask how much of something is needed to completely fill the object. It is measured in cubic units, such as cubic inches. Here are some formulas for the volumes of basic three-dimensional geometric figures:

- For a regular prism whose sides are all rectangles, the volume is $l \times w \times h$, where w is the width, l is the length, and h is the height of the prism
- For a cube, which is a prism whose faces are all squares of the same size, the volume is s^3
- The volume of a sphere of radius r is given by $\frac{4}{3}\pi r^3$
- The volume of a cylinder whose base has a radius of r and which has a height of h is given by $\pi r^2 h$

Word Problems

Word problems can appear daunting, but don't let the verbiage psych you out. No matter the scenario or specifics, the key to answering them is to translate the words into a math problem. Always keep in mind what the question is asking and what operations could lead to that answer.

Translating Words into Math

When asked to rewrite a mathematical expression as a situation or translated from a word problem into an expression, look for a series of key words indicating addition, subtraction, multiplication, or division:

Addition: add, altogether, together, plus, increased by, more than, in all, sum, and total

Subtraction: minus, less than, difference, decreased by, fewer than, remain, and take away

Multiplication: *times, twice, of, double,* and *triple*

Division: divided by, cut up, half, quotient of, split, and shared equally

Identifying and utilizing the proper units for the scenario requires knowing how to apply the conversion rates for money, length, volume, and mass. For example, given a scenario that requires subtracting 8 inches from $2\frac{1}{2}$ feet, both values should first be expressed in the same unit (they could be expressed $\frac{2}{3}$ft & $2\frac{1}{2}$ft, or 8in and 30in). The desired unit for the answer may also require converting back to another unit.

Consider the following scenario: A parking area along the river is only wide enough to fit one row of cars and is $\frac{1}{2}$ kilometers long. The average space needed per car is 5 meters. How many cars can be parked along the river? First, all measurements should be converted to similar units: $\frac{1}{2}$km = 500m. The operation(s) needed should be identified. Because the problem asks for the number of cars, the total space should be divided by the space per car. 500 meters divided by 5 meters per car yields a total of 100 cars. Written as an expression, the meters unit cancels and the cars unit is left: $\frac{500m}{5m/car}$ the same as $500m \times \frac{1\,car}{5m}$ yields 100 cars.

When dealing with problems involving elapsed time, breaking the problem down into workable parts is helpful. For example, suppose the length of time between 1:15pm and 3:45pm must be determined. From 1:15pm to 2:00pm is 45 minutes (knowing there are 60 minutes in an hour). From 2:00pm to 3:00pm is 1 hour. From 3:00pm to 3:45pm is 45 minutes. The total elapsed time is 45 minutes plus 1 hour plus 45 minutes. This sum produces 1 hour and 90 minutes. 90 minutes is over an hour, so this is converted to 1 hour (60 minutes) and 30 minutes. The total elapsed time can now be expressed as 2 hours and 30 minutes.

Example 1

Alexandra made $96 during the first 3 hours of her shift as a temporary worker at a law office. She will continue to earn money at this rate until she finishes in 5 more hours. How much does Alexandra make per hour? How much will Alexandra have made at the end of the day?

The hourly rate can be figured by dividing $96 by 3 hours to get $32 per hour. Now her total pay can be figured by multiplying $32 per hour by 8 hours, which comes out to $256.

Example 2

Bob had $20 and Tom had $4. After selling 4 ice cream cones to Bob, Tom has as much money as Bob.

The cost of an ice cream cone is an unknown quantity and can be represented by a variable (x). The amount of money Bob has after his purchase is four times the cost of an ice cream cone subtracted from his original

$$\$20 \rightarrow 20 - 4x$$

The amount of money Tom has after his sale is four times the cost of an ice cream cone added to his original

$$\$4 \rightarrow 4x + 4$$

After the sale, the amount of money that Bob and Tom have is equal

$$\rightarrow 20 - 4x = 4x + 4$$

Solving for x yields $x = 2$.

Data Analysis

Representing Data

Most statistics involve collecting a large amount of data, analyzing it, and then making decisions based on previously known information. These decisions also can be measured through additional data collection and then analyzed. Therefore, the cycle can repeat itself over and over. Representing the data visually is a large part of the process, and many plots on the real number line exist that allow this to be

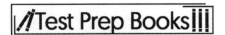
done. For example, a **dot plot** uses dots to represent data points above the number line. Also, a **histogram** represents a data set as a collection of rectangles, which illustrate the frequency distribution of the data. Finally, a **box plot** (also known as a **box and whisker plot**) plots a data set on the number line by segmenting the distribution into four quartiles that are divided equally in half by the median.

Here's an example of a box plot, a histogram, and a dot plot for the same data set:

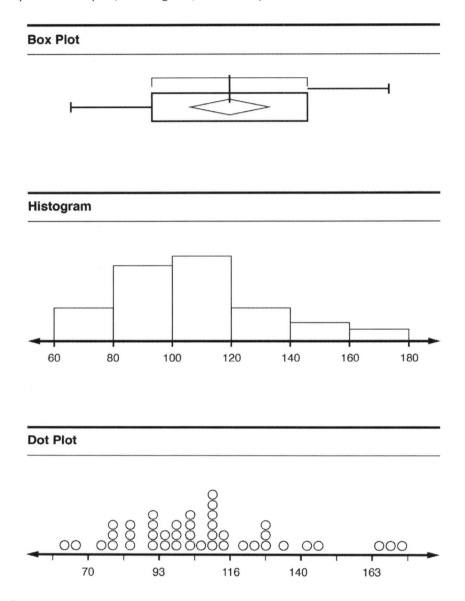

Comparing Data

Comparing data sets within statistics can mean many things. The first way to compare data sets is by looking at the center and spread of each set. The **center** of a data set can mean two things: median or mean. The **median** is the value that's halfway into each data set, and it splits the data into two intervals. The **mean** is the average value of the data within a set. It's calculated by adding up all of the data in the set and dividing the total by the number of data points. **Outliers** can significantly impact the mean. Additionally, two completely different data sets can have the same mean. For example, a data set with

30

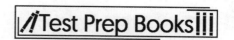

values ranging from 0 to 100 and a data set with values ranging from 44 to 56 can both have means of 50. The first data set has a much wider range, which is known as the **spread** of the data. This measures how varied the data is within each set. Spread can be defined further as either interquartile range or standard deviation.

The **interquartile range (IQR)** is the range of the middle 50 percent of the data set. This range can be seen in the large rectangle on a box plot. The **standard deviation** (s or σ) quantifies the amount of variation with respect to the mean. A lower standard deviation shows that the data set doesn't differ greatly from the mean. A larger standard deviation shows that the data set is spread out farther from the mean. The formula used for standard deviation depends on whether it's being used for a population or a sample (a subset of a population). The formula for sample standard deviation is:

$$s = \sqrt{\frac{\sum (x - \bar{x})^2}{n - 1}}$$

In this formula, s represents the standard deviation value, x is each value in the data set, $\bar{x}$ is the sample mean, and n is the total number of data points in the set. Note that sample standard deviations use *one less than the total* in the denominator. The population standard deviation formula is similar:

$$\sigma = \sqrt{\frac{\sum (x - \mu)^2}{N}}$$

For population standard deviations, sigma (σ) represents the standard deviation, x represents each value in the data set, mu (μ) is the population mean, and N is the total number of data points for the population.

Interpreting Data

The shape of a data set is another way to compare two or more sets of data. If a data set isn't symmetric around its mean, it's said to be **skewed.** If the tail to the left of the mean is longer, it's said to be skewed to the left. In this case, the mean is less than the median. Conversely, if the tail to the right of the mean is longer, it's said to be *skewed to the right* and the mean is greater than the median. When classifying a data set according to its shape, its overall *skewness* is being discussed. If the mean and median are equal, the data set isn't skewed; it is **symmetric**.

An outlier is a data point that lies a great distance away from the majority of the data set. It also can be labeled as an extreme value. Technically, an outlier is any value that falls 1.5 times the IQR above the upper quartile or 1.5 times the IQR below the lower quartile. The effect of outliers in the data set is seen visually because they affect the mean. If there's a large difference between the mean and mode, outliers are the cause. The mean shows bias towards the outlying values. However, the median won't be affected as greatly by outliers.

Normal Distribution

A **normal distribution** of data follows the shape of a bell curve, and the data set's median, mean, and mode are equal. Therefore, 50 percent of its values are less than the mean and 50 percent are greater than the mean. Data sets that follow this shape can be generalized using normal distributions. Normal distributions are described as **frequency distributions** in which the data set is plotted as percentages rather than true data points. A **relative frequency distribution** is one where the y-axis is between zero and 1, which is the same as 0% to 100%. Within a standard deviation, 68 percent of the values are within

1 standard deviation of the mean, 95 percent of the values are within 2 standard deviations of the mean, and 99.7 percent of the values are within 3 standard deviations of the mean. The number of standard deviations that a data point falls from the mean is called the **z-score.** The formula for the z-score is $Z = \frac{x - \mu}{\sigma}$, where μ is the mean, σ is the standard deviation, and x is the data point.

This formula is used to fit any data set that resembles a normal distribution to a standard normal distribution in a process known as **standardizing**. Here is a normal distribution with labeled z-scores:

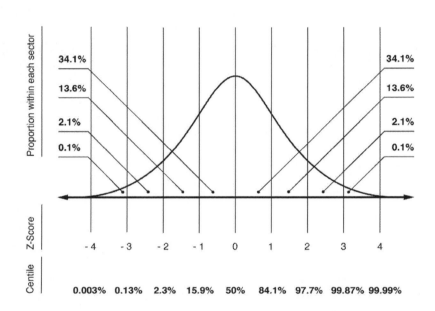

Population percentages can be estimated using normal distributions. For example, the probability that a data point will be less than the mean, or that the z-score will be less than 0, is 50%. Similarly, the probability that a data point will be within 1 standard deviation of the mean, or that the z-score will be between −1 and 1, is about 68.2%. When using a z-table, the left column states how many standard deviations (to one decimal place) away from the mean the point is, and the row heading states the second decimal place. The entries in the table corresponding to each column and row give the probability, which is equal to the area.

Areas Under the Curve
The area under the curve of a standard normal distribution is equal to 1. Areas under the curve can be estimated using the z-score and a table. The area is equal to the probability that a data point lies in that region in decimal form. For example, the area under the curve from $z = -1$ to $z = 1$ is 0.682.

Algebra

Computation with Integers and Negative Rational Numbers

Integers are the whole numbers together with their negatives. They include numbers like 5, 24, 0, –6, and 15. They do not include fractions or numbers that have digits after the decimal point.

Rational numbers are all numbers that can be written as a fraction using integers. A **fraction** is written as $\frac{x}{y}$ and represents the quotient of x being divided by y. More practically, it means dividing the whole into y equal parts, then taking x of those parts.

Examples of rational numbers include $\frac{1}{2}$ and $\frac{5}{4}$. The **numerator** is the number on the top of the fraction, while the **denominator** is the number on the bottom. Because every integer can be written as a fraction with a denominator of 1, (e.g., $\frac{3}{1} = 3$), every integer is also a rational number.

When adding integers and negative rational numbers, there are some basic rules to determine if the solution is negative or positive:

Adding two positive numbers results in a positive number:

$$3.3 + 4.8 = 8.1$$

Adding two negative numbers results in a negative number:

$$(-8) + (-6) = -14$$

Adding one positive and one negative number requires taking the absolute values and finding the difference between them. Then, the sign of the number that has the higher absolute value for the final solution is used.

For example, $(-9) + 11$, has a difference of absolute values of 2. The final solution is 2 because 11 has the higher absolute value. Another example is $9 + (-11)$, which has a difference of absolute values of 2. The final solution is –2 because 11 has the higher absolute value.

When subtracting integers and negative rational numbers, one has to change the problem to adding the opposite and then apply the rules of addition.

Subtracting two positive numbers is the same as adding one positive and one negative number.

For example, $4.9 - 7.1$ is the same as $4.9 + (-7.1)$. The solution is –2.2 since the absolute value of –7.1 is greater. Another example is $8.5 - 6.4$ which is the same as $8.5 + (-6.4)$. The solution is 2.1 since the absolute value of 8.5 is greater.

Subtracting a positive number from a negative number results in negative value.

For example, $(-12) - 7$ is the same as $(-12) + (-7)$ with a solution of –19.

Subtracting a negative number from a positive number results in a positive value.

For example, $12 - (-7)$ is the same as $12 + 7$ with a solution of 19.

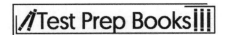

For multiplication and division of integers and rational numbers, if both numbers are positive or both numbers are negative, the result is a positive value.

For example, $(-1.7)(-4)$ has a solution of 6.8, since both numbers are negative values.

If one number is positive and another number is negative, the result is a negative value.

For example, $(-15) \div 5$ has a solution of -3 since there is one negative number.

The Use of Absolute Values

The **absolute value** represents the distance a number is from 0. The *absolute value symbol* is | | with a number between the bars. The $|10| = 10$ and the $|-10| = 10$.

When simplifying an algebraic expression, the value of the absolute value expression is determined first, much like parentheses in the order of operations. See the example below:

$$|8 - 12| + 5 = |-4| + 5 = 4 + 5 = 9$$

Ordering

Exponents are shorthand for longer multiplications or divisions. The exponent is written to the upper right of a number. In the expression 2^3, the exponent is 3. The number with the exponent is called the **base**.

When the exponent is a whole number, it means to multiply the base by itself as many times as the number in the exponent. So,

$$2^3 = 2 \times 2 \times 2 = 8$$

If the exponent is a negative number, it means to take the reciprocal of the positive exponent:

$$2^{-3} = \frac{1}{2^3} = \frac{1}{8}$$

When the exponent is 0, the result is always 1: $2^0 = 1, 5^0 = 1$, and so on.

When the exponent is 2, the number is **squared**, and when the exponent is 3, it is **cubed**.

When working with longer expressions, parentheses are used to show the order in which the operations should be performed. Operations inside the parentheses should be completed first. Thus, $(3 - 1) \div 2$ means one should first subtract 1 from 3, and then divide that result by 2.

The **order of operations** gives an order for how a mathematical expression is to be simplified:

- Parentheses
- Exponents
- Multiplication
- Division
- Addition
- Subtraction

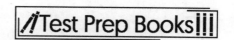

To help remember this, many students like to use the mnemonic PEMDAS. Some students associate this word with a phrase to help them, such as "Pirates Eat Many Donuts at Sea." Here is a quick example:

$$\text{Evaluate } 2^2 \times (3 - 1) \div 2 + 3.$$

$$\text{Parentheses: } 2^2 \times 2 \div 2 + 3.$$

$$\text{Exponents: } 4 \times 2 \div 2 + 3$$

$$\text{Multiply: } 8 \div 2 + 3.$$

$$\text{Divide: } 4 + 3.$$

$$\text{Addition: } 7$$

Evaluation of Simple Formulas and Expressions

To evaluate simple formulas and expressions, the first step is to substitute the given values in for the variable(s). Then, the order of operations is used to simplify.

Example 1
Evaluate $\frac{1}{2}x^2 - 3, x = 4$.

The first step is to substitute in 4 for x in the expression:

$$\frac{1}{2}(4)^2 - 3$$

Then, the order of operations is used to simplify.

The exponent comes first, $\frac{1}{2}(16) - 3$, then the multiplication $8 - 3$, and then, after subtraction, the solution is 5.

Example 2
Evaluate $4|5 - x| + 2y, x = 4, y = -3$.

The first step is to substitute 4 in for x and −3 in for y in the expression:

$$4|5 - 4| + 2(-3)$$

Then, the absolute value expression is simplified, which is:

$$|5 - 4| = |1| = 1$$

The expression is $4(1) + 2(-3)$ which can be simplified using the order of operations.

First is the multiplication, $4 + (-6)$; then addition yields an answer of −2.

Example 3

Find the perimeter of a rectangle with a length of 6 inches and a width of 9 inches.

The first step is substituting in 6 for the length and 9 for the width in the perimeter of a rectangle formula,

$$P = 2(6) + 2(9)$$

Then, the order of operations is used to simplify.

First is multiplication (resulting in $12 + 18$) and then addition for a solution of 30 inches.

Adding and Subtracting Monomials and Polynomials

To add or subtract polynomials, add the coefficients of terms with the same exponent. For instance:

$$(-2x^2 + 3x + 1) + (4x^2 - x)$$

$$(-2 + 4)x^2 + (3 - 1)x + 1 = 2x^2 + 2x + 1$$

Multiplying and Dividing Monomials and Polynomials

To multiply polynomials, each term of the first polynomial multiplies each term of the second polynomial, and adds up the results. Here's an example:

$$(3x^4 + 2x^2)(2x^2 + 3)$$

$$3x^4 \times 2x^2 + 3x^4 \times 3 + 2x^2 \times 2x^2 + 2x^2 \times 3$$

Then, add like terms with a result of:

$$6x^6 + 9x^4 + 4x^4 + 6x^2 = 6x^6 + 13x^4 + 6x^2$$

A polynomial with two terms is called a **binomial**. Another way of remember the rule for multiplying two binomials is to use the acronym *FOIL*: multiply the *First* terms together, then the *Outside* terms (terms on the far left and far right), then the *Inner* terms, and finally the *Last* two terms. For longer polynomials, there is no such convenient mnemonic, so remember to multiply each term of the first polynomial by each term of the second, and add the results.

To divide one polynomial by another, the procedure is similar to long division. At each step, one needs to figure out how to get the term of the dividend with the highest exponent as a multiple of the divisor. The divisor is multiplied by the multiple to get that term, which goes in the quotient. Then, the product of this term is subtracted with the dividend from the divisor and repeat the process. This sounds rather abstract, so it may be easiest to see the procedure by describing it while looking at an example.

Example

$$(4x^3 + x^2 - x + 4) \div (2x - 1)$$

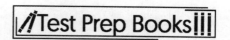

The first step is to set up the problem for long division:

$$2x - 1 \;\big)\; \overline{4x^3 + x^2 - x + 4}$$

Divide the first term of the divisor on the left by the first term of the numerator under the bar and place the result over the bar:

$$\begin{array}{r} 2x^2 \quad\quad\quad\quad \\ 2x - 1 \;\big)\; \overline{4x^3 + x^2 - x + 4} \end{array}$$

Next, multiply that new term by the divisor and place it beneath the numerator:

$$\begin{array}{r} 2x^2 \quad\quad\quad\quad \\ 2x - 1 \;\big)\; \overline{4x^3 + x^2 - x + 4} \\ 4x^3 - 2x^2 \quad\quad\quad \end{array}$$

Subtract it from the numerator to find the difference, a new polynomial:

$$\begin{array}{r} 2x^2 \quad\quad\quad\quad \\ 2x - 1 \;\big)\; \overline{4x^3 + x^2 - x + 4} \\ -\quad \underline{4x^3 - 2x^2 \quad\quad\quad} \\ 3x^2 - x + 4 \end{array}$$

The same steps are repeated until there are no more x terms in the quotient above the bar or the subtraction step leaves no remainder.

Divide the first term of the new polynomial by the first term of the divisor, multiply that by divisor, and subtract from the new polynomial:

$$2x - 1 \overline{\smash{\big)}\ 4x^3 + x^2 - x + 4} \quad \Bigg\uparrow \quad 2x^2 + \frac{3}{2}x + \frac{1}{4}$$

$$\begin{array}{r} 2x^2 + \dfrac{3}{2}x + \dfrac{1}{4} \\[2mm] 2x - 1 \overline{\smash{\big)}\ 4x^3 + x^2 - x + 4} \\[1mm] -\ \underline{4x^3 - 2x^2} \\[1mm] 3x^2 - x + 4 \\[1mm] -\ \underline{3x^2 - \dfrac{3}{2}x} \\[1mm] \dfrac{1}{2}x + 4 \\[1mm] -\ \underline{\dfrac{1}{2}x - \dfrac{1}{4}} \\[1mm] \dfrac{17}{4} \end{array}$$

In this case, the problem doesn't divide evenly, so the answer is the quotient, plus the remainder divided by the divisor ($2x - 1$):

$$2x^2 + \frac{3}{2}x + \frac{1}{4} + \frac{17}{4(2x - 1)}$$

The Evaluation of Positive Rational Roots and Exponents

There are a few rules for working with exponents. For any numbers a, b, m, n, the following hold true:

$$a^1 = a$$

$$1^a = 1$$

$$a^0 = 1$$

$$a^m \times a^n = a^{m+n}$$

$$a^m \div a^n = a^{m-n}$$

$$(a^m)^n = a^{m \times n}$$

$$(a \times b)^m = a^m \times b^m$$

$$(a \div b)^m = a^m \div b^m$$

Any number, including a fraction, can be an exponent. The same rules apply.

38

Simplifying Algebraic Fractions

A **rational expression** is a fraction with a polynomial in the numerator and denominator. The denominator polynomial cannot be zero. An example of a rational expression is:

$$\frac{3x^4 - 2}{-x + 1}$$

The same rules for working with addition, subtraction, multiplication, and division with rational expressions apply as when working with regular fractions.

The first step is to find a common denominator when adding or subtracting. This can be done just as with regular fractions. For example, if $\frac{a}{b} + \frac{c}{d}$, then a common denominator can be found by multiplying to find the following fractions: $\frac{ad}{bd}, \frac{cb}{db}$.

A **complex fraction** is a fraction in which the numerator and denominator are themselves fractions, of the form $\frac{\left(\frac{a}{b}\right)}{\left(\frac{c}{d}\right)}$. These can be simplified by following the usual rules for the order of operations, or by remembering that dividing one fraction by another is the same as multiplying by the reciprocal of the divisor. This means that any complex fraction can be rewritten using the following form:

$$\frac{\left(\frac{a}{b}\right)}{\left(\frac{c}{d}\right)} = \frac{a}{b} \times \frac{d}{c}$$

The following problem is an example of solving a complex fraction:

$$\frac{\left(\frac{5}{4}\right)}{\left(\frac{3}{8}\right)} = \frac{5}{4} \times \frac{8}{3} = \frac{40}{12} = \frac{10}{3}$$

Factoring

Factors for polynomials are similar to factors for integers—they are numbers, variables, or polynomials that, when multiplied together, give a product equal to the polynomial in question. One polynomial is a factor of a second polynomial if the second polynomial can be obtained from the first by multiplying by a third polynomial.

$6x^6 + 13x^4 + 6x^2$ can be obtained by multiplying together $(3x^4 + 2x^2)(2x^2 + 3)$. This means $2x^2 + 3$ and $3x^4 + 2x^2$ are factors of,

$$6x^6 + 13x^4 + 6x^2$$

In general, finding the factors of a polynomial can be tricky. However, there are a few types of polynomials that can be factored in a straightforward way.

If a certain monomial is in each term of a polynomial, it can be factored out. There are several common forms polynomials take, which if you recognize, you can solve. The first example is a perfect square trinomial. To factor this polynomial, first expand the middle term of the expression:

$$x^2 + 2xy + y^2$$

$$x^2 + xy + xy + y^2$$

Factor out a common term in each half of the expression (in this case x from the left and y from the right):

$$x(x + y) + y(x + y)$$

Then the same can be done again, treating $(x + y)$ as the common factor:

$$(x + y)(x + y) = (x + y)^2$$

Therefore, the formula for this polynomial is:

$$x^2 + 2xy + y^2 = (x + y)^2$$

Next is another example of a perfect square trinomial. The process is the similar, but notice the difference in sign:

$$x^2 - 2xy + y^2$$

$$x^2 - xy - xy + y^2$$

Factor out the common term on each side:

$$x(x - y) - y(x - y)$$

Factoring out the common term again:

$$(x - y)(x - y) = (x - y)^2$$

Thus:

$$x^2 - 2xy + y^2 = (x - y)^2$$

The next is known as a difference of squares. This process is effectively the reverse of binomial multiplication:

$$x^2 - y^2$$

$$x^2 - xy + xy - y^2$$

$$x(x - y) + y(x - y)$$

$$(x + y)(x - y)$$

Therefore:

$$x^2 - y^2 = (x + y)(x - y)$$

40

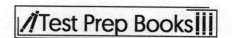

The following two polynomials are known as the sum or difference of cubes. These are special polynomials that take the form of $x^3 + y^3$ or $x^3 - y^3$. The following formula factors the sum of cubes:

$$x^3 + y^3 = (x + y)(x^2 - xy + y^2)$$

Next is the difference of cubes, but note the change in sign. The formulas for both are similar, but the order of signs for factoring the sum or difference of cubes can be remembered by using the acronym SOAP, which stands for "same, opposite, always positive." The first sign is the same as the sign in the first expression, the second is opposite, and the third is always positive. The next formula factors the difference of cubes:

$$x^3 - y^3 = (x - y)(x^2 + xy + y^2)$$

The following two examples are expansions of cubed binomials. Similarly, these polynomials always follow a pattern:

$$x^3 + 3x^2y + 3xy^2 + y^3 = (x + y)^3$$

$$x^3 - 3x^2y + 3xy^2 - y^3 = (x - y)^3$$

These rules can be used in many combinations with one another. For example, the expression $3x^3 - 24$ has a common factor of 3, which becomes:

$$3(x^3 - 8)$$

A difference of cubes still remains which can then be factored out:

$$3(x - 2)(x^2 + 2x + 4)$$

There are no other terms to be pulled out, so this expression is completely factored.

When factoring polynomials, a good strategy is to multiply the factors to check the result. Let's try another example:

$$4x^3 + 16x^2$$

Both sides of the expression can be divided by 4, and both contain x^2, because $4x^3$ can be thought of as $4x^2(x)$, so the common term can simply be factored out:

$$4x^2(x + 4)$$

It sometimes can be necessary to rewrite the polynomial in some clever way before applying the above rules. Consider the problem of factoring $x^4 - 1$. This does not immediately look like any of the previous polynomials. However, it's possible to think of this polynomial as $x^4 - 1 = (x^2)^2 - (1^2)^2$, and now it can be treated as a difference of squares to simplify this:

$$(x^2)^2 - (1^2)^2$$

$$(x^2)^2 - x^2 1^2 + x^2 1^2 - (1^2)^2$$

$$x^2(x^2 - 1^2) + 1^2(x^2 - 1^2)$$

$$(x^2 + 1^2)(x^2 - 1^2)$$

$$(x^2 + 1)(x^2 - 1)$$

Solving Linear Equations and Inequalities

The simplest equations to solve are **linear equations**, which have the form $ax + b = 0$. These have the solution $x = -\frac{b}{a}$.

For instance, in the equation $\frac{1}{3}x - 4 = 0$, it can be determined that $\frac{1}{3}x = 4$ by adding 4 on each side. Next, both sides of the equation are multiplied by 3 to get $x = 12$.

Solving an inequality is very similar to solving equations, with one important issue to keep track of: if multiplying or dividing both sides of an inequality by a negative number, the direction of the inequality *flips*.

For example, consider the inequality $-4x < 12$. Solving this inequality requires the division of –4. When the negative four is divided, the less-than sign changes to a greater-than sign. The solution becomes $x > -3$.

Example
$-4x - 3 \leq -2x + 1$

2x is added to both sides, and 3 is added to both sides, leaving $-2x \leq 4$.

$-2x \leq 4$ is multiplied by $-\frac{1}{2}$, which means flipping the direction of the inequality.

This gives $x \geq -2$.

An **absolute inequality** is an inequality that is true for all real numbers. An inequality that is only true for some real numbers is called **conditional**.

In addition to the inequalities above, there are also **double inequalities** where three quantities are compared to one another, such as:
$$3 \leq x + 4 < 5$$

The rules for double inequalities include always performing any operations to every part of the inequality and reversing the direction of the inequality when multiplying or dividing by a negative number.

When solving equations and inequalities, the solutions can be checked by plugging the answer back in to the original problem. If the solution makes a true statement, the solution is correct.

Solving Quadratic Equations by Factoring

Solving quadratic equations is a little trickier. If they take the form $ax^2 - b = 0$, then the equation can be solved by adding b to both sides and dividing by a to get:

$$x^2 = \frac{b}{a}$$

Using the sixth rule above, the solution is $x = \pm\sqrt{\frac{b}{a}}$. Note that this is actually two separate solutions, unless b happens to be 0.

42

If a quadratic equation has no constant—so that it takes the form $ax^2 + bx = 0$—then the x can be factored out to get:

$$x(ax + b) = 0$$

Then, the solutions are $x = 0$, together with the solutions to $ax + b = 0$. Both factors x and $(ax + b)$ can be set equal to zero to solve for x because one of those values must be zero for their product to equal zero. For an equation $ab = 0$ to be true, either $a = 0$, or $b = 0$.

A given quadratic equation $x^2 + bx + c$ can be factored into $(x + A)(x + B)$, where $A + B = b$, and $AB = c$. Finding the values of A and B can take time, but such a pair of numbers can be found by guessing and checking. Looking at the positive and negative factors for c offers a good starting point.

For example, in $x^2 - 5x + 6$, the factors of 6 are 1, 2, and 3. Now, $(-2)(-3) = 6$, and $-2 - 3 = -5$. In general, however, this may not work, in which case another approach may need to be used.

A quadratic equation of the form $x^2 + 2xb + b^2 = 0$ can be factored into:

$$(x + b)^2 = 0$$

Similarly, $x^2 - 2xy + y^2 = 0$ factors into:

$$(x - y)^2 = 0$$

In general, the constant term may not be the right value to be factored this way. A more general method for solving these quadratic equations must then be found. The following two methods will work in any situation.

Completing the Square

The first method is called **completing the square**. The idea here is that in any equation $x^2 + 2xb + c = 0$, something could be added to both sides of the equation to get the left side to look like $x^2 + 2xb + b^2$, meaning it could be factored into:

$$(x + b)^2 = 0$$

<u>Example</u>
$x^2 + 6x - 1 = 0$

The left-hand side could be factored if the constant were equal to 9, since:

$$x^2 + 6x + 9 = (x + 3)^2$$

To get a constant of 9 on the left, 10 needs to be added to both sides.

That changes the equation to:

$$x^2 + 6x + 9 = 10$$

Factoring the left gives:

$$(x + 3)^2 = 10$$

Then, the square root of both sides can be taken (remembering that this introduces a $\pm$):

$$x + 3 = \pm\sqrt{10}$$

Finally, 3 is subtracted from both sides to get two solutions:

$$x = -3 \pm \sqrt{10}$$

The Quadratic Formula

The first method of completing the square can be used in finding the second method, the quadratic formula. It can be used to solve any quadratic equation. This formula may be the longest method for solving quadratic equations and is commonly used as a last resort after other methods are ruled out.

It can be helpful in memorizing the formula to see where it comes from, so here are the steps involved.

The most general form for a quadratic equation is:

$$ax^2 + bx + c = 0$$

First, dividing both sides by a leaves us with:

$$x^2 + \frac{b}{a}x + \frac{c}{a} = 0$$

To complete the square on the left-hand side, c/a can be subtracted on both sides to get:

$$x^2 + \frac{b}{a}x = -\frac{c}{a}$$

$(\frac{b}{2a})^2$ is then added to both sides.

This gives:

$$x^2 + \frac{b}{a}x + (\frac{b}{2a})^2 = (\frac{b}{2a})^2 - \frac{c}{a}$$

The left can now be factored and the right-hand side simplified to give:

$$(x + \frac{b}{2a})^2 = \frac{b^2 - 4ac}{4a}$$

Taking the square roots gives:

$$x + \frac{b}{2a} = \pm\frac{\sqrt{b^2 - 4ac}}{2a}$$

Solving for x yields the quadratic formula:

$$x = \frac{-b \pm \sqrt{b^2 - 4ac}}{2a}$$

It isn't necessary to remember how to get this formula, but memorizing the formula itself is the goal.

If an equation involves taking a root, then the first step is to move the root to one side of the equation and everything else to the other side. That way, both sides can be raised to the index of the radical in order to remove it, and solving the equation can continue.

Solving Verbal Problems Presented in an Algebraic Context

There is a four-step process in problem-solving that can be used as a guide:

- Understand the problem and determine the unknown information.
- Translate the verbal problem into an algebraic equation.
- Solve the equation by using inverse operations.
- Check the work and answer the given question.

<u>Example</u>

Three times the sum of a number plus 4 equals the number plus 8. What is the number?

The first step is to determine the unknown, which is the number, or x.

The second step is to translate the problem into the equation, which is:

$$3(x + 4) = x + 8$$

The equation can be solved as follows:

$3x + 12 = x + 8$	Apply the distributive property
$3x = x - 4$	Subtract 12 from both sides of the equation
$2x = -4$	Subtract x from both sides of the equation
$x = -2$	Divide both sides of the equation by 2

The final step is checking the solution. Plugging the value for x back into the equation yields the following problem:

$$3(-2) + 12 = -2 + 8.$$

Using the order of operations shows that a true statement is made: $6 = 6$

Geometry

Simple Geometry Problems

There are many key facts related to geometry that are applicable. The sum of the measures of the angles of a triangle are 180°, and for a quadrilateral, the sum is 360°. Rectangles and squares each have four right angles. A **right angle** has a measure of 90°.

Perimeter

The **perimeter** is the distance around a figure or the sum of all sides of a polygon.

The **formula for the perimeter of a square** is four times the length of a side. For example, the following square has side lengths of 5 feet:

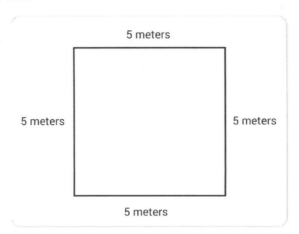

The perimeter is 20 feet because 4 times 5 is 20.

The **formula for a perimeter of a rectangle** is the sum of twice the length and twice the width. For example, if the length of a rectangle is 10 inches and the width 8 inches, then the perimeter is 36 inches because:

$$P = 2l + 2w = 2(10) + 2(8) = 20 + 16 = 36 \text{ inches}$$

Area

The area is the amount of space inside of a figure, and there are formulas associated with area.

The area of a triangle is the product of one-half the base and height. For example, if the base of the triangle is 2 feet and the height 4 feet, then the area is 4 square feet. The following equation shows the formula used to calculate the area of the triangle:

$$A = \frac{1}{2}bh = \frac{1}{2}(2)(4) = 4 \text{ square feet}$$

The area of a square is the length of a side squared. For example, if a side of a square is 7 centimeters, then the area is 49 square centimeters. The formula for this example is $A = s^2 = 7^2 = 49$ square centimeters. An example is if the rectangle has a length of 6 inches and a width of 7 inches, then the area is 42 square inches:

$$A = lw = 6(7) = 42 \text{ square inches}$$

The area of a trapezoid is one-half the height times the sum of the bases. For example, if the length of the bases are 2.5 and 3 feet and the height 3.5 feet, then the area is 9.625 square feet. The following formula shows how the area is calculated:

$$A = \frac{1}{2}h(b_1 + b_2) = \frac{1}{2}(3.5)(2.5 + 3)$$

$$\frac{1}{2}(3.5)(5.5) = 9.625 \text{ square feet}$$

The perimeter of a figure is measured in single units, while the area is measured in square units.

Distribution of a Quantity into its Fractional Parts

A quantity may be broken into its fractional parts. For example, a toy box holds three types of toys for kids. $\frac{1}{3}$ of the toys are Type A and $\frac{1}{4}$ of the toys are Type B. With that information, how many Type C toys are there?

First, the sum of Type A and Type B must be determined by finding a common denominator to add the fractions. The lowest common multiple is 12, so that is what will be used. The sum is:

$$\frac{1}{3} + \frac{1}{4} = \frac{4}{12} + \frac{3}{12} = \frac{7}{12}$$

This value is subtracted from 1 to find the number of Type C toys. The value is subtracted from 1 because 1 represents a whole. The calculation is:

$$1 - \frac{7}{12} = \frac{12}{12} - \frac{7}{12} = \frac{5}{12}$$

This means that $\frac{5}{12}$ of the toys are Type C. To check the answer, add all fractions together, and the result should be 1.

Plane Geometry

Locations on the plane that have no width or breadth are called **points**. These points usually will be denoted with capital letters such as P.

Any pair of points A, B on the plane will determine a unique straight line between them. This line is denoted AB. Sometimes to emphasize a line is being considered, this will be written as $\overleftrightarrow{AB}$.

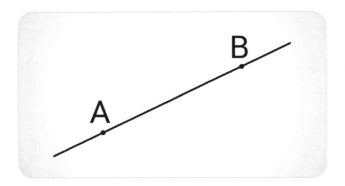

If the Cartesian coordinates for A and B are known, then the distance $d(A, B)$ along the line between them can be measured using the **distance formula**, which states that if $A = (x_1, y_1)$ and $B = (x_2, y_2)$, then the distance between them is:

$$d(A, B) = \sqrt{(x_2 - x_1)^2 + (y_2 - y_1)^2}$$

The part of a line that lies between A and B is called a **line segment**. It has two endpoints, one at A and one at B. **Rays** also can be formed. Given points A and B, a *ray* is the portion of a line that starts at one of these points, passes through the other, and keeps on going. Therefore, a ray has a single endpoint, but the other end goes off to infinity.

Given a pair of points A and B, a circle centered at A and passing through B can be formed. This is the set of points whose distance from A is exactly $d(A, B)$. The radius of this circle will be $d(A, B)$.

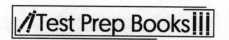

The **circumference** of a circle is the distance traveled by following the edge of the circle for one complete revolution, and the length of the circumference is given by $2\pi r$, where r is the radius of the circle. The formula for circumference is $C = 2\pi r$.

When two lines cross, they form an *angle*. The point where the lines cross is called the **vertex** of the angle. The angle can be named by either just using the vertex, $\angle A$, or else by listing three points $\angle BAC$, as shown in the diagram below.

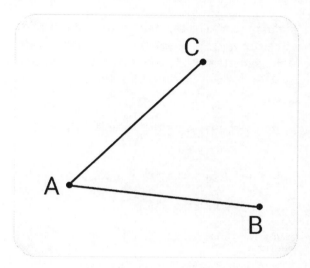

The measurement of an angle can be given in degrees or in radians. In degrees, a full circle is 360 degrees, written 360°. In radians, a full circle is 2π radians.

Given two points on the circumference of a circle, the path along the circle between those points is called an **arc of the circle**. For example, the arc between B and C is denoted by a thinner line:

The length of the path along an arc is called the **arc length**. If the circle has radius r, then the arc length is given by multiplying the measure of the angle in radians by the radius of the circle.

Two lines are said to be **parallel** if they never intersect. If the lines are AB and CD, then this is written as $AB \parallel CD$.

If two lines cross to form four quarter-circles, that is, 90° angles, the two lines are **perpendicular**. If the point at which they cross is B, and the two lines are AB and BC, then this is written as $AB \perp BC$.

A **polygon** is a closed figure (meaning it divides the plane into an inside and an outside) consisting of a collection of line segments between points. These points are called the **vertices** of the polygon. These line segments must not overlap one another. Note that the number of sides is equal to the number of angles, or vertices of the polygon. The angles between line segments meeting one another in the polygon are called **interior angles**.

A **regular polygon** is a polygon whose edges are all the same length and whose interior angles are all of equal measure.

A **triangle** is a polygon with three sides. A **quadrilateral** is a polygon with four sides.

A **right triangle** is a triangle that has one 90° angle.

The sum of the interior angles of any triangle must add up to 180°.

An **isosceles triangle** is a triangle in which two of the sides are the same length. In this case, it will always have two congruent interior angles. If a triangle has two congruent interior angles, it will always be isosceles.

An **equilateral triangle** is a triangle whose sides are all the same length and whose angles are all equivalent to one another, equal to 60°. Equilateral triangles are examples of regular polygons. Note that equilateral triangles are also isosceles.

A **rectangle** is a quadrilateral whose interior angles are all 90°. A rectangle has two sets of sides that are equal to one another.

A **square** is a rectangle whose width and height are equal. Therefore, squares are regular polygons.

A **parallelogram** is a quadrilateral in which the opposite sides are parallel and equivalent to each other.

Transformations of a Plane

Given a figure drawn on a plane, many changes can be made to that figure, including **rotation**, **translation**, and **reflection**. Rotations turn the figure about a point, translations slide the figure, and reflections flip the figure over a specified line. When performing these transformations, the original figure is called the **pre-image**, and the figure after transformation is called the **image**.

More specifically, *translation* means that all points in the figure are moved in the same direction by the same distance. In other words, the figure is slid in some fixed direction. Of course, while the entire figure is slid by the same distance, this does not change any of the measurements of the figures involved. The result will have the same distances and angles as the original figure.

In terms of Cartesian coordinates, a translation means a shift of each of the original points (x, y) by a fixed amount in the x and y directions, to become $(x + a, y + b)$.

Another procedure that can be performed is called *reflection*. To do this, a line in the plane is specified, called the **line of reflection**. Then, take each point and flip it over the line so that it is the same distance from the line but on the opposite side of it. This does not change any of the distances or angles involved, but it does reverse the order in which everything appears.

To reflect something over the x-axis, the points (x, y) are sent to $(x, -y)$. To reflect something over the y-axis, the points (x, y) are sent to the points $(-x, y)$. Flipping over other lines is not something easy to express in Cartesian coordinates. However, by drawing the figure and the line of reflection, the distance to the line and the original points can be used to find the reflected figure.

Example: Reflect this triangle with vertices $(-1, 0)$, $(2, 1)$, and $(2, 0)$ over the y-axis. The pre-image is shown below.

To do this, flip the *x* values of the points involved to the negatives of themselves, while keeping the *y* values the same. The image is shown here.

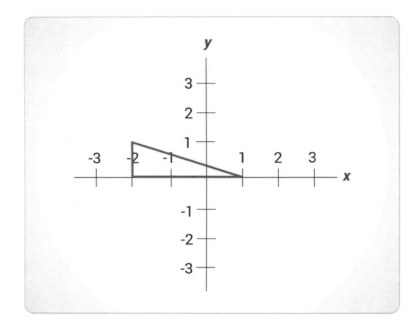

The new vertices will be (1, 0), (−2, 1), and (−2, 0).

Another procedure that does not change the distances and angles in a figure is *rotation*. In this procedure, pick a center point, then rotate every vertex along a circle around that point by the same angle. This procedure is also not easy to express in Cartesian coordinates, and this is not a requirement on this test. However, as with reflections, it's helpful to draw the figures and see what the result of the rotation would look like. This transformation can be performed using a compass and protractor.

Each one of these transformations can be performed on the coordinate plane without changes to the original dimensions or angles.

If two figures in the plane involve the same distances and angles, they are called **congruent figures**. In other words, two figures are congruent when they go from one form to another through reflection, rotation, and translation, or a combination of these.

Remember that rotation and translation will give back a new figure that is identical to the original figure, but reflection will give back a mirror image of it.

To recognize that a figure has undergone a rotation, check to see that the figure has not been changed into a mirror image, but that its orientation has changed (that is, whether the parts of the figure now form different angles with the *x* and *y* axes).

To recognize that a figure has undergone a translation, check to see that the figure has not been changed into a mirror image, and that the orientation remains the same.

To recognize that a figure has undergone a reflection, check to see that the new figure is a mirror image of the old figure.

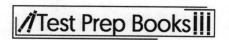

Keep in mind that sometimes a combination of translations, reflections, and rotations may be performed on a figure.

Dilation

A **dilation** is a transformation that preserves angles, but not distances. This can be thought of as stretching or shrinking a figure. If a dilation makes figures larger, it is called an **enlargement**. If a dilation makes figures smaller, it is called a **reduction**. The easiest example is to dilate around the origin. In this case, multiply the x and y coordinates by a **scale factor**, k, sending points (x, y) to (kx, ky).

As an example, draw a dilation of the following triangle, whose vertices will be the points (−1, 0), (1, 0), and (1, 1).

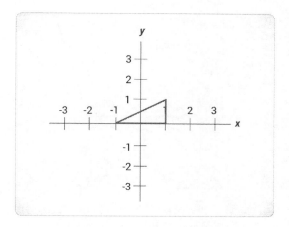

For this problem, dilate by a scale factor of 2, so the new vertices will be (−2, 0), (2, 0), and (2, 2).

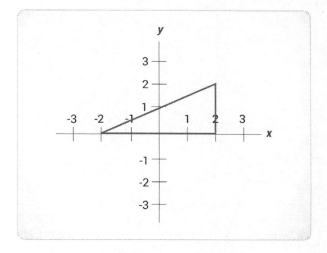

Note that after a dilation, the distances between the vertices of the figure will have changed, but the angles will remain the same. The two figures that are obtained by dilation, along with possibly translation, rotation, and reflection, are all *similar* to one another. Another way to think of this is that similar figures have the same number of vertices and edges, and their angles are all the same. Similar figures have the same basic shape but are different in size.

Symmetry

Using the types of transformations above, if an object can undergo these changes and not appear to have changed, then the figure is symmetrical. If an object can be split in half by a line and flipped over that line to lie directly on top of itself, it is said to have **line symmetry**. An example of both types of figures is seen below.

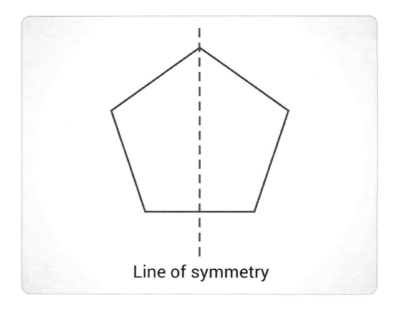

Line of symmetry

If an object can be rotated about its center to any degree smaller than 360, and it lies directly on top of itself, the object is said to have **rotational symmetry**. An example of this type of symmetry is shown below. The pentagon has an order of 5.

The rotational symmetry lines in the figure above can be used to find the angles formed at the center of the pentagon. Knowing that all of the angles together form a full circle, at 360 degrees, the figure can be split into 5 angles equally. By dividing the 360° by 5, each angle is 72°.

Given the length of one side of the figure, the perimeter of the pentagon can also be found using rotational symmetry. If one side length was 3 cm, that side length can be rotated onto each other side length four times. This would give a total of 5 side lengths equal to 3 cm. To find the perimeter, or distance around the figure, multiply 3 by 5. The perimeter of the figure would be 15 cm.

If a line cannot be drawn anywhere on the object to flip the figure onto itself or rotated less than or equal to 180 degrees to lay on top of itself, the object is asymmetrical. Examples of these types of figures are shown below.

No line of symmetry

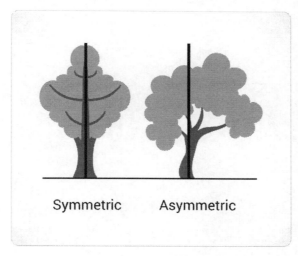

Symmetric   Asymmetric

Perimeters and Areas

The **perimeter of a polygon** is the total length of a trip around the whole polygon, starting and ending at the same point. It is found by adding up the lengths of each line segment in the polygon. For a rectangle with sides of length x and y, the perimeter will be $2x + 2y$.

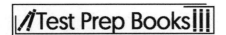
The area of a polygon is the area of the region that it encloses. Regarding the area of a rectangle with sides of length x and y, the area is given by xy. For a triangle with a base of length b and a height of length h, the area is $\frac{1}{2}bh$.

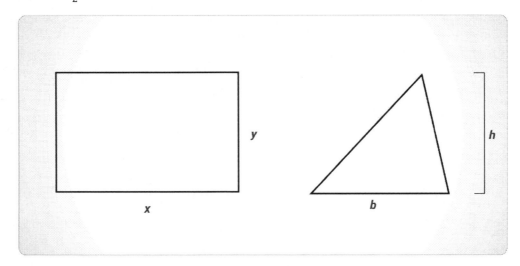

To find the areas of more general polygons, it is usually easiest to break up the polygon into rectangles and triangles. For example, find the area of the following figure whose vertices are (−1, 0), (−1, 2), (1, 3), and (1, 0).

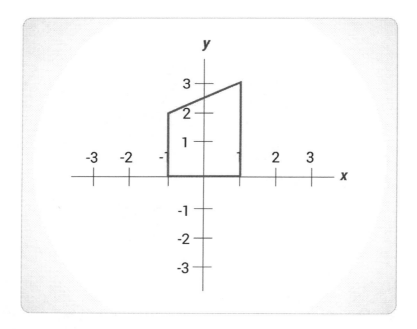

Separate this into a rectangle and a triangle as shown:

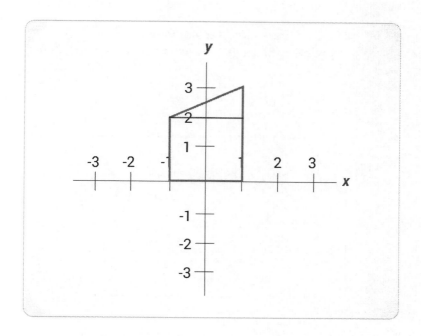

The rectangle has a height of 2 and a width of 2, so it has a total area of $2 \times 2 = 4$. The triangle has a width of 2 and a height of 1, so it has an area of:

$$\frac{1}{2}2 \times 1 = 1$$

Therefore, the entire quadrilateral has an area of $4 + 1 = 5$.

As another example, suppose someone wants to tile a rectangular room that is 10 feet by 6 feet using triangular tiles that are 12 inches by 6 inches. How many tiles would be needed? To figure this, first find the area of the room, which will be $10 \times 6 = 60$ square feet. The dimensions of the triangle are 1 foot by ½ foot, so the area of each triangle is:

$$\frac{1}{2} \times 1 \times \frac{1}{2} = \frac{1}{4} \text{ square feet}$$

Notice that the dimensions of the triangle had to be converted to the same units as the rectangle. Now, take the total area divided by the area of one tile to find the answer:

$$\frac{60}{\frac{1}{4}} = 60 \times 4 = 240 \text{ tiles required}$$

Volumes and Surface Areas

Geometry in three dimensions is similar to geometry in two dimensions. The main new feature is that three points now define a unique *plane* that passes through each of them. Three dimensional objects can be made by putting together two-dimensional figures in different surfaces. Below, some of the possible three-dimensional figures will be provided, along with formulas for their volumes and surface areas.

A rectangular prism is a box whose sides are all rectangles meeting at 90° angles. Such a box has three dimensions: length, width, and height. If the length is x, the width is y, and the height is z, then the volume is given by $V = xyz$.

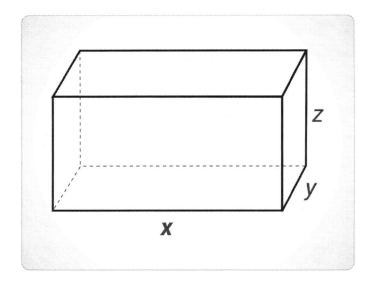

The surface area will be given by computing the surface area of each rectangle and adding them together. There are a total of six rectangles. Two of them have sides of length x and y, two have sides of length y and z, and two have sides of length x and z. Therefore, the total surface area will be given by:

$$SA = 2xy + 2yz + 2xz$$

A **rectangular pyramid** is a figure with a rectangular base and four triangular sides that meet at a single vertex. If the rectangle has sides of length x and y, then the volume will be given by:

$$V = \frac{1}{3}xyh$$

To find the surface area, the dimensions of each triangle need to be known. However, these dimensions can differ depending on the problem in question. Therefore, there is no general formula for calculating total surface area.

A **sphere** is a set of points all of which are equidistant from some central point. It is like a circle, but in three dimensions. The volume of a sphere of radius r is given by:

$$V = \frac{4}{3}\pi r^3$$

The surface area is given by $A = 4\pi r^2$.

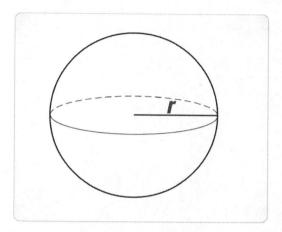

The Pythagorean Theorem

The Pythagorean theorem is an important result in geometry. It states that for right triangles, the sum of the squares of the two shorter sides will be equal to the square of the longest side (also called the **hypotenuse**). The longest side will always be the side opposite to the 90° angle. If this side is called c, and the other two sides are a and b, then the Pythagorean theorem states that $c^2 = a^2 + b^2$. Since lengths are always positive, this also can be written as:

$$c = \sqrt{a^2 + b^2}$$

A diagram to show the parts of a triangle using the Pythagorean theorem is below.

As an example of the theorem, suppose that Shirley has a rectangular field that is 5 feet wide and 12 feet long, and she wants to split it in half using a fence that goes from one corner to the opposite corner. How long will this fence need to be? To figure this out, note that this makes the field into two right triangles, whose hypotenuse will be the fence dividing it in half. Therefore, the fence length will be given by:

$$\sqrt{5^2 + 12^2} = \sqrt{169} = 13 \text{ feet long}$$

Similar Figures and Proportions

Sometimes, two figures are similar, meaning they have the same basic shape and the same interior angles, but they have different dimensions. If the ratio of two corresponding sides is known, then that ratio, or scale factor, holds true for all of the dimensions of the new figure.

Here is an example of applying this principle. Suppose that Lara is 5 feet tall and is standing 30 feet from the base of a light pole, and her shadow is 6 feet long. How high is the light on the pole? To figure this, it helps to make a sketch of the situation:

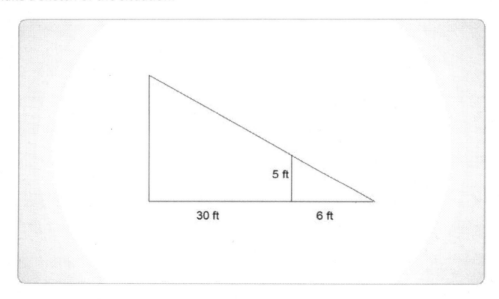

The light pole is the left side of the triangle. Lara is the 5-foot vertical line. Notice that there are two right triangles here, and that they have all the same angles as one another. Therefore, they form similar triangles. So, figure the ratio of proportionality between them.

The bases of these triangles are known. The small triangle, formed by Lara and her shadow, has a base of 6 feet. The large triangle formed by the light pole along with the line from the base of the pole out to the end of Lara's shadow is $30 + 6 = 36$ feet long. So, the ratio of the big triangle to the little triangle will be $\frac{36}{6} = 6$. The height of the little triangle is 5 feet. Therefore, the height of the big triangle will be $6 \times 5 = 30$ feet, meaning that the light is 30 feet up the pole.

Notice that the perimeter of a figure changes by the ratio of proportionality between two similar figures, but the area changes by the **square of the ratio**. This is because if the length of one side is doubled, the area is quadrupled.

As an example, suppose two rectangles are similar, but the edges of the second rectangle are three times longer than the edges of the first rectangle. The area of the first rectangle is 10 square inches. How much more area does the second rectangle have than the first?

To answer this, note that the area of the second rectangle is $3^2 = 9$ times the area of the first rectangle, which is 10 square inches. Therefore, the area of the second rectangle is going to be $9 \times 10 = 90$ square inches. This means it has $90 - 10 = 80$ square inches more area than the first rectangle.

As a second example, suppose X and Y are similar right triangles. The hypotenuse of X is 4 inches. The area of Y is $\frac{1}{4}$ the area of X. What is the hypotenuse of Y?

First, realize the area has changed by a factor of $\frac{1}{4}$. The area changes by a factor that is the *square* of the ratio of changes in lengths, so the ratio of the lengths is the square root of the ratio of areas. That means that the ratio of lengths must be $\sqrt{\frac{1}{4}} = \frac{1}{2}$, and the hypotenuse of Y must be:

$$\frac{1}{2} \times 4 = 2 \text{ inches}$$

Volumes between similar solids change like the cube of the change in the lengths of their edges. Likewise, if the ratio of the volumes between similar solids is known, the ratio between their lengths is known by finding the cube root of the ratio of their volumes.

For example, suppose there are two similar rectangular pyramids X and Y. The base of X is 1 inch by 2 inches, and the volume of X is 8 inches. The volume of Y is 64 inches. What are the dimensions of the base of Y?

To answer this, first find the ratio of the volume of Y to the volume of X. This will be given by $\frac{64}{8} = 8$. Now the ratio of lengths is the cube root of the ratio of volumes, or $\sqrt[3]{8} = 2$. So, the dimensions of the base of Y must be 2 inches by 4 inches.

Practice Quiz

1. At the store, Jan buys $90 of apples and oranges. Apples cost $1 each and oranges cost $2 each. If Jan buys the same number of apples as oranges, how many oranges did she buy?
    a. 20
    b. 25
    c. 30
    d. 35

2. A box with rectangular faces is 5 feet long, 6 feet wide, and 3 feet high. What is its volume?
    a. 60 cubic feet
    b. 75 cubic feet
    c. 90 cubic feet
    d. 100 cubic feet

3. A train traveling 50 miles per hour takes a trip of 3 hours. If a map has a scale of 1 inch per 10 miles, how many inches apart are the train's starting point and ending point on the map?
    a. 10
    b. 12
    c. 13
    d. 15

4. A traveler takes an hour to drive to a museum, spends 3 hours and 30 minutes there, and takes half an hour to drive home. What percentage of this time was spent driving?
    a. 15%
    b. 30%
    c. 40%
    d. 50%

5. A truck is carrying three cylindrical barrels. Their bases have a diameter of 2 feet, and they have a height of 3 feet. What is the total volume of the three barrels in cubic feet?
    a. 3π
    b. 9π
    c. 12π
    d. 15π

See answers on next page

Answer Explanations

1. C: One apple/orange pair costs $3 total. Jan therefore bought $\frac{90}{3} = 30$ total pairs, and hence 30 oranges.

2. C: The volume of a box with rectangular sides is the length times width times height, so:

$$5 \times 6 \times 3 = 90 \text{ cubic feet}$$

3. D: First, the train's journey in the real world is:

$$3 \text{ h} \times 50 \frac{\text{mi}}{\text{h}} = 150 \text{ mi}$$

On the map, 1 inch corresponds to 10 miles, so that is equivalent to:

$$150 \text{ mi} \times \frac{1 \text{ in}}{10 \text{ mi}} = 15 \text{ in}$$

Therefore, the start and end points are 15 inches apart on the map.

4. B: The total trip time is:

$$1 + 3.5 + 0.5 = 5 \text{ hours}$$

The total time driving is:

$$1 + 0.5 = 1.5 \text{ hours}$$

So, the fraction of time spent driving is $\frac{1.5}{5}$, or $\frac{3}{10}$. To convert this to a percentage, multiply the top and bottom by 10 to make the denominator 100. We find $\frac{3}{10} \times \frac{10}{10} = \frac{30}{10}$. Since the denominator is 100, the numerator is our percentage: 30%.

5. B: The formula for the volume of a cylinder is $\pi r^2 h$, where r is the radius and h is the height. The diameter is twice the radius, so these barrels have a radius of 1 foot. That means each barrel has a volume of:

$$\pi \times 1^2 \times 3 = 3\pi \text{ ft}^3$$

Since there are three of them, the total is:

$$3 \times 3\pi = 9\pi \text{ ft}^3$$

Literary Analysis

Style, Tone, and Mood

Style, tone, and mood are often thought to be the same thing. Though they're closely related, there are important differences to keep in mind. The easiest way to do this is to remember that style "creates and affects" tone and mood. More specifically, style is how the writer uses words to create the desired tone and mood for their writing.

Style
Style can include any number of technical writing choices. A few examples of style choices include:

- Sentence Construction: When presenting facts, does the writer use shorter sentences to create a quicker sense of the supporting evidence, or do they use longer sentences to elaborate and explain the information?

- Technical Language: Does the writer use jargon to demonstrate their expertise in the subject, or do they use ordinary language to help the reader understand things in simple terms?

- Formal Language: Does the writer refrain from using contractions such as *won't* or *can't* to create a more formal tone, or do they use a colloquial, conversational style to connect to the reader?

- Formatting: Does the writer use a series of shorter paragraphs to help the reader follow a line of argument, or do they use longer paragraphs to examine an issue in great detail and demonstrate their knowledge of the topic?

On the test, examine the writer's style and how their writing choices affect the way the text comes across.

Tone
Tone refers to the writer's attitude toward the subject matter. Tone conveys how the writer feels about characters, situations, events, ideas, etc. For example, the tone conveys how the writer feels about their characters and the situations in which they're involved.

A lot of nonfiction writing has a neutral tone, which is an important tone for the writer to take. A neutral tone demonstrates that the writer is presenting a topic impartially and letting the information speak for itself. On the other hand, nonfiction writing can be just as effective and appropriate if the tone isn't neutral. For instance, take this example involving seat belts:

> Seat belts save more lives than any other automobile safety feature. Many studies show that airbags save lives as well; however, not all cars have airbags. For instance, some older cars don't. Furthermore, air bags aren't entirely reliable. For example, studies show that in 15% of accidents airbags don't deploy as designed, but, on the other hand, seat belt malfunctions are extremely rare. The number of highway fatalities has plummeted since laws requiring seat belt usage were enacted.

64

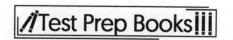

In this passage, the writer mostly chooses to retain a neutral tone when presenting information. If the writer would instead include their own personal experience of losing a friend or family member in a car accident, the tone would change dramatically. The tone would no longer be neutral and would show that the writer has a personal stake in the content, allowing them to interpret the information in a different way. When analyzing tone, consider what the writer is trying to achieve in the text and how they *create* the tone using style.

Mood

Mood refers to the feelings and atmosphere that the writer's words create for the reader. Like tone, many nonfiction texts can have a neutral mood. To return to the previous example, if the writer would choose to include information about a person they know being killed in a car accident, the text would suddenly carry an emotional component that is absent in the previous example. Depending on how they present the information, the writer can create a sad, angry, or even hopeful mood. When analyzing the mood, consider what the writer wants to accomplish and whether the best choice was made to achieve that end.

Consistency

Whatever style, tone, and mood the writer uses, good writing should remain consistent throughout. If the writer chooses to include the tragic, personal experience above, it would affect the style, tone, and mood of the entire text. It would seem out of place for such an example to be used in the middle of a neutral, measured, and analytical text. To adjust the rest of the text, the writer needs to make additional choices to remain consistent. For example, the writer might decide to use the word *tragedy* in place of the more neutral *fatality*, or they could describe a series of car-related deaths as an *epidemic*. Adverbs and adjectives such as *devastating* or *horribly* could be included to maintain this consistent attitude toward the content. When analyzing writing, look for sudden shifts in style, tone, and mood, and consider whether the writer would be wiser to maintain the prevailing strategy.

Identify the Position and Purpose

When it comes to an author's writing, readers should always identify a position or stance. No matter how objective a text may seem, readers should assume the author has preconceived beliefs. One can reduce the likelihood of accepting an invalid argument by looking for multiple articles on the topic, including those with varying opinions. If several opinions point in the same direction and are backed by reputable peer-reviewed sources, it's more likely the author has a valid argument. Positions that run contrary to widely held beliefs and existing data should invite scrutiny. There are exceptions to the rule, so be a careful consumer of information.

Though themes, symbols, and motifs are buried deep within the text and can sometimes be difficult to infer, an author's purpose is usually obvious from the beginning. There are four purposes of writing: to inform, to persuade, to describe, and to entertain. Informative writing presents facts in an accessible way. Persuasive writing appeals to emotions and logic to inspire the reader to adopt a specific stance. Be wary of this type of writing, as it can mask a lack of objectivity with powerful emotion. Descriptive writing is designed to paint a picture in the reader's mind, while texts that entertain are often narratives designed to engage and delight the reader.

The various writing styles are usually blended, with one purpose dominating the rest. A persuasive text, for example, might begin with a humorous tale to make readers more receptive to the persuasive message, or a recipe in a cookbook designed to inform might be preceded by an entertaining anecdote that makes the recipes more appealing.

Identify Passage Characteristics

Writing can be classified under four passage types: narrative, expository, descriptive (sometimes called technical), and persuasive. Though these types are not mutually exclusive, one form tends to dominate the rest. By recognizing the *type* of passage you're reading, you gain insight into *how* you should read. When reading a narrative intended to entertain, sometimes you can read more quickly through the passage if the details are discernible. A technical document, on the other hand, might require a close read, because skimming the passage might cause the reader to miss salient details.

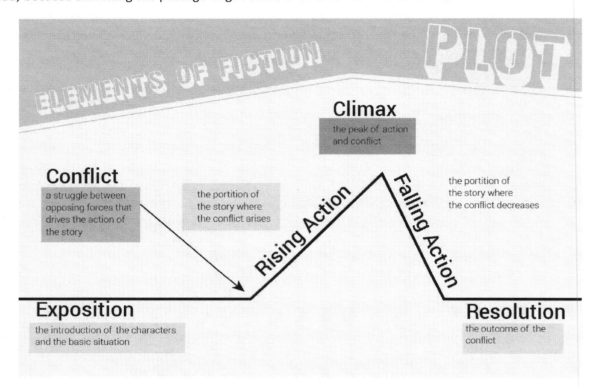

1. Narrative writing, at its core, is the art of storytelling. For a narrative to exist, certain elements must be present. First, it must have characters. While many characters are human, characters could be defined as anything that thinks, acts, and talks like a human. For example, many recent movies, such as *Lord of the Rings* and *The Chronicles of Narnia*, include animals, fantasy creatures, and even trees that behave like humans. Narratives also must have a plot or sequence of events. Typically, those events follow a standard plot diagram, but recent trends start *in medias res* or in the middle (nearer the climax). In this instance, foreshadowing and flashbacks often fill in plot details. Finally, along with characters and a plot, there must also be conflict. Conflict is usually divided into two types: internal and external. Internal conflict indicates the character is in turmoil. Think of an angel on one shoulder and the devil on the other, arguing it out. Internal conflicts are presented through the character's thoughts. External conflicts are visible. Types of external conflict include person versus person, person versus nature, person versus technology, person versus the supernatural, or person versus fate.

2. Expository writing is detached and to the point, while other types of writing — persuasive, narrative, and descriptive — are livelier. Since expository writing is designed to instruct or inform, it usually

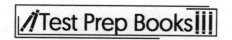
involves directions and steps written in second person ("you" voice) and lacks any persuasive or narrative elements. Sequence words such as *first*, *second*, and *third*, or *in the first place, secondly*, and *lastly* are often given to add fluency and cohesion. Common examples of expository writing include instructor's lessons, cookbook recipes, and repair manuals.

3. Due to its empirical nature, technical writing is filled with steps, charts, graphs, data, and statistics. The goal of technical writing is to advance understanding in a field through the scientific method. Experts such as teachers, doctors, or mechanics use words unique to the profession in which they operate. These words, which often incorporate acronyms, are called **jargon**. Technical writing is a type of expository writing but is not meant to be understood by the general public. Instead, technical writers assume readers have received a formal education in a particular field of study and need no explanation as to what the jargon means. Imagine a doctor trying to understand a diagnostic reading for a car or a mechanic trying to interpret lab results. Only professionals with proper training will fully comprehend the text.

4. Persuasive writing is designed to change opinions and attitudes. The topic, stance, and arguments are found in the thesis, positioned near the end of the introduction. Later supporting paragraphs offer relevant quotations, paraphrases, and summaries from primary or secondary sources, which are then interpreted, analyzed, and evaluated. The goal of persuasive writers is not to stack quotes, but to develop original ideas by using sources as a starting point. Good persuasive writing makes powerful arguments with valid sources and thoughtful analysis. Poor persuasive writing is riddled with bias and logical fallacies. Sometimes logical and illogical arguments are sandwiched together in the same text. Therefore, readers should display skepticism when reading persuasive arguments.

Influences of Historical Context

Studying historical literature is fascinating. It reveals a snapshot in time of people, places, and cultures; a collective set of beliefs and attitudes that no longer exist. Writing changes as attitudes and cultures evolve. Beliefs previously considered immoral or wrong may be considered acceptable today. Researching the historical period of an author gives the reader perspective. The dialogue in Jane Austen's *Pride and Prejudice*, for example, is indicative of social class during the Regency era. Similarly, the stereotypes and slurs in *The Adventures of Huckleberry Finn* were a result of common attitudes and beliefs in the late 1800s, attitudes now found to be reprehensible.

Recognizing Cultural Themes

Regardless of culture, place, or time, certain themes are universal to the human condition. Because humans experience joy, rage, jealousy, and pride, certain themes span centuries. For example, Shakespeare's *Macbeth,* as well as modern works like *The 50th Law* by rapper 50 Cent and Robert Greene or the Netflix series *House of Cards* all feature characters who commit atrocious acts because of ambition. Similarly, *The Adventures of Huckleberry Finn*, published in the 1880s, and *The Catcher in the Rye*, published in the 1950s, both have characters who lie, connive, and survive on their wits.

Moviegoers know whether they are seeing an action, romance or horror film, and are often disappointed if the movie doesn't fit into the conventions of a particular category. Similarly, categories or genres give readers a sense of what to expect from a text. Some of the most basic genres in literature include books, short stories, poetry, and drama. Many genres can be split into sub-genres. For example, the sub-genres of historical fiction, realistic fiction, and fantasy all fit under the fiction genre.

Each genre has a unique way of approaching a particular theme. Books and short stories use plot, characterization, and setting, while poems rely on figurative language, sound devices, and symbolism. Dramas reveal plot through dialogue and the actor's voice and body language.

Paragraph Comprehension

Topic Versus the Main Idea

It is very important to know the difference between the topic and the main idea of the text. Even though these two are similar because they both present the central point of a text, they have distinctive differences. A **topic** is the subject of the text; This can usually be described in a concise one- to two-word phrase. On the other hand, the **main idea** is more detailed and provides the author's central point of the text. It can be expressed through a complete sentence and can be found in the beginning, middle, or end of a paragraph. In most nonfiction books, the first sentence of the passage usually (but not always) states the main idea. Take a look at the passage below to review the topic versus the main idea:

Cheetahs

Cheetahs are one of the fastest mammals on land, reaching up to 70 miles an hour over short distances. Even though cheetahs can run as fast as 70 miles an hour, they usually only have to run half that speed to catch up with their choice of prey. Cheetahs cannot maintain a fast pace over long periods of time because they will overheat their bodies. After a chase, cheetahs need to rest for approximately 30 minutes prior to eating or returning to any other activity.

In the example above, the topic of the passage is "Cheetahs" simply because that is the subject of the text. The main idea of the text is "Cheetahs are one of the fastest mammals on land but can only maintain this fast pace for short distances." While it covers the topic, it is more detailed and refers to the text in its entirety. The text continues to provide additional details called **supporting details,** which will be discussed in the next section.

Supporting Details

Supporting details help readers better develop and understand the main idea. Supporting details answer questions like *who, what, where, when, why,* and *how.* Different types of supporting details include examples, facts and statistics, anecdotes, and sensory details.

Persuasive and informative texts often use supporting details. In persuasive texts, authors attempt to make readers agree with their point of view, and supporting details are often used as "selling points." If authors make a statement, they should support the statement with evidence in order to adequately persuade readers. Informative texts use supporting details such as examples and facts to inform readers. Take another look at the previous "Cheetahs" passage to find examples of supporting details:

Cheetahs

Cheetahs are one of the fastest mammals on land, reaching up to 70 miles an hour over short distances. Even though cheetahs can run as fast as 70 miles an hour, they usually only have to run half that speed to catch up with their choice of prey. Cheetahs cannot maintain a fast pace over long periods of time because they will overheat their bodies. After a chase, cheetahs need to rest for approximately 30 minutes prior to eating or returning to any other activity.

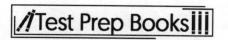

In the example above, supporting details include:

- Cheetahs reach up to 70 miles per hour over short distances.
- They usually only have to run half that speed to catch up with their prey.
- Cheetahs will overheat their bodies if they exert a high speed over longer distances.
- Cheetahs need to rest for 30 minutes after a chase.

Look at the diagram below (applying the cheetah example) to help determine the hierarchy of topic, main idea, and supporting details.

Drawing Conclusions

When drawing conclusions about texts or passages, readers should do two main things: 1) Use the information that they already know and 2) Use the information they have learned from the text or passage. Authors write with an intended purpose, and it is the reader's responsibility to understand and form logical conclusions of authors' ideas. It is important to remember that the reader's conclusions should be supported by information directly from the text. Readers cannot simply form conclusions based off of only information they already know.

There are several ways readers can draw conclusions from authors' ideas, such as note taking, text evidence, text credibility, writing a response to text, directly stated information versus implications, outlining, summarizing, and paraphrasing. Let's take a look at each important strategy to help readers draw logical conclusions.

Note Taking

When readers take notes throughout texts or passages, they are jotting down important facts or points that the author makes. Note taking is a useful record of information that helps readers understand the text or passage and respond to it. When taking notes, readers should keep lines brief and filled with pertinent information so that they are not rereading a large amount of text, but rather just key points, elements, or words. After readers have completed a text or passage, they can refer to their notes to help them form a conclusion about the author's ideas in the text or passage.

Text Evidence

Text evidence is the information readers find in a text or passage that supports the main idea or point(s) in a story. In turn, text evidence can help readers draw conclusions about the text or passage. The information should be taken directly from the text or passage and placed in quotation marks. Text evidence provides readers with information to support ideas about the text so that they do not rely simply on their own thoughts. Details should be precise, descriptive, and factual. Statistics are a great piece of text evidence because they provide readers with exact numbers and not just a generalization. For example, instead of saying "Asia has a larger population than Europe," authors could provide detailed information such as, "In Asia there are over 4 billion people, whereas in Europe there are a little over 750 million." More definitive information provides better evidence to readers to help support their conclusions about texts or passages.

Text Credibility

Credible sources are important when drawing conclusions because readers need to be able to trust what they are reading. Authors should always use credible sources to help gain the trust of their readers. A text is **credible** when it is believable and the author is objective and unbiased. If readers do not trust an author's words, they may simply dismiss the text completely. For example, if an author writes a persuasive essay, he or she is outwardly trying to sway readers' opinions to align with their own. Readers may agree or disagree with the author, which may, in turn, lead them to believe that the author is credible or not credible. Also, readers should keep in mind the source of the text. If readers review a journal about astronomy, would a more reliable source be a NASA employee or a medical doctor? Overall, text credibility is important when drawing conclusions, because readers want reliable sources that support the decisions they have made about the author's ideas.

Writing a Response to Text

Once readers have determined their opinions and validated the credibility of a text, they can then reflect on the text. Writing a response to a text is one way readers can reflect on the given text or passage. When readers write responses to a text, it is important for them to rely on the evidence within the text to support their opinions or thoughts. Supporting evidence such as facts, details, statistics, and quotes directly from the text are key pieces of information readers should reflect upon or use when writing a response to text.

Directly Stated Information Versus Implications

Engaged readers should constantly self-question while reviewing texts to help them form conclusions. Self-questioning is when readers review a paragraph, page, passage, or chapter and ask themselves, "Did I understand what I read?," "What was the main event in this section?," "Where is this taking

70

place?," and so on. Authors can provide clues or pieces of evidence throughout a text or passage to guide readers toward a conclusion. This is why active and engaged readers should read the text or passage in its entirety before forming a definitive conclusion. If readers do not gather all the pieces of evidence needed, then they may jump to an illogical conclusion.

At times, authors directly state conclusions while others simply imply them. Of course, it is easier if authors outwardly provide conclusions to readers because it does not leave any information open to interpretation. On the other hand, implications are things that authors do not directly state but can be assumed based off of information they provided. If authors only imply what may have happened, readers can form a menagerie of ideas for conclusions. For example, look at the following statement: "Once we heard the sirens, we hunkered down in the storm shelter." In this statement, the author does not directly state that there was a tornado, but clues such as "sirens" and "storm shelter" provide insight to the readers to help form that conclusion.

Outlining

An outline is a system used to organize writing. When reading texts, outlining is important because it helps readers organize important information in a logical pattern using roman numerals. Usually, outlines start with the main idea(s) and then branch out into subgroups or subsidiary thoughts of subjects. Not only do outlines provide a visual tool for readers to reflect on how events, characters, settings, or other key parts of the text or passage relate to one another, but they can also lead readers to a stronger conclusion.

The sample below demonstrates what a general outline looks like.

I. Main Topic 1
    a. Subtopic 1
    b. Subtopic 2
        1. Detail 1
        2. Detail 2
II. Main Topic 2
    a. Subtopic 1
    b. Subtopic 2
        1. Detail 1
        2. Detail 2

Summarizing

At the end of a text or passage, it is important to summarize what the readers read. Summarizing is a strategy in which readers determine what is important throughout the text or passage, shorten those ideas, and rewrite or retell it in their own words. A summary should identify the main idea of the text or passage. Important details or supportive evidence should also be accurately reported in the summary. If writers provide irrelevant details in the summary, it may cloud the greater meaning of the summary in the text. When summarizing, writers should not include their opinions, quotes, or what they thought the author should have said. A clear summary provides clarity of the text or passage to the readers. Let's review the checklist of items writers should include in their summary.

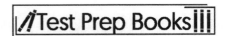
Summary Checklist

- Title of the story
- Someone: Who is or are the main character(s)?
- Wanted: What did the character(s) want?
- But: What was the problem?
- So: How did the character(s) solve the problem?
- Then: How did the story end? What was the resolution?

Paraphrasing

Another strategy readers can use to help them fully comprehend a text or passage is paraphrasing. Paraphrasing is when readers take the author's words and put them into their own words. When readers and writers paraphrase, they should avoid copying the text—that is plagiarism. It is also important to include as many details as possible when restating the facts. Not only will this help readers and writers recall information, but by putting the information into their own words, they demonstrate whether or not they fully comprehend the text or passage. Look at the example below showing an original text and how to paraphrase it.

> *Original Text*: Fenway Park is home to the beloved Boston Red Sox. The stadium opened on April 20, 1912. The stadium currently seats over 37,000 fans, many of whom travel from all over the country to experience the iconic team and nostalgia of Fenway Park.

> *Paraphrased*: On April 20, 1912, Fenway Park opened. Home to the Boston Red Sox, the stadium now seats over 37,000 fans. Many spectators travel to watch the Red Sox and experience the spirit of Fenway Park.

Paraphrasing, summarizing, and quoting can often cross paths with one another. Review the chart below showing the similarities and differences between the three strategies.

Paraphrasing	Summarizing	Quoting
Uses own words	Puts main ideas into own words	Uses words that are identical to text
References original source	References original source	Requires quotation marks
Uses own sentences	Shows important ideas of source	Uses author's own words and ideas

Inferences in a Text

Readers should be able to make **inferences**. Making an inference requires the reader to read between the lines and look for what is implied rather than what is explicitly stated. That is, using information that is known from the text, the reader is able to make a logical assumption about information that is not explicitly stated but is probably true.

Read the following passage:

> "Hey, do you wanna meet my new puppy?" Jonathan asked.
>
> "Oh, I'm sorry but please don't—" Jacinta began to protest, but before she could finish, Jonathan had already opened the passenger side door of his car and a perfect white ball of fur came bouncing towards Jacinta.
>
> "Isn't he the cutest?" beamed Jonathan.
>
> "Yes—achoo!—he's pretty—aaaachooo!!—adora—aaa—aaaachoo!" Jacinta managed to say in between sneezes. "But if you don't mind, I—I—achoo!—need to go inside."

Which of the following can be inferred from Jacinta's reaction to the puppy?
   a. She hates animals.
   b. She is allergic to dogs.
   c. She prefers cats to dogs.
   d. She is angry at Jonathan.

An inference requires the reader to consider the information presented and then form their own idea about what is probably true. Based on the details in the passage, what is the best answer to the question? Important details to pay attention to include the tone of Jacinta's dialogue, which is overall polite and apologetic, as well as her reaction itself, which is a long string of sneezes. Answer choices (a) and (d) both express strong emotions ("hates" and "angry") that are not evident in Jacinta's speech or actions. Answer choice (c) mentions cats, but there is nothing in the passage to indicate Jacinta's feelings about cats. Answer choice (b), "she is allergic to dogs," is the most logical choice. Based on the fact that she began sneezing as soon as a fluffy dog approached her, it makes sense to guess that Jacinta might be allergic to dogs. Using the clues in the passage, it is reasonable to guess that this is true even though Jacinta never directly states, "Sorry, I'm allergic to dogs!"

Making inferences is crucial for readers of literature because literary texts often avoid presenting complete and direct information to readers about characters' thoughts or feelings, or they present this information in an unclear way, leaving it up to the reader to interpret clues given in the text. In order to make inferences while reading, readers should ask themselves:

- What details are being presented in the text?
- Is there any important information that seems to be missing?
- Based on the information that the author *does* include, what else is probably true?
- Is this inference reasonable based on what is already known?

Apply Information

A natural extension of being able to make an inference from a given set of information is also being able to apply that information to a new context. This is especially useful in non-fiction or informative writing. Considering the facts and details presented in the text, readers should consider how the same information might be relevant in a different situation. The following is an example of applying an inferential conclusion to a different context:

> Often, individuals behave differently in large groups than they do as individuals. One example of this is the psychological phenomenon known as the bystander effect. According to the

bystander effect, the more people who witness an accident or crime occur, the less likely each individual bystander is to respond or offer assistance to the victim. A classic example of this is the murder of Kitty Genovese in New York City in the 1960s. Although there were over thirty witnesses to her killing by a stabber, none of them intervened to help Kitty or contact the police.

Considering the phenomenon of the bystander effect, what would probably happen if somebody tripped on the stairs in a crowded subway station?
    a. Everybody would stop to help the person who tripped
        b. Bystanders would point and laugh at the person who tripped
        c. Someone would call the police after walking away from the station
        d. Few if any bystanders would offer assistance to the person who tripped

This question asks readers to apply the information they learned from the passage, which is an informative paragraph about the bystander effect. According to the passage, this is a concept in psychology that describes the way people in groups respond to an accident—the more people are present, the less likely any one person is to intervene. While the passage illustrates this effect with the example of a woman's murder, the question asks readers to apply it to a different context—in this case, someone falling down the stairs in front of many subway passengers. Although this specific situation is not discussed in the passage, readers should be able to apply the general concepts described in the paragraph. The definition of the bystander effect includes any instance of an accident or crime in front of a large group of people. The question asks about a situation that falls within the same definition, so the general concept should still hold true: in the midst of a large crowd, few individuals are likely to actually respond to an accident. In this case, answer choice (d) is the best response.

Author's Use of Language

Authors utilize a wide range of techniques to tell a story or communicate information. Readers should be familiar with the most common of these techniques. Techniques of writing are also commonly known as **rhetorical devices**.

Types of Appeals

In non-fiction writing, authors employ argumentative techniques to present their opinion to readers in the most convincing way. Persuasive writing usually includes at least one type of **appeal**: an appeal to logic (*logos*), emotion (*pathos*), or credibility and trustworthiness (*ethos*). When a writer appeals to logic, they are asking readers to agree with them based on research, evidence, and an established line of reasoning. An author's argument might also appeal to readers' emotions, perhaps by including personal stories and **anecdotes** (a short narrative of a specific event). A final type of appeal, appeal to authority, asks the reader to agree with the author's argument on the basis of their expertise or credentials. Consider three different approaches to arguing the same opinion:

<u>Logic (Logos)</u>
This is an example of an appeal to logic:

> Our school should abolish its current ban on campus cell phone use. The ban was adopted last year as an attempt to reduce class disruptions and help students focus more on their lessons. However, since the rule was enacted, there has been no change in the number of disciplinary problems in class. Therefore, the rule is ineffective and should be done away with.

74

The author uses evidence to disprove the logic of the school's rule (the rule was supposed to reduce discipline problems, but the number of problems has not been reduced; therefore, the rule is not working) and call for its repeal.

Emotion (Pathos)

An author's argument might also appeal to readers' emotions, perhaps by including personal stories and anecdotes. The next example presents an appeal to emotion. By sharing the personal anecdote of one student and speaking about emotional topics like family relationships, the author invokes the reader's empathy in asking them to reconsider the school rule.

> Our school should abolish its current ban on campus cell phone use. If students aren't able to use their phones during the school day, many of them feel isolated from their loved ones. For example, last semester, one student's grandmother had a heart attack in the morning. However, because he couldn't use his cell phone, the student didn't know about his grandmother's accident until the end of the day—when she had already passed away, and it was too late to say goodbye. By preventing students from contacting their friends and family, our school is placing undue stress and anxiety on students.

Credibility (Ethos)

Finally, an appeal to authority includes a statement from a relevant expert. In this case, the author uses a doctor in the field of education to support the argument. All three examples begin from the same opinion—the school's phone ban needs to change—but rely on different argumentative styles to persuade the reader.

> Our school should abolish its current ban on campus cell phone use. According to Dr. Bartholomew Everett, a leading educational expert, "Research studies show that cell phone usage has no real impact on student attentiveness. Rather, phones provide a valuable technological resource for learning. Schools need to learn how to integrate this new technology into their curriculum." Rather than banning phones altogether, our school should follow the advice of experts and allow students to use phones as part of their learning.

Rhetorical Questions

Another commonly used argumentative technique is asking rhetorical questions, questions that do not actually require an answer but that push the reader to consider the topic further.

> I wholly disagree with the proposal to ban restaurants from serving foods with high sugar and sodium contents. Do we really want to live in a world where the government can control what we eat? I prefer to make my own food choices.

Here, the author's rhetorical question prompts readers to put themselves in a hypothetical situation and imagine how they would feel about it.

Figurative Language

Literary texts also employ rhetorical devices. Figurative language like simile and metaphor is a type of rhetorical device commonly found in literature. In addition to rhetorical devices that play on the *meanings* of words, there are also rhetorical devices that use the *sounds* of words. These devices are most often found in poetry but may also be found in other types of literature and in non-fiction writing like speech texts.

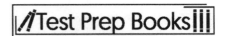

Alliteration and **assonance** are both varieties of sound repetition. Other types of sound repetition include: anaphora, repetition that occurs at the beginning of the sentences; epiphora, repetition occurring at the end of phrases; antimetabole, repetition of words in reverse order; and antiphrasis, a form of denial of an assertion in a text.

Alliteration refers to the repetition of the first sound of each word. Recall Robert Burns' opening line:

> My love is like a red, red rose

This line includes two instances of alliteration: "love" and "like" (repeated *L* sound), as well as "red" and "rose" (repeated *R* sound). Next, assonance refers to the repetition of vowel sounds, and can occur anywhere within a word (not just the opening sound). Here is the opening of a poem by John Keats:

> When I have fears that I may cease to be
>
> Before my pen has glean'd my teeming brain

Assonance can be found in the words "fears," "cease," "be," "glean'd," and "teeming," all of which stress the long *E* sound. Both alliteration and assonance create a harmony that unifies the writer's language.

Another sound device is **onomatopoeia**, or words whose spelling mimics the sound they describe. Words such as "crash," "bang," and "sizzle" are all examples of onomatopoeia. Use of onomatopoetic language adds auditory imagery to the text.

Readers are probably most familiar with the technique of **pun**. A pun is a play on words, taking advantage of two words that have the same or similar pronunciation. Puns can be found throughout Shakespeare's plays, for instance:

> Now is the winter of our discontent
> Made glorious summer by this son of York

These lines from *Richard III* contain a play on words. Richard III refers to his brother, the newly crowned King Edward IV, as the "son of York," referencing their family heritage from the house of York. However, while drawing a comparison between the political climate and the weather (times of political trouble were the "winter," but now the new king brings "glorious summer"), Richard's use of the word "son" also implies another word with the same pronunciation, "sun"—so Edward IV is also like the sun, bringing light, warmth, and hope to England. Puns are a clever way for writers to suggest two meanings at once.

Counterarguments

If an author presents a differing opinion or a counterargument in order to refute it, the reader should consider how and why the information is being presented. It is meant to strengthen the original argument and shouldn't be confused with the author's intended conclusion, but it should also be considered in the reader's final evaluation.

Authors can also use bias if they ignore the opposing viewpoint or present their side in an unbalanced way. A strong argument considers the opposition and finds a way to refute it. Critical readers should look for an unfair or one-sided presentation of the argument and be skeptical, as a bias may be present. Even if this bias is unintentional, if it exists in the writing, the reader should be wary of the validity of the

76

argument. Readers should also look for the use of stereotypes, which refer to specific groups. Stereotypes are often negative connotations about a person or place and should always be avoided. When a critical reader finds stereotypes in a piece of writing, they should be critical of the argument, and consider the validity of anything the author presents. Stereotypes reveal a flaw in the writer's thinking and may suggest a lack of knowledge or understanding about the subject.

Meaning of Words in Context

There will be many occasions in one's reading career in which an unknown word or a word with multiple meanings will pop up. There are ways of determining what these words or phrases mean that do not require the use of the dictionary, which is especially helpful during a test where one may not be available. Even outside of the exam, knowing how to derive an understanding of a word via context clues will be a critical skill in the real world. The context is the circumstances in which a story or a passage is happening and can usually be found in the series of words directly before or directly after the word or phrase in question. The clues are the words that hint towards the meaning of the unknown word or phrase.

There may be questions that ask about the meaning of a particular word or phrase within a passage. There are a couple ways to approach these kinds of questions:

1. Define the word or phrase in a way that is easy to comprehend (using context clues).
2. Try out each answer choice in place of the word.

To demonstrate, here's an example from *Alice in Wonderland*:

> Alice was beginning to get very tired of sitting by her sister on the bank, and of having nothing to do: once or twice she <u>peeped</u> into the book her sister was reading, but it had no pictures or conversations in it, "and what is the use of a book," thought Alice, "without pictures or conversations?"

Q: As it is used in the selection, the word <u>peeped</u> means:

Using the first technique, before looking at the answers, define the word *peeped* using context clues and then find the matching answer. Then, analyze the entire passage in order to determine the meaning, not just the surrounding words.

To begin, imagine a blank where the word should be and put a synonym or definition there: "once or twice she _____ into the book her sister was reading." The context clue here is the book. It may be tempting to put *read* where the blank is, but notice the preposition word, *into*. One does not read *into* a book, one simply reads a book, and since reading a book requires that it is seen with a pair of eyes, then *look* would make the most sense to put into the blank: "once or twice she <u>looked </u>into the book her sister was reading."

Once an easy-to-understand word or synonym has been supplanted, readers should check to make sure it makes sense with the rest of the passage. What happened after she looked into the book? She thought to herself how a book without pictures or conversations is useless. This situation in its entirety makes sense.

Now check the answer choices for a match:
   a. To make a high-pitched cry
   b. To smack
   c. To look curiously
   d. To pout

Since the word was already defined, Choice *C* is the best option.

Using the second technique, replace the figurative blank with each of the answer choices and determine which one is the most appropriate. Remember to look further into the passage to clarify that they work, because they could still make sense out of context.
   a. Once or twice, she <u>made a high pitched cry</u> into the book her sister was reading
   b. Once or twice, she <u>smacked</u> into the book her sister was reading
   c. Once or twice, she <u>looked curiously</u> into the book her sister was reading
   d. Once or twice, she <u>pouted</u> into the book her sister was reading

For Choice *A*, it does not make much sense in any context for a person to cry into a book, unless maybe something terrible has happened in the story. Given that afterward Alice thinks to herself how useless a book without pictures is, this option does not make sense within context.

For Choice *B*, smacking a book someone is reading may make sense if the rest of the passage indicates a reason for doing so. If Alice was angry or her sister had shoved it in her face, then maybe smacking the book would make sense within context. However, since whatever she does with the book causes her to think, "what is the use of a book without pictures or conversations?" then answer Choice *B* is not an appropriate answer. Answer Choice *C* fits well within context, given her subsequent thoughts on the matter. Answer Choice *D* does not make sense in context or grammatically, as people do not "pout into" things.

This is a simple example to illustrate the techniques outlined above. There may, however, be a question in which all of the definitions are correct and also make sense out of context, in which the appropriate context clues will really need to be honed in on in order to determine the correct answer. For example, here is another passage from *Alice in Wonderland*:

> ... but when the Rabbit actually took a watch out of its waistcoat pocket, and looked at it, and then hurried on, Alice <u>started</u> to her feet, for it flashed across her mind that she had never before seen a rabbit with either a waistcoat-pocket or a watch to take out of it, and burning with curiosity, she ran across the field after it, and was just in time to see it pop down a large rabbit-hole under the hedge.

Q: As it is used in the passage, the word started means _____.
   a. to turn on
   b. to begin
   c. to move quickly
   d. to be surprised

All of these words qualify as a definition of *start*, but using context clues, the correct answer can be identified using one of the two techniques above. It's easy to see that one does not turn on, begin, or be surprised to one's feet. The selection also states that she "ran across the field after it," indicating that she was in a hurry. Therefore, to move quickly would make the most sense in this context.

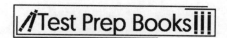

The same strategies can be applied to vocabulary that may be completely unfamiliar. In this case, focus on the words before or after the unknown word in order to determine its definition. Take this sentence, for example:

> Sam was such a <u>miser</u> that he forced Andrew to pay him twelve cents for the candy, even though he had a large inheritance and he knew his friend was poor.

Unlike with assertion questions, for vocabulary questions, it may be necessary to apply some critical thinking skills when something isn't explicitly stated within the passage. Think about the implications of the passage, or what the text is trying to say. With this example, it is important to realize that it is considered unusually stingy for a person to demand so little money from someone instead of just letting their friend have the candy, especially if this person is already wealthy. Hence, a <u>miser</u> is a greedy or stingy individual.

Questions about complex vocabulary may not be explicitly asked, but this is a useful skill to know. If there is an unfamiliar word while reading a passage and its definition goes unknown, it is possible to miss out on a critical message that could inhibit the ability to appropriately answer the questions. Practicing this technique in daily life will sharpen this ability to derive meanings from context clues with ease.

Practice Quiz

Directions: Assume each passage below to be true. Then, pick the answer choice that best answers the question.

1. Samuel teaches at a high school in one of the biggest cities in the United States. His students come from diverse family backgrounds. Samuel observes that the best students in his class are from homes where parental supervision is minimal. The parents of the bottom five students are the most involved, by a large margin. There are 24 students in his class.

What is true about the students that Samuel teaches?
    a. They are not a diverse group of students.
    b. The students with the most involved parents have the worst academic performance.
    c. The best students in his class have the most parental supervision.
    d. Only five students have parents that provide minimal supervision.

2. A famous children's author recently published a historical fiction novel under a pseudonym; however, it did not sell as many copies as her children's books. In her earlier years, she had majored in history and earned a graduate degree in Antebellum American History, which is the time frame of her new novel. Critics praised this newest work far more than the children's series that made her famous. In fact, her new novel was nominated for the prestigious Albert J. Beveridge Award but still isn't selling like her children's books, which fly off the shelves because of her name alone.

What made the children's author famous?
    a. Being nominated for a prestigious award
    b. Her historical fiction novel
    c. Her children's series
    d. Using a pseudonym for her new novel

3. Reggie had been preparing for his part in the play for several months. His mother had even knitted him a costume. That night when he went on stage, his entire family and all his friends were there to watch, and he was mortified when his costume split in half. Afterwards, his mother admitted that she was not the best of seamstresses.

When did Reggie's costume split in half?
    a. While he was preparing for the play
    b. While his mother was knitting it
    c. During the play
    d. After the play

4. The reason for different breeds of dogs is that there were specific needs that humans wanted to fill with their animals. For example, scent hounds are known for their extraordinary ability to track game through scent. These breeds are also known for their endurance in seeking deer and other prey. Therefore, early hunters took dogs that displayed these abilities and bred them to encourage these traits.

What is the main purpose of the passage?
    a. To explain the abilities and traits of scent hounds
    b. To describe early hunting techniques
    c. To explain one of the needs of humans that was filled by breeding dogs
    d. To show that scent hounds are the best breed for hunting

5. The RV was a great purchase for our family and brought us all closer together. Every morning we would wake up, eat breakfast, and break camp. We laughed at our own comical attempts to back The Beast into spaces that seemed impossibly small. When things inevitably went wrong and we couldn't solve the problems on our own, we discovered the incredible helpfulness and friendliness of the RV community. We even made some new friends in the process.

According the passage, what did the family discover?

    a.   The best way to back an RV into small spaces

    b.   That the RV community is friendly and helpful

    c.   That as a family they could solve problems on their own

    d.   That it's impossible to make friends when you break camp each morning

See answers on next page

Answer Explanations

1. B: Choice *B* is correct. The passage states that the parents of the bottom five students are the most involved. Choice *A* is incorrect. The passage states that Samuel's students come from diverse backgrounds. Choice *C* is incorrect. Samuel has observed that the best students have minimal parental supervision, not the most supervision. Choice *D* is incorrect. The passage does not give the number of students who have minimal supervision. It only states that the best students have minimal supervision. Five is the number of the students who have the most involved parents. There are 19 other students in the class, but even with this information, we cannot determine how many students have minimal supervision. Some parents might be right in the middle, providing moderate supervision.

2. C: It is stated in the passage that her new work was praised far more than the children's series that made her famous. Therefore, Choice *C* is correct. Choice *A* is incorrect. She was nominated for the Albert J. Beveridge Award, but this is not what made her famous. Choice *B* is incorrect. Although critics praised her new historical fiction novel more than they praised her children's series, it's the children's series, not the new novel, that made her famous. Choice *D* is incorrect. The author did not become famous for using a pseudonym. She was already famous for her children's series before she wrote a new novel under a pseudonym.

3. C: Choice *C* is correct. The passage states that on the night he went on stage he was mortified when his costume split in half. Choice *A* is incorrect. His costume did not split in half while he was preparing for the play. Choice *B* is incorrect. It did not split open while his mother was knitting it. Choice *D* is incorrect. After the play, his mother admitted that she was not a good seamstress, but this is not when the costume split in half.

4. C: The passage begins by stating that the reason that there are different breeds of dogs is that humans needed to use animals to fill specific needs. It goes on the explain why scent hounds are good for hunting, and it ends by stating that early hunters bred the dogs to encourage their traits. Therefore, the best answer choice is Choice *C*. The passage is explaining one of the needs—hunting—that was filled by breeding dogs with excellent hunting abilities. Choice *A* is incorrect. Although the traits are described, they aren't the main purpose of the passage. These descriptions are used to demonstrate one reason why humans began to breed dogs. Choice *B* is incorrect. Early hunters bred dogs with certain abilities, but early hunting techniques are not discussed. Choice *D* is incorrect. The purpose of the passage is not to show that scent hounds are the best hunting breed. The passage does not state which breed is the best for hunting.

5. B: Choice *B* is correct. Things inevitably went wrong for the family and there were problems they couldn't solve on their own, and this is how they discovered that the RV community is incredibly helpful and friendly. This can also be proof that Choice *C* is incorrect. Choice *A* is incorrect. The passage never states that the family learned how to back the RV into small spaces. Choice *D* is incorrect. Making friends and breaking camp daily are both mentioned in the passage, but a connection is never made between the two. In fact, the passage states that the family made new friends.

Mechanical Comprehension

The *Mechanical Comprehension (MC)* section tests a candidate's knowledge of mechanics and physical principles. These include concepts of force, energy, and work, and how they're used to predict the functioning of tools and machines. This knowledge is important for a successful career in the military. A good score on the MC test shows that a candidate has a solid background for learning how to use tools and machines properly. This is extremely important for the efficient, safe completion of most tasks a future soldier, sailor, or airman must undertake during their service.

The test problems in the MC section of the exam focus on understanding physical principles, but they are *qualitative* in nature rather than *quantitative*. This means the problems involve predicting the *behavior* of a system (such as the direction it moves) rather than calculating a specific measurement (such as its velocity). The figure below shows a sample problem similar to those on the MC test:

Mechanical Comprehension Sample Test Problem

Question 1.

Extending the reach of this crane will shift its

- ○ **A.** total weight
- ○ **B.** allowable speed
- ○ **C.** center of gravity
- ○ **D.** center of buoyancy

The sample problem pictures a system of a crane lifting a weight, and below the picture is a question. On the exam, it's *very important* to read these questions *carefully*. This question involves completing the following sentence: *Extending the reach of this crane will shift its _____.* After the sentence, four possible answers are provided.

The correct answer is *C, center of gravity*. In this sample problem, it's easy to guess the correct answer simply by eliminating the rest. Answer *A* is incorrect because moving the load out along the crane's boom won't change its weight, just like moving a bodybuilder's arm that's holding a dumbbell won't change the combined weight of the bodybuilder and the dumbbell. Answer *B* is incorrect because the crane isn't moving. That leaves Answers *C* and *D*, but *D* is incorrect because buoyancy is only involved in systems with a liquid (the buoyancy of air is negligible). Therefore, through the process of elimination, *C* is the correct answer.

Review of Physics and Mechanical Principles

The proper use of tools and machinery depends on an understanding of basic physics, which includes the study of motion and the interactions of *mass*, *force*, and *energy*. These terms are used every day, but their exact meanings are difficult to define. In fact, they're usually defined in terms of each other.

The matter in the universe (atoms and molecules) is characterized in terms of its **mass**, which is measured in kilograms in the **International System of Units (SI)**. The amount of mass that occupies a given volume of space is termed **density**.

Mass occupies space, but it's also a component that inversely relates to acceleration when a force is applied to it. This **force** is the application of *energy* to an object with the intent of changing its position (mainly its acceleration).

To understand acceleration, it's necessary to relate it to displacement and velocity. The **displacement** of an object is simply the distance it travels. The **velocity** of an object is the distance it travels in a unit of time, such as miles per hour or meters per second:

$$Velocity = \frac{Distance\ Traveled}{Time\ Required}$$

There's often confusion between the words "speed" and "velocity." Velocity includes speed *and* direction. For example, a car traveling east and another traveling west can have the same speed of 30 miles per hour (mph), but their velocities are different. If movement eastward is considered positive, then movement westward is negative. Thus, the eastbound car has a velocity of 30 mph while the westbound car has a velocity of −30 mph.

The fact that velocity has a **magnitude** (speed) and a direction makes it a vector quantity. A **vector** is an arrow pointing in the direction of motion, with its length proportional to its magnitude.

Vectors can be added geometrically as shown below. In this example, a boat is traveling east at 4 *knots* (nautical miles per hour) and there's a current of 3 knots (thus a slow boat and a very fast current). If the boat travels in the same direction as the current, it gets a "lift" from the current and its speed is 7 knots. If the boat heads *into* the current, it has a forward speed of only 1 knot (4 knots – 3 knots = 1 knot) and makes very little headway. As shown in the figure below, the current is flowing north across the boat's path. Thus, for every 4 miles of progress the boat makes eastward, it drifts 3 miles to the north.

Working with Velocity Vectors

Distance traveled in one hour = 5 nautical miles

Current = 3 knots

Boat Speed = 4 knots

The total distance traveled is calculated using the **Pythagorean Theorem** for a right triangle, which should be memorized as follows:

$$a2 + b2 = c2 \text{ or } c = \sqrt{a^2 + b^2}$$

Of course, the problem above was set up using a Pythagorean triple (3, 4, 5), which made the calculation easy.

Another example where velocity and speed are different is with a car traveling around a bend in the road. The speed is constant along the road, but the direction (and therefore the velocity) changes continuously.

The **acceleration** of an object is the change in its velocity in a given period of time:

$$Acceleration = \frac{Change\ in\ Velocity}{Time\ Required}$$

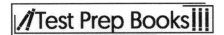
For example, a car starts at rest and then reaches a velocity of 70 mph in 8 seconds. What's the car's acceleration in feet per second squared? First, the velocity must be converted from miles per hour to feet per second:

$$70\,\frac{miles}{hour} \times \frac{5,280\,feet}{mile} \times \frac{hour}{3600\,seconds} = 102.67\,feet/second$$

Starting from rest, the acceleration is:

$$Acceleration = \frac{102.67\,\dfrac{feet}{second} - 0\,\dfrac{feet}{second}}{8\,seconds} = 12.8\,feet/second^2$$

Newton's Laws

Isaac Newton's three laws of motion describe how the acceleration of an object is related to its mass and the forces acting on it. The three laws are:

- Unless acted on by a force, a body at rest tends to remain at rest; a body in motion tends to remain in motion with a constant velocity and direction.

- A force that acts on a body accelerates it in the direction of the force. The larger the force, the greater the acceleration; the larger the mass, the greater its inertia (resistance to movement and acceleration).

- Every force acting on a body is resisted by an equal and opposite force.

To understand Newton's laws, it's necessary to understand forces. These forces can push or pull on a mass, and they have a magnitude and a direction. Forces are represented by a vector, which is the arrow lined up along the direction of the force with its tip at the point of application. The magnitude of the force is represented by the length of the vector.

The figure below shows a mass acted on or "pushed" by two equal forces (shown here by vectors of the same length). Both vectors "push" along the same line through the center of the mass, but in opposite directions. What happens?

A Mass Acted on by Equal and Opposite Forces

According to Newton's third law, every force on a body is resisted by an equal and opposite force. In the figure above, Force 1 acts on the left side of the mass. The mass pushes back. Force 2 acts on the right side, and the mass pushes back against this force too. The net force on the mass is zero, so according to Newton's first law, there's no change in the **momentum** (the mass times its velocity) of the mass. Therefore, if the mass is at rest before the forces are applied, it remains at rest. If the mass is in motion with a constant velocity, its momentum doesn't change. So, what happens when the net force on the mass isn't zero, as shown in the figure below?

A Mass Acted on by Unbalanced Forces

Mass

Notice that the forces are vector quantities and are added geometrically the same way that velocity vectors are manipulated.

Here in the figure above, the mass is pulled by two forces acting to the right, so the mass accelerates in the direction of the net force. This is described by Newton's second law:

Force = Mass x Acceleration

The force (measured in *newtons*) is equal to the product of the mass (measured in kilograms) and its acceleration (measured in meters per second squared or meters per second, per second). A better way to look at the equation is dividing through by the mass:

Acceleration = Force/Mass

This form of the equation makes it easier to see that the acceleration of an object varies directly with the net force applied and inversely with the mass. Thus, as the mass increases, the acceleration is reduced for a given force. To better understand, think of how a baseball accelerates when hit by a bat. Now imagine hitting a cannonball with the same bat and the same force. The cannonball is more massive than the baseball, so it won't accelerate very much when hit by the bat.

In addition to forces acting on a body by touching it, gravity acts as a force at a distance and causes all bodies in the universe to attract each other. The **force of gravity (F_g)** is proportional to the masses of the two objects (*m* and *M*) and inversely proportional to the square of the distance (r^2) between them (and *G* is the proportionality constant). This is shown in the following equation:

$$F_g = G \frac{mM}{r^2}$$

The force of gravity is what causes an object to fall to Earth when dropped. Understanding gravity helps explain the difference between mass and weight. Mass is a property of an object that remains the same while it's intact, no matter where it's located. A 10-kilogram cannonball has the same mass on Earth as it does on the moon. On Earth, it *weighs* 98.1 newtons because of the attractive force of gravity, so it accelerates at 9.81 m/s². However, on the moon, the same cannonball has a weight of only about 16 newtons. This is because the gravitational attraction on the moon is approximately one-sixth that on Earth. Although Earth still attracts the body on the moon, it's so far away that its force is negligible.

For Americans, there's often confusion when talking about mass because the United States still uses "pounds" as a measurement of weight. In the traditional system used in the United States, the unit of mass is called a **slug**. It's derived by dividing the weight in pounds by the acceleration of gravity (32 feet/s²); however, it's rarely used today. To avoid future problems, test takers should continue using SI units and *remember to express mass in kilograms and weight in Newtons*.

Another way to understand Newton's second law is to think of it as an object's change in momentum, which is defined as the product of the object's mass and its velocity:

$$Momentum = Mass \times Velocity$$

Which of the following has the greater momentum: a pitched baseball, a softball, or a bullet fired from a rifle?

A bullet with a mass of 5 grams (0.005 kilograms) is fired from a rifle with a muzzle velocity of 2200 mph. Its momentum is calculated as:

$$2200 \frac{miles}{hour} \times \frac{5,280\ feet}{mile} \times \frac{m}{3.28\ feet} \times \frac{hour}{3600\ seconds} \times 0.005kg = 4.92 \frac{kg.m}{seconds}$$

A softball has a mass between 177 grams and 198 grams and is thrown by a college pitcher at 50 miles per hour. Taking an average mass of 188 grams (0.188 kilograms), a softball's momentum is calculated as:

$$50 \frac{miles}{hour} \times \frac{5280\ feet}{mile} \times \frac{m}{3.28\ ft} \times \frac{hour}{3600\ seconds} \times 0.188kg = 4.19 \frac{kg.m}{seconds}$$

That's only slightly less than the momentum of the bullet. Although the speed of the softball is considerably less, its mass is much greater than the bullet's.

A professional baseball pitcher can throw a 145-gram baseball at 100 miles per hour. A similar calculation (try doing it!) shows that the pitched hardball has a momentum of about 6.48 kg.m/seconds. That's more momentum than a speeding bullet!

So why is the bullet more harmful than the hard ball? It's because the force that it applies acts on a much smaller area.

Instead of using acceleration, Newton's second law is expressed here as the change in momentum (with the delta symbol "Δ" meaning "change"):

$$Force = \frac{\Delta\ Momentum}{\Delta\ Time} = \frac{\Delta\ (Mass \times Velocity)}{\Delta\ Time} = Mass \times \frac{\Delta\ Velocity}{\Delta\ Time}$$

The rapid application of force is called **impulse**. Another way of stating Newton's second law is in terms of the impulse, which is the force multiplied by its time of application:

$$Impluse = Force \times \Delta\ Time = Mass \times \Delta\ Velocity$$

In the case of the rifle, the force created by the pressure of the charge's explosion in its shell pushes the bullet, accelerating it until it leaves the barrel of the gun with its **muzzle velocity** (the speed the bullet has when it leaves the muzzle). After leaving the gun, the bullet doesn't accelerate because the gas pressure is exhausted. The bullet travels with a constant velocity in the direction it's fired (ignoring the force exerted against the bullet by friction and drag).

Similarly, the pitcher applies a force to the ball by using their muscles when throwing. Once the ball leaves the pitcher's fingers, it doesn't accelerate and the ball travels toward the batter at a constant speed (again ignoring friction and drag). The speed is constant, but the velocity can change if the ball travels along a curve.

Projectile Motion

According to Newton's first law, if no additional forces act on the bullet or ball, it travels in a straight line. This is also true if the bullet is fired in outer space. However, here on Earth, the force of gravity continues to act so the motion of the bullet or ball is affected.

What happens when a bullet is fired from the top of a hill using a rifle held perfectly horizontal? Ignoring air resistance, its horizontal velocity remains constant at its muzzle velocity. Its vertical velocity (which is zero when it leaves the gun barrel) increases because of gravity's acceleration. Each passing second, the bullet traces out the same distance horizontally while increasing distance vertically (shown in the figure below). In the end, the projectile traces out a **parabolic curve**.

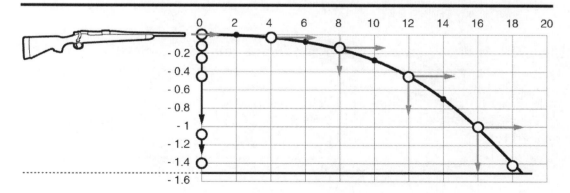

Projectile Path for a Bullet Fired Horizontally from a Hill (Ignoring Air Resistance)

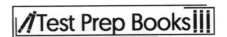
This vertical, downward acceleration is why a pitcher must put an arc on the ball when throwing across home plate. Otherwise, the ball will fall at the batter's feet.

It's also interesting to note that if an artillery crew simultaneously drops one cannonball and fires another one horizontally, the two cannonballs will hit the ground at the same time since both balls are accelerating at the same rate and experience the same changes in vertical velocity.

What if air resistance is taken into account? This is best answered by looking at the horizontal and vertical motions separately.

The horizontal velocity is no longer constant because the initial velocity of the projectile is continually reduced by the resistance of the air. This is a complex problem in fluid mechanics, but it's sufficient to note that that the projectile doesn't fly as far before landing as predicted from the simple theory.

The vertical velocity is also reduced by air resistance. However, unlike the horizontal motion where the propelling force is zero after the cannonball is fired, the downward force of gravity acts continuously. The downward velocity increases every second due to the acceleration of gravity. As the velocity increases, the resisting force (called **drag**) increases with the square of the velocity. If the projectile is fired or dropped from a sufficient height, it reaches a terminal velocity such that the upward drag force equals the downward force of gravity. When that occurs, the projectile falls at a constant rate.

This is the same principle that's used for a parachute. Its drag (caused by its shape that scoops up air) is sufficient enough to slow down the fall of the parachutist to a safe velocity, thus avoiding a fatal crash on the ground.

So, what's the bottom line? If the vertical height isn't too great, a real projectile will fall short of the theoretical point of impact. However, if the height of the fall is significant and the drag of the object results in a small terminal fall velocity, then the projectile can go further than the theoretical point of impact.

What if the projectile is launched from a moving platform? In this case, the platform's velocity is added to the projectile's velocity. That's why an object dropped from the mast of a moving ship lands at the base of the mast rather than behind it. However, to an observer on the shore, the object traces out a parabolic arc.

Angular Momentum

In the previous examples, all forces acted through the center of the mass, but what happens if the forces aren't applied through the same line of action, like in the figure below?

A Mass Acted on by Forces Out of Line with Each Other

90

When this happens, the two forces create **torque** and the mass rotates around its center of gravity. In the figure above, the center of gravity is the center of the rectangle ("Center of Mass"), which is determined by the two, intersecting main diagonals. The center of an irregularly shaped object is found by hanging it from two different edges, and the center of gravity is at the intersection of the two "plumb lines."

Newton's second law still applies when the forces form a moment pair, but it must be expressed in terms of angular acceleration and the moment of inertia. The **moment of inertia** is a measure of the body's resistance to rotation, similar to the mass's resistance to linear acceleration. The more compact the body, the less the moment of inertia and the faster it rotates, much like how an ice skater spinning with outstretched arms will speed up as the arms are brought in close to the body.

The concept of torque is important in understanding the use of wrenches and is likely to be on the test. The concept of torque and moment/lever arm will be taken up again below, when the physics of simple machines is presented.

Energy and Work

The previous examples of moving boats, cars, bullets, and baseballs are examples of simple systems that are thought of as particles with forces acting through their center of gravity. They all have one property in common: *energy*. The energy of the system results from the forces acting on it and is considered its ability to do work.

Work or the energy required to do work (which are the same) is calculated as the product of force and distance traveled along the line of action of the force. It's measured in *foot-pounds* in the traditional system (which is still used in workshops and factories) and in *newton meters (N·m)* in the International System of Units (SI), which is the preferred system of measurement today.

Potential and Kinetic Energy

Energy can neither be created nor destroyed, but it can be converted from one form to another. There are many forms of energy, but it's useful to start with mechanical energy and potential energy.

The **potential energy** of an object is equal to the work that's required to lift it from its original elevation to its current elevation. This is calculated as the weight of the object or its downward force (mass times the acceleration of gravity) multiplied by the distance (*y*) it is lifted above the reference elevation or "datum." This is written:

$$PE = mgy$$

The mechanical or **kinetic energy** of a system is related to its mass and velocity:

$$KE = \frac{1}{2}mv^2$$

The **total energy** is the sum of the kinetic energy and the potential energy, both of which are measured in foot-pounds or newton meters.

If a weight with a mass of 10 kilograms is raised up a ladder to a height of 10 meters, it has a potential energy of:

$$10\ m\ x\ 10\ kg\ x\ 9.81\ m/s^2\ =\ 981\ N\ m$$

This is approximately 1000 newton meters if the acceleration of gravity (9.81 m/s²) is rounded to 10 m/s², which is accurate enough for most earth-bound calculations. It has zero kinetic energy because it's at rest, with zero velocity.

If the weight is dropped from its perch, it accelerates downward so that its velocity and kinetic energy increase as its potential energy is "used up" or, more precisely, converted to kinetic energy.

When the weight reaches the bottom of the ladder, just before it hits the ground, it has a kinetic energy of 981 N·m (ignoring small losses due to air resistance). The velocity can be solved by using the following:

$$981\ N \times m = \frac{1}{2}10\ kg \times v^2 \quad or \quad v = 14.01\ m/s$$

When the 10-kilogram weight hits the ground, its potential energy (which was measured *from* the ground) and its velocity are both zero, so its kinetic energy is also zero. What's happened to the energy? It's dissipated into heat, noise, and kicking up some dust. It's important to remember that energy can neither be created nor destroyed, so it can only change from one form to another.

The conversion between potential and kinetic energy works the same way for a pendulum. If it's raised and held at its highest position, it has maximum potential energy but zero kinetic energy.

Potential and Kinetic Energy for a Swinging Pendulum

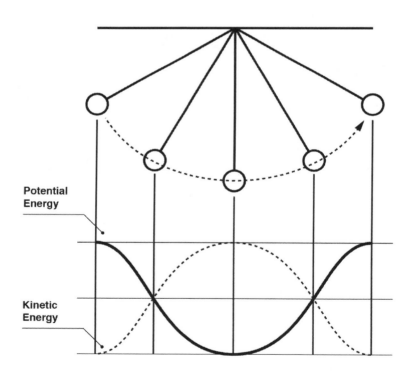

When the pendulum is released from its highest position (see left side of the figure above), it swings down so that its kinetic energy increases as its potential energy decreases. At the bottom of its swing, the pendulum is moving at its maximum velocity with its maximum kinetic energy. As the pendulum swings past the bottom of its path, its velocity slows down as its potential energy increases.

Work

The released potential energy of a system can be used to do *work*.

For instance, most of the energy lost by letting a weight fall freely can be recovered by hooking it up to a pulley to do work by pulling another weight back up (as shown in the figure below).

Using the Energy of a Falling Weight to Raise Another Weight

High PE

In other words, the potential energy expended to lower the weight is used to do the work of lifting another object. Of course, in a real system, there are losses due to friction. The action of pulleys will be discussed later in this study guide.

Since *energy* is defined as *the capacity to do work*, energy and work are measured in the same units:

$$Energy = Work = Force \times Distance$$

Force is measured in **newtons (N).** Distance is measured in meters. The units of work are **newton meters (N·m)**. The same is true for kinetic energy and potential energy.

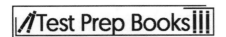

Another way to store energy is to compress a spring. Energy is stored in the spring by stretching or compressing it. The work required to shorten or lengthen the spring is given by the equation:

$$F = k \times d$$

Here, "d" is the length in meters and "k" is the resistance of the spring constant (measured in N×m), which is a constant as long as the spring isn't stretched past its elastic limit. The resistance of the spring is constant, but the force needed to compress the spring increases with each millimeter it's pushed.

The potential energy stored in the spring is equal to the work done to compress it, which is the total force times the change in length. Since the resisting force of the spring increases as its displacement increases, the average force must be used in the calculation:

$$W = PE = F \times d = \frac{1}{2}(F_i + F_f)d \times d$$

$$\frac{1}{2}(0 + F_f)d \times d = \frac{1}{2}Fd^2$$

The potential energy in the spring is stored by locking it into place, and the work energy used to compress it is recovered when the spring is unlocked. It's the same when dropping a weight from a height—the energy doesn't have to be wasted. In the case of the spring, the energy is used to propel an object.

Potential and Kinetic Energy of a Spring

Compress Spring with Force = k * d

Compress Spring with Potential Force = k * d

Stored PE

Energy of released spring transferred to the ball

Pushing a block horizontally along a rough surface requires work. In this example, the work needs to overcome the force of friction, which opposes the direction of the motion and equals the weight of the block times a **friction factor (f)**. The friction factor is greater for rough surfaces than smooth surfaces, and it's usually greater *before* the motion starts than after it has begun to slide. These terms are illustrated in the figure below.

Pushing a Block Horizontally Against the Force of Friction

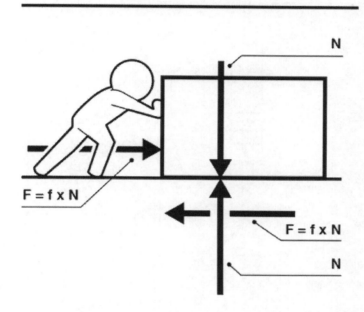

When pushing a block, there's no increase in potential energy since the block's elevation doesn't change. Expending the energy to overcome friction is "wasted" in the generation of heat. Yet, to move a block from point A to point B, an energy cost must be paid. However, friction isn't always a hindrance. In fact, it's the force that makes the motion of a wheel possible.

Heat energy can also be created by burning organic fuels, such as wood, coal, natural gas, and petroleum. All of these are derived from plant matter that's created using solar energy and photosynthesis. The chemical energy or *"heat"* liberated by the combustion of these fuels is used to warm buildings during the winter or even melt metal in a foundry. The heat is also used to generate steam, which can drive engines or turn turbines to generate electric energy.

In fact, work and heat are interchangeable. This fact was first recognized by gun founders when they were boring out cast, brass cannon blanks. The cannon blanks were submerged in a water bath to reduce friction, yet as the boring continued, the water bath boiled away!

Later, the amount of work needed to raise the temperature of water was measured by an English physicist (and brewer) named James Prescott Joule. The way that Joule measured the mechanical equivalent of heat is illustrated in the figure below. This setup is similar to the one in the figure above with the pulley, except instead of lifting another weight, the falling weight's potential energy is converted to the mechanical energy of the rotating vertical shaft. This turns the paddles, which churns the water to increase its temperature. Through a long series of repeated measurements, Joule showed that 4186 N·m of work was necessary to raise the temperature of one kilogram of water by one degree Celsius, no matter how the work was delivered.

Device Measuring the Mechanical Energy Needed to Increase the Temperature of Water

Vertical shaft

Thermometer
$\Delta T + 1° =$
4186 N•m

Rotating paddles

Water bath
Containing
1 kg of Water

Falling weight

In recognition of this experiment, the newton meter is also called a *"joule."* Linking the names for work and heat to the names of two great physicists is appropriate because heat and work being interchangeable is of the greatest practical importance. These two men were part of a very small, select group of scientists for whom units of measurement have been named: Marie Curie for radioactivity, Blaise Pascal for pressure, James Watt for power, Andre Ampere for electric current, and only a few others.

Just as mechanical work is converted into heat energy, heat energy is converted into mechanical energy in the reverse process. An example of this is a closely fitting piston supporting a weight and mounted in a cylinder where steam enters from the bottom.

In this example, water is heated into steam in a boiler, and then the steam is drawn off and piped into a cylinder. Steam pressure builds up in the piston, exerting a force in all directions. This is counteracted by the tensile strength of the cylinder; otherwise, it would burst. The pressure also acts on the exposed face of the piston, pushing it upwards against the load (displacing it) and thus doing work.

Work developed from the pressure acting over the area exerts a force on the piston as described in the following equation:

$$Work = Pressure \times Piston\ Area \times Displacement$$

Here, the work is measured in newton meters, the pressure in newtons per square meter or **pascals (Pa)**, and the piston displacement is measured in meters.

Since the volume enclosed between the cylinder and piston increases with the displacement, the work can also be expressed as:

$$Work = Pressure \times \Delta Volume$$

For example, a 10-kilogram weight is set on top of a piston-cylinder assembly with a diameter of 25 centimeters. The area of the cylinder is:

$$Area = \frac{\pi \times d^2}{4} = 0.785 \times 0.25^2 = .049\ m^2$$

If the acceleration due to gravity is approximately 10 m/s², and the area is rounded to .05 meters squared, then the pressure needed to counteract the weight of the 10-kilogram weight is estimated as:

$$P = \frac{F}{A} \approx 10\ \times \frac{10}{0.05} = 2000\ \frac{N}{m^2} = 2000\ Pa = 2\ KPa$$

If steam with a pressure slightly greater than this value is piped into the cylinder, it slowly lifts the load. If steam at a much higher pressure is suddenly admitted to the cylinder, it throws the load into the air. This is the principle used to steam-catapult airplanes off the deck of an aircraft carrier.

Power

Power is defined as the rate at which work is done, or the time it takes to do a given amount of work. In the International System of Units (SI), work is measured in *newton meters (N·m)* or **joules (J)**. Power is measured in joules/second or **watts (W)**.

For example, to raise a 1-kilogram mass one meter off the ground, it takes approximately 10 newton meters of work (approximating the gravitational acceleration of 9.81 m/s² as 10 m/s²). To do the work in 10 seconds, it requires 1 watt of power. Doing it in 1 second requires 10 watts of power. Essentially, *doing it faster means dividing by a smaller number*, and that means greater power.

Although SI units are preferred for technical work throughout the world, the old traditional (or English) unit of measuring power is still used. Introduced by *James Watt* (the same man for whom the SI unit of power "watt" is named), the unit of **horsepower (HP)** rated the power of the steam engines that he and his partner (Matthew Boulton) manufactured and sold to mine operators in 18th century England. The mine operators used these engines to pump water out of flooded facilities in the beginning of the Industrial Revolution.

To provide a measurement that the miners would be familiar with, Watt and Boulton referenced the power of their engines with the "power of a horse."

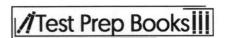

Watt's measurements showed that, on average, a well-harnessed horse could lift a 330-pound weight 100 feet up a well in one minute (330 pounds is the weight of a 40-gallon barrel filled to the brim). Remembering that power is expressed in terms of energy or work per unit time, horsepower came to be measured as:

$$1 \; HP = \frac{100 \; feet \times 330 \; pounds}{1 \; minute} \times \frac{1 \; minute}{60 \; seconds} = 550 \; foot \; pounds/second$$

A horse that pulled the weight up faster, or pulled up more weight in the same time, was a more *powerful* horse than Watt's "average horse."

Hundreds of millions of engines of all types have been built since Watt and Boulton started manufacturing their products, and the unit of *horsepower* has been used throughout the world to this day. Of course, modern technicians and engineers still need to convert horsepower to watts to work with SI units. An approximate conversion is *1 HP = 746 W*.

Take for example a 2016 CTS-V Cadillac rated at 640 HP. If a **megawatt (MW)** is one million watts, that means the Cadillac has almost half a megawatt of power as shown by this conversion:

$$640 \; HP \times \frac{746 \; W}{1 \; HP} = 477,440 \; W = 477.4 \; kW$$

The power of the Cadillac is comparable to that of the new Westinghouse AP–1000 Nuclear Power Plant, which is rated at 1100 MW or the equivalent of 2304 Cadillacs (assuming no loss in power). That would need a very big parking lot and a tremendous amount of gasoline!

A question that's often asked is, "How much energy is expended by running an engine for a fixed amount of time?" This is important to know when planning how much fuel is needed to run an engine. For instance, how much energy is expended in running the new Cadillac at maximum power for 30 minutes?

In this case, the energy expenditure is approximately 240 kilowatt hours. This must be converted to joules, using the conversion factor that one watt equals one joule per second:

$$240,000 \; W \; hours \times \frac{3600 \; seconds}{1 \; hour} = 8.64(10)^8 \; joules$$

So how much gasoline is burned? Industrial tests show that a gallon of gasoline is rated to contain about 1.3×10^8 joules of energy. That's 130 million joules per gallon. The gallons of gasoline are obtained by dividing:

$$\frac{8.64(10)^8 J}{1.3(10)^8 \; J/gallon} = 6.65 \; gallons \times \frac{3.8 \; liters}{gallon} = 25.3 \; liters$$

The calculation has now come full circle. It began with power. Power equals energy divided by time. Power multiplied by time equals the energy needed to run the machine, which came from burning fuel.

Fluids

In addition to the behavior of solid particles acted on by forces, it is important to understand the behavior of fluids. Fluids include both liquids and gasses. The best way to understand fluid behavior is to contrast it with the behavior of solids, as shown in the figure below.

First, consider a block of ice, which is solid water. If it is set down inside a large box it will exert a force on the bottom of the box due to its weight as shown on the left, in Part A of the figure. The solid block exerts a pressure on the bottom of the box equal to its total weight divided by the area of its base:

$$Pressure = Weight\ of\ block/Area\ of\ base$$

That pressure acts only in the area directly under the block of ice.

If the same mass of ice is melted, it behaves much differently. It still has the same weight as before because its mass hasn't changed. However, the volume has decreased because liquid water molecules are more tightly packed together than ice molecules, which is why ice floats (it is less dense).

The Behavior of Solids and Liquids Compared

A

Forces exerted by a block of ice on its container

B

Forces exerted by a water on its container

The melted ice (now water) conforms to the shape of the container. This means that the fluid exerts pressure not only on the base, but on the sides of the box at the water line and below. Actually, pressure in a liquid is exerted in all directions, but all the forces in the interior of the fluid cancel each other out, so that a net force is only exerted on the walls. Note also that the pressure on the walls increases with the depth of the water.

The fact that the liquid exerts pressure in all directions is part of the reason some solids float in liquids. Consider the forces acting on a block of wood floating in water, as shown in the figure below.

Floatation of a Block of Wood

Buoyant Force

The block of wood is submerged in the water and pressure acts on its bottom and sides as shown. The weight of the block tends to force it down into the water. The force of the pressure on the left side of the block just cancels the force of the pressure on the right side.

There is a net upward force on the bottom of the block due to the pressure of the water acting on that surface. This force, which counteracts the weight of the block, is known as the *buoyant force*.

The block will sink to a depth such that the buoyant force of the water (equal to the weight of the volume displaced) just matches the total weight of the block. This will happen if two conditions are met:

- The body of water is deep enough to float the block
- The density of the block is less than the density of the water

If the body of water is not deep enough, the water pressure on the bottom side of the block won't be enough to develop a buoyant force equal to the block's weight. The block will be "beached" just like a boat caught at low tide.

If the density of the block is greater than the density of the fluid, the buoyant force acting on the bottom of the boat will not be sufficient to counteract the total weight of the block. That's why a solid steel block will sink in water.

If steel is denser than water, how can a steel ship float? The steel ship floats because it's hollow. The volume of water displaced by its steel shell (hull) is heavier than the entire weight of the ship and its contents (which includes a lot of empty space). In fact, there's so much empty space within a steel ship's

100

hull that it can bob out of the water and be unstable at sea if some of the void spaces (called ballast tanks) aren't filled with water. This provides more weight and balance (or "trim") to the vessel.

The discussion of buoyant forces on solids holds for liquids as well. A less dense liquid can float on a denser liquid if they're **immiscible** (do not mix). For instance, oil can float on water because oil isn't as dense as the water. Fresh water can float on salt water for the same reason.

Pascal's law states that a change in pressure, applied to an enclosed fluid, is transmitted undiminished to every portion of the fluid and to the walls of its containing vessel. This principle is used in the design of hydraulic jacks, as shown in the figure below.

A force (F_1) is exerted on a small "driving" piston, which creates pressure on the hydraulic fluid. This pressure is transmitted through the fluid to a large cylinder. While the pressure is the same everywhere in the oil, the pressure action on the area of the larger cylinder creates a much higher upward force (F_2).

Illustration of a Hydraulic Jack Exemplifying Pascal's Law

Looking again at the figure above, suppose the diameter of the small cylinder is 5 centimeters and the diameter of the large cylinder is 80 centimeters. If a force of 20 newtons (N) is exerted on the small driving piston, what's the value of the upward force F_2? In other words, what weight can the large piston support?

The pressure within the system is created from the force F_1 acting over the area of the piston:

$$P = \frac{F_1}{A} = \frac{20 \ N}{\pi \ (0.05 \ m)^2/4} = 10,185 \ Pa$$

The same pressure acts on the larger piston, creating the upward force, F_2:

$$F_2 = P \times A = 10{,}185\,Pa \times \pi \times (0.8\,m)^2/4 = 5120\,N$$

Because a liquid has no internal shear strength, it can be transported in a pipe or channel between two locations. A fluid's "rate of flow" is the volume of fluid that passes a given location in a given amount of time and is expressed in $m^3/second$. The **flow rate (Q)** is determined by measuring the **area of flow (A)** in m^2, and the **flow velocity (v)** in m/s:

$$Q = v \times A$$

This equation is called the **Continuity Equation**. It's one of the most important equations in engineering and should be memorized. For example, what is the flow rate for a pipe with an inside diameter of 1200 millimeters running full with a velocity of 1.6 m/s (measured by a *sonic velocity meter*)?

Using the Continuity Equation, the flow is obtained by keeping careful track of units:

$$Q = v \times A = 1.6\frac{m}{s} \times \frac{\pi}{4} \times \left(\frac{1200\,mm}{1000\,mm/m}\right)^2 = 1.81\,m^3/second$$

For more practice, imagine that a pipe is filling a storage tank with a diameter of 100 meters. How long does it take for the water level to rise by 2 meters?

Since the flow rate (Q) is expressed in m³/second, and volume is measured in m³, then the time in seconds to supply a volume (V) is V/Q. Here, the volume required is:

$$Volume\ Required = Base\ Area \times Depth = \frac{\pi}{4}100^2 \times 2\,m = 15{,}700\,m^3$$

Thus, the time to fill the tank another 2 meters is 15,700 m^3 divided by 1.81 m^3/s = 8674 seconds or 2.4 hours.

It's important to understand that, for a given flow rate, a smaller pipe requires a higher velocity.

The energy of a flow system is evaluated in terms of potential and kinetic energy, the same way the energy of a falling weight is evaluated. The total energy of a fluid flow system is divided into potential energy of elevation, and pressure and the kinetic energy of velocity. **Bernoulli's Equation** states that, for a constant flow rate, the total energy of the system (divided into components of elevation, pressure, and velocity) remains constant. This is written as:

$$Z + \frac{P}{\rho g} + \frac{v^2}{2g} = Constant$$

Each of the terms in this equation has dimensions of meters. The first term is the **elevation energy**, where Z is the elevation in meters. The second term is the **pressure energy**, where P is the pressure, ρ is the density, and g is the acceleration of gravity. The dimensions of the second term are also in meters. The third term is the **velocity energy**, also expressed in meters.

For a fixed elevation, the equation shows that, as the pressure increases, the velocity decreases. In the other case, as the velocity increases, the pressure decreases.

The use of the Bernoulli Equation is illustrated in the figure below. The total energy is the same at Sections 1 and 2. The area of flow at Section 1 is greater than the area at Section 2. Since the flow rate is the same at each section, the velocity at Point 2 is higher than at Point 1:

$$Q = V_1 \times A_1 = V_2 \times A_2, \qquad V_2 = V_1 \times \frac{A_1}{A_2}$$

Finally, since the total energy is the same at the two sections, the pressure at Point 2 is less than at Point 1. The tubes drawn at Points 1 and 2 would actually have the water levels shown in the figure; the pressure at each point would support a column of water of a height equal to the pressure divided by the unit weight of the water ($h = P/\rho g$).

An Example of Using the Bernoulli Equation

$$Q = V_1 \times A_1 = V_2 \times A_2 \qquad V_2 = V_1 \times \frac{A_1}{A_2}$$

Machines

Now that the basic physics of work and energy have been discussed, the common machines used to do the work can be discussed in more detail.

A **machine** is a device that: transforms energy from one form to another, multiplies the force applied to do work, changes the direction of the resultant force, or increases the speed at which the work is done.

The details of how energy is converted into work by a system are extremely complicated but, no matter how complicated the "linkage" between the components, every system is composed of certain elemental or simple machines. These are discussed briefly in the following sections.

Levers

The simplest machine is a **lever**, which consists of two pieces or components: a **bar** (or beam) and a **fulcrum** (the pivot-point around which motion takes place). As shown below, the *effort* acts at a distance (L_1) from the fulcrum and the *load* acts at a distance (L_2) from the fulcrum.

Components of a Lever

These lengths L_1 and L_2 are called **lever arms**. When the lever is balanced, the load (R) times its lever arm (L_2) equals the effort (F) times its lever arm (L_1). The force needed to lift the load is:

$$F = R \times \frac{L_2}{L_1}$$

This equation shows that as the lever arm L_1 is increased, the force required to lift the resisting load (R) is reduced. This is why Archimedes, one of the leading ancient Greek scientists, said, "Give me a lever long enough, and a place to stand, and I can move the Earth."

The ratio of the moment arms is the so-called "mechanical advantage" of the simple lever; the effort is multiplied by the mechanical advantage. For example, a 100-kilogram mass (a weight of approximately

104

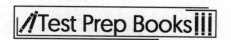

1000 N) is lifted with a lever like the one in the figure below, with a total length of 3 meters, and the fulcrum situated 50 centimeters from the left end. What's the force needed to balance the load?

$$F = 1000 \; N \times \frac{0.5 \; meters}{2.5 \; meters} = 200 \; N$$

Depending on the location of the load and effort with respect to the fulcrum, three "classes" of lever are recognized. In each case, the forces can be analyzed as described above.

The Three Classes of Levers

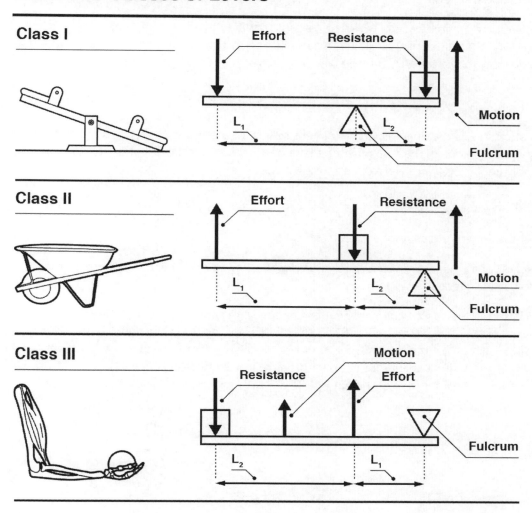

As seen in the figure, a *Class I* lever has the fulcrum positioned between the effort and the load. Examples of Class I levers include see-saws, balance scales, crow bars, and scissors. As explained above, the force needed to balance the load is $F = R \times (L_2/L_1)$, which means that the mechanical advantage is L_2/L_1. The crane boom shown back in the first figure in this section was a Class I lever, where the tower acted as the fulcrum and the counterweight on the left end of the boom provided the effort.

For a *Class II* lever, the load is placed between the fulcrum and the effort. A wheel barrow is a good example of a Class II lever. The mechanical advantage of a Class II lever is $(L_1 + L_2)/L_2$.

For a *Class III* lever, the effort is applied at a point between the fulcrum and the load, which increases the speed at which the load is moved. A human arm is a Class III lever, with the elbow acting as the fulcrum. The mechanical advantage of a Class III lever is $(L_1 + L_2)/L_1$.

Wheels and Axles

The **wheel and axle** is a special kind of lever. The *axle*, to which the load is applied, is set perpendicular to the *wheel* through its center. Effort is then applied along the rim of the wheel, either with a cable running around the perimeter or with a *crank* set parallel to the axle.

The mechanical advantage of the wheel and axle is provided by the moment arm of the perimeter cable or crank. Using the center of the axle (with a radius of r) as the fulcrum, the resistance of the load (L) is just balanced by the effort (F) times the wheel radius:

$$F \times R = L \times r \quad \text{or} \quad F = L \times \frac{r}{R}$$

This equation shows that increasing the wheel's radius for a given shaft reduces the required effort to carry the load. Of course, the axle must be made of a strong material or it'll be twisted apart by the applied torque. This is why steel axles are used.

Gears, Belts, and Cams

The functioning of a wheel and axle can be modified with the use of gears and belts. **Gears** are used to change the direction or speed of a wheel's motion.

The direction of a wheel's motion can be changed by using *beveled gears*, with the shafts set at right angles to each other, as shown in part *A* in the figure below.

The speed of a wheel can be changed by meshing together *spur gears* with different diameters. A small gear (A) is shown driving a larger gear (B) in the middle section *(B)* in the figure below. The gears rotate in opposite directions; if the driver, Gear A, moves clockwise, then Gear B is driven counter-clockwise. Gear B rotates at half the speed of the driver, Gear A. In general, the change in speed is given by the ratio of the number of teeth in each gear:

$$\frac{Rev_{Gear\ B}}{Rev_{Gear\ A}} = \frac{Number\ of\ Teeth\ in\ A}{Number\ of\ Teeth\ in\ B}$$

Rather than meshing the gears, **belts** are used to connect them as shown in part *(C)*.

Gear and Belt Arrangements

A

Bevel gears used to change the direction of shaft rotation

90°

65°

B

Spur Gears (A 'driving' B) used to change the shaft rotation speed

40 Teeth

B

20 Teeth

A

C

Spur gears driven by a belt/chain

Gears can change the speed and direction of the axle rotation, but the rotary motion is maintained. To convert the rotary motion of a gear train into linear motion, it's necessary to use a *cam* (a type of off-centered wheel shown in the figure below, where rotary shaft motion lifts the valve in a vertical direction.

Conversion of Rotary to Vertical Linear Motion with a Cam

Pulleys

A **pulley** looks like a wheel and axle, but provides a mechanical advantage in a different way. A *fixed pulley* was shown previously as a way to capture the potential energy of a falling weight to do useful work by lifting another weight. As shown in part *A* in the figure below, the fixed pulley is used to change the direction of the downward force exerted by the falling weight, but it doesn't provide any mechanical advantage.

The lever arm of the falling weight (A) is the distance between the rim of the fixed pulley and the center of the axle. This is also the length of the lever arm acting on the rising weight (B), so the ratio of the two arms is 1:0, meaning there's no mechanical advantage. In the case of a wheel and axle, the mechanical advantage is the ratio of the wheel radius to the axle radius.

A *moving pulley*, which is really a Class II lever, provides a mechanical advantage of 2:1 as shown below on the right side of the figure *(B)*.

Fixed-Block Versus Moving-Block Pulleys

A

Single Fixed Block with No Mechanical Advantage

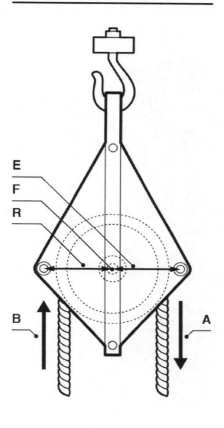

B

Single Moving Block with 2:1 Mechanical Advantage

As demonstrated by the rigs in the figure below, using a wider moving block with multiple sheaves can achieve a greater mechanical advantage.

Single-Acting and Double-Acting Block and Tackles

Hook

Cheek
Either face

Pin

Strap

Shell
Entire outer
part

Shallow

Sheave

Breech

A
Single-sheave
Moving Block

B
Two-sheave
Moving Block

The mechanical advantage of the multiple-sheave block and tackle is approximated by counting the number of ropes going to and from the moving block. For example, there are two ropes connecting the moving block to the fixed block in part *A* of the figure above, so the mechanical advantage is 2:1. There are three ropes connecting the moving and fixed blocks in part *B*, so the mechanical advantage is 3:1. The advantage of using a multiple-sheave block is the increased hauling power obtained, but there's a cost; the weight of the moving block must be overcome, and a multiple-sheave block is significantly heavier than a single-sheave block.

Ramps
The **ramp** (or inclined plane) has been used since ancient times to move massive, extremely heavy objects up to higher positions, such as in the pyramids of the Middle East and Central America.

For example, to lift a barrel straight up to a height (*H*) requires a force equal to its weight (*W*). However, the force needed to lift the barrel is reduced by rolling it up a ramp, as shown below. So, if the surface of the ramp is *D* meters long and *H* meters high, the force (*F*) required to roll the weight (*W*) up the ramp is:

$$F = \frac{H}{D} \times W$$

Definition Sketch for a Ramp or Inclined Plane

For a fixed height and weight, the longer the ramp, the less force must be applied. Remember, though, that the useful work done (in *N-m*) is the same in either case and is equal to *W* × *H*.

Wedges

If an incline or ramp is imagined as a right triangle like in the figure above, then a **wedge** would be formed by placing two inclines (ramps) back-to-back (or an isosceles triangle). A wedge is one of the six simple machines and is used to cut or split material. It does this by being driven for its full length into the material being cut. This material is then forced apart by a distance equal to the base of the wedge. Axes, chisels, and knives work on the same principle.

Screws

Screws are used in many applications, including vises and jacks. They are also used to fasten wood and other materials together. A screw is thought of as an inclined plane wrapped around a central cylinder. To visualize this, one can think of a barbershop pole, or cutting the shape of an incline (right triangle) out of a sheet of paper and wrapping it around a pencil (as in part *A* in the figure below). Threads are made from steel by turning round stock on a lathe and slowly advancing a cutting tool (a wedge) along it, as shown in part *B*.

Definition Sketch for a Screw and Its Use in a Car Jack

A — Theoretical formation of a thread

B — Cutting a steel screw thread on a lathe

C — Use of a screw in a car jack

The application of a simple screw in a car jack is shown in part *C* in the figure above. The mechanical advantage of the jack is derived from the pitch of the screw winding. Turning the handle of the jack one revolution raises the screw by a height equal to the *screw pitch (p)*. If the handle has a length *R*, the distance the handle travels is equal to the circumference of the circle it traces out.

The theoretical mechanical advantage of the jack's screw is:

$$MA = \frac{F}{L} = \frac{p}{2\pi R} \quad \text{so} \quad F = L \times \frac{p}{2\pi R}$$

For example, the theoretical force (*F*) required to lift a car with a mass (*L*) of 5000 kilograms, using a jack with a handle 30 centimeters long and a screw pitch of 0.5 cm, is given as:

$$F \cong 50{,}000\ N \times \frac{0.5\ cm}{6.284 * 30\ cm} \cong 130\ N$$

The theoretical value of mechanical advantage doesn't account for friction, so the actual force needed to turn the handle is higher than calculated.

Practice Quiz

1. Velocity is a measure of which of the following?
   a. Speed with direction
   b. The change in speed over the change in time
   c. Acceleration with direction
   d. All of the above

2. Which of the following is true of an object at rest on Earth?
   a. It has no forces acting upon it.
   b. It has no gravity acting upon it.
   c. It is in transition.
   d. It is in equilibrium.

3. The law of the conservation of energy states which of the following?
   a. Energy should be stored in power cells for future use.
   b. Energy will replenish itself once exhausted.
   c. Energy cannot be created or destroyed.
   d. Energy should be saved because it can run out.

4. At what point in its swing does a pendulum have the most potential energy?
   a. At the top of its swing, just before going into motion
   b. At the bottom of its swing, in full motion
   c. Halfway between the top of its swing and the bottom of its swing
   d. It has the same amount of potential energy throughout its path

5. What is the force that opposes motion?
   a. Reactive force
   b. Responsive force
   c. Friction
   d. Momentum

See answers on next page

Answer Explanations

1. A: Velocity is a measure of speed with direction. To calculate velocity, find the distance covered and the time it took to cover that distance; change in position over the change in time. A standard measurement for velocity is in meters per second (m/s). The change in velocity over change in time is acceleration, while acceleration with direction has no specific name.

2. D: An object at rest has forces acting upon it, including gravitational, normal, and frictional forces. All of these forces are in balance with each other and cause no movement in the object's position. This is equilibrium. An object in constant motion is also considered to be in equilibrium or a state of balanced forces.

3. C: This is a fundamental law of thermodynamics. Energy can only transfer, transform, or travel. The amount of energy in a system is always the same.

4. A: Potential energy represents the energy possessed by an object by virtue of its position. An object's gravitational potential energy can be found as a simple function of its height or by what distance it drops. Out of all of the answer choices, Choice A has the pendulum at its highest point. Choice B demonstrates when the pendulum has the most kinetic energy. Choice C has more potential energy than Choice B but less than Choice A. Choice D is incorrect, because the height of the pendulum changes during its swing, therefore its potential energy is changing.

5. C: The force that opposes motion is called *friction*. It also provides the resistance necessary for walking, running, braking, etc. In order for something to slide down a ramp, it must be acted upon by a force stronger than that of friction. Choices A and B are not actual terms, and Choice D is the measure of mass multiplied by velocity ($p = mv$).

Aviation and Nautical Information Test (ANIT)

Aviation History

The history of aviation dates back to ancient times. Beginning in the fifth century BCE, ancient Greeks constructed bird-like wings and jumped from great heights, commonly resulting in death or serious injury. Ancient Chinese and Japanese inventors first developed man-carrying kites for military purposes. Like the ancient Greeks, the man-carrying kites were inherently dangerous, and governments typically forced prisoners to carry out the missions. Additionally, Chinese scientists were the first to discover that hot air rises, and they launched balloon-powered sky lanterns to terrify enemy forces during combat.

Europeans' interest in aviation soared during the Renaissance (fourteenth to seventeenth century). Most notably, Leonardo da Vinci studied the flight of various animals and sketched numerous designs of novel aircraft, including ornithopters, rotorcrafts, gliders, and parachutes. At the beginning of the eighteenth century, Sir Isaac Newton developed one of the earliest theories of air resistance, laying the foundation for the modern field of aerodynamics. The tail end of the eighteenth century featured numerous breakthroughs, particularly after Henry Cavendish discovered hydrogen gas. On November 21, 1783, brothers Joseph-Michel and Jacques-Étienne Montgolfier launched the world's first manned hydrogen-filled balloon, which successfully flew and safely landed in France. This historic achievement popularized ballooning across Europe, and industrious military leaders immediately sought to capitalize on the benefits of air travel.

After the ballooning craze swept across Europe, the United States spurred further aeronautic innovation during the American Civil War (1861–1865). To gain an edge over the Confederate rebels, Abraham Lincoln appointed Thaddeus Lowe as the nation's first Chief Aeronaut and tasked him with developing aerial reconnaissance assets. Prior to this appointment, Lowe had constructed massive balloons with the intention of making a transatlantic voyage and experimented with novel methods of manufacturing hydrogen gas. As Chief Aeronaut, Lowe established the Union Army Balloon Corps, and he invented portable hydrogen gas generators so the balloons could be filled within combat zones. Combat aerial reconnaissance provided Union forces with critical intelligence about the movement of enemy troops, and during battles, the balloonists assisted Union artillery in targeting fortified Confederate positions. Lowe also oversaw the conversion of ships into balloon carriers, the forerunner of modern aircraft carriers. Additionally, the Union Army Balloon Corps forever altered the history of aeronautics due to the impression these specialized forces had on a highly influential official observer, Ferdinand von Zeppelin, who was stationed with Lowe during the Peninsular Campaign (1862).

Inspired by what he saw in the American Civil War, Ferdinand von Zeppelin became obsessed with the possibility of constructing a large and rigid airship with superior military capabilities. Specifically, Zeppelin's concept essentially amounted to a balloon of unprecedented size powered by multiple gasbag engines, all contained in a stronger and more flexible aluminum structure. Furthermore, Zeppelin acquired a more efficient type of purified hydrogen gas to maximize the aircraft's power-to-weight ratio and several tools to optimize steering. During the early twentieth century, Zeppelin's airships facilitated the development of the world's first commercial airline service, and they became so ubiquitous that all rigid airships were referred to as **zeppelins**. Germany also effectively used zeppelins for naval reconnaissance and bombing campaigns against Britain during World War I (1914–1918). Despite their considerable successes, the zeppelins suffered from a lack of suitable munitions and vulnerability to ground fire.

Following Germany's defeat, the Allied Powers mostly prohibited Germany from constructing more zeppelins under the terms of the Treaty of Versailles, which temporarily stalled the industry. Still, zeppelins remained popular in Europe for several decades until the infamous Hindenburg explosion in 1937. The Hindenburg accident occurred as a result of German engineers replacing nonflammable helium gas with flammable hydrogen due to an American prohibition on exporting helium to Nazi Germany. In addition to inflicting a devastating blow to Nazi propaganda, the Hindenburg accident marked the official end of the zeppelin as a commercial and military aircraft.

While balloons and zeppelins captured the public's imagination, other scientists and inventors focused on developing a fixed-wing aircraft known as the **airplane**. Sir George Cayley is widely credited as the father of the airplane due to his critical discoveries in physics and aeronautics during the early nineteenth century. Among other achievements, Cayley was the first to identify the four distinct forces that have an effect on air travel (drag, lift, thrust, and weight), and he developed the concept of a modern fixed-wing airplane with systems specifically designed for control, lift, and propulsion. Although Cayley never built a functional airplane, he played an essential role in advancing the forerunners of airplanes, such as gliders, steerable parachutes, and triplanes.

The invention of steam engines in the mid-nineteenth century marked a momentous shift in the history of aviation. Compared to early prototypes, airplanes with aerial steam carriages had significantly greater power-to-weight ratios, which led to the construction of fixed-wing airplanes powered by propellers. With the support of the Aeronautical Society of Great Britain, John Stringfellow built a monoplane with a steam engine and conducted the first unmanned steam-powered flight in 1848. Stringfellow's experiments with steam-powered monoplanes and gliders enhanced aeronauts' understanding of wings' aspect ratio, particularly in terms of demonstrating the superior efficacy of long and thin wings.

Two other prominent members of the Aeronautical Society of Great Britain, Francis Herbert Wenham and John Browning, later invented the first functional wind tunnel in 1871. Wind tunnels effectively simulated the conditions of air travel by using steam engines to blow air through an enclosed tunnel. As a result, aeronauts could conduct extremely detailed tests of model airplanes. Additionally, tests were much simpler and safer because the airplanes remained stationary in the wind tunnel as the artificial wind simulated the effect of an airplane flying through the air. Many important discoveries wouldn't have been possible without the wind tunnel. For example, during the late 1870s, Horatio Phillips conducted wind tunnel experiments that uncovered new principles of aerodynamic lift, resulting in the creation of modern aerofoil sections (cross-sections of wings). Wind tunnels have remained an essential part of aeronautic studies, greatly contributing to the invention of supersonic aircraft during the Cold War (1947–1991).

As the field of aerodynamics blossomed during the tail end of the nineteenth century, American and European inventors competed in a daring competition to perfect manned air travel. Some of the most influential pioneers included John Joseph Montgomery leveraging groundbreaking aeronautic theories to create manned gliders in 1883; Otto Lilienthal making more than 2000 untethered flights in a heavier-than-air aircraft in the 1890s; and Octave Chanute perfecting the design for a biplane glider. The United States helped spur these developments by pouring money into Samuel Pierpont Langley's research. Langley never successfully piloted one of his inventions, but he shattered the world record for longest distance traveled by an unmanned heavier-than-air aircraft. Furthermore, Langley effectively demonstrated his counterintuitive theory that airplanes required less propulsion as their speed increased due to induced drag.

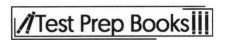

Orville and Wilbur Wright were also gliding pioneers at the turn of the twentieth century. With their experience flying gliders and extensive mechanical skills, the Wright brothers made history when they became the first pilots to successfully fly a motor-powered airplane. To accomplish this feat, they overcame several aviation challenges related to power and control by inventing and implementing a three-axis control system. This type of control system enhanced the steering and balance of airplanes in flight. Following an extensive series of tests in their homemade wind tunnel, the Wright brothers launched their trailblazing Wright Flyer in Kitty Hawk, North Carolina, on December 17, 1903. Despite this paradigm-shifting aeronautic success, they struggled to acquire patents on their control system and gain international recognition for their accomplishment. Still, their success inarguably ushered in a new era of aviation, and by the beginning of World War I, numerous global powers deployed motor-powered and fixed-wing manned airplanes for military purposes.

Italy first used airplanes in bombing campaigns and reconnaissance missions during the Italian-Turkish War (1911–1913). Several other nations quickly mirrored Italy's military strategy in the run-up to World War I (1914–1918). Three cutting-edge innovations transformed aerial combat in this period. First, a German engineer and aeronaut, Hugo Junkers, developed the world's first aircraft entirely constructed with metal, which vastly improved the durability of airplanes in combat. Second, a French fighter pilot, Roland Garros, placed a fixed machine gun to his plane to improve combat performance. Third, a French and German engineer independently developed a synchronization gear to optimize and synchronize the deployment of aircraft guns, which was particularly important to avoid interference between the propeller and guns.

Germany, Italy, Britain, and France pioneered the manufacturing of the new all-metal fighter pilots during World War I, and planes played a crucial role in combat by the end of the conflict. The development and proliferation of fighter planes naturally resulted in extensive aerial combat for the first time in history, and pilots with at least five victories in these "dogfights" were known as **flying aces**. One of the most renowned aces was a German pilot named Manfred von Richthofen who earned the nickname "Red Baron" for his unparalleled skill in air-to-air combat. Over the course of World War I, the Red Baron shot down eighty Allied planes.

Advancements continued at a furious pace during the interwar period, which led to a series of new aeronautic milestones. The United States and Soviet Union both joined the European powers as leading manufacturers of advanced aircraft. In addition, Spanish aeronautic engineers invented the world's first functional rotorcraft called the **autogyro,** which resembled a modern helicopter except the rotor lacked power and developed lift via autorotation. A few years after the Spaniards' success, Soviet engineers constructed a single-rotor helicopter. In addition, several countries built airplanes that broke world records for size and weight. For example, Germany's Dornier Do X, constructed in 1929, had a wingspan of 48 meters. The Dornier Do X transported 169 people on one voyage, which remained the world record for two decades.

Aircraft constructed during the interwar period were also outfitted with a variety of new tools, including flight instruments installed in cockpits. Flight instruments allowed pilots to gather flight data in real time, including information related to altitude, speed, direction, and atmospheric conditions. Of similar importance was the invention of jet engines in Germany and Britain. Jet engines used internal combustion to generate thrust, which allowed airplanes to achieve significantly faster speed and carry larger loads.

Aviation also cemented itself as a popular part of mainstream culture all over the world during the interwar period. Veteran pilots showcased their skills across the United States and Europe in air shows and barnstorming exhibitions that featured stunts and races. Amelia Earhart earned international acclaim for her performance as a barnstormer, and she later became the first female pilot to successfully cross the Atlantic and the Pacific Oceans. Several other impressive feats were accomplished during this period. Members of the US Army Air Service flew for 175 days to complete the first successful circumnavigation of the globe by air travel in 1924. Charles Lindbergh achieved another milestone in aviation when he flew the famed Spirit of St. Louis from New York to Paris in 1927. Lindbergh's 33.5-hour-long journey was the first nonstop transatlantic flight. One year later, an Australian pilot named Charles Kingsford Smith completed the first transpacific flight by flying from the United States to Europe.

World War II (1939–1945) marked another watershed moment in aviation history. Global powers heavily invested in the mass manufacturing of aircraft as part of their total war strategy. In particular, the United States, Soviet Union, Britain, Germany, and Japan established massive air forces with extensive capabilities. The battle for air superiority took on an even more important role in World War II. The Battle of Britain (1940) represented the first large-scale military campaign that predominantly featured air-to-air combat. The legendary British Spitfires ultimately held off the deadly German Luftwaffe, which kept Britain in the war. The American and Japanese navies also fought unprecedented battles as the combatants deployed new aircraft carriers to launch aerial attacks in the Pacific Ocean. For example, American bombers sank three Japanese aircraft carriers at the Battle of Midway (1942), which represented a pivotal turning point in World War II.

Airplanes were also outfitted with more precise and deadly munitions. For example, the US Army Air Forces (USAAF) relentlessly firebombed Tokyo between 1944 and 1945, resulting in the total annihilation of Japanese military infrastructure in Tokyo as well as approximately 100,000 civilian deaths and 270,000 destroyed buildings. The United States also used a B-29 bomber to drop two atomic bombs on the Japanese cities of Nagasaki and Hiroshima, which effectively brought an end to hostilities.

Aircraft design and technology changed dramatically during World War II. Cantilever monoplanes replaced biplanes because the use of a single wing reduced drag and boosted performance. Jet engines and rocket engines both became increasingly common in aircraft as the conflict progressed. Helicopters were also deployed for the first time and served a variety of niche roles in the conflict, ranging from search-and-rescue missions to reconnaissance. Likewise, flight instruments improved as cockpits implemented power-assisted flight controls and blind flying instruments. Additionally, air forces enjoyed far greater communication capabilities due to the implementation of radio and radar tools.

Pilot demographics were also transformed due to the extreme demand for skilled labor during World War II. Most famously, the USAAF hired African American pilots and airmen for the first time. These predominantly fighter groups, known as the **Tuskegee Airmen**, flew 1578 combat missions and were credited with destroying more than 260 enemy aircraft. Similarly, Soviet women served as combat pilots in an all-female regiment commonly referred to as the **Night Witches,** and these female pilots dropped more than 3000 tons of munitions on strategic German positions.

Given the importance and prevalence of aircraft in World War II, commercial aviation boomed in the conflict's aftermath. New jet airliners were equipped with advanced turbine engines, which enabled airplanes to fly farther and faster with more passengers than ever before. The mass manufacturing of the American-made Boeing 707 and DC-8 radically improved passengers' flying experience, and ex-military planes were converted into cargo planes. In 1969, Air France and British Airways introduced the Concorde, a supersonic passenger airliner with a maximum speed greater than Mach 2, meaning it could fly twice the speed of sound. That same year, Boeing produced the Boeing 747, one of the largest and

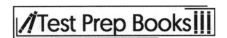

most successful commercial jets to ever fly. Most recently, the Learjet and Gulfstream revolutionized private business travel. Overall, jets spurred globalization as people and goods traveled all over the world in record time, frequency, and quantity.

The Cold War (1947–1991) spurred further aeronautic innovation as the United States and Soviet Union battled for global supremacy, resulting in numerous record-breaking aeronautic feats. In 1947, an American pilot named Chuck Yeager broke the sound barrier while flying a Bell X-1, a rocket-powered aircraft. During the late 1940s and 1950s, the United States and Soviet Union built supersonic interceptor aircraft to defend against nuclear bombers. In 1967, the American-made X-15, an experimental hypersonic and rocket-powered aircraft, shattered the air speed record when it reached Mach 6.7 (4543 mph). Another highly classified aircraft, the Lockheed SR-71 ("Blackbird"), was also produced during the 1960s. The Blackbird was one of the most effective reconnaissance aircraft in the history of the US Air Force (USAF), largely because it was so fast that its primary method of evasion was to outrace the threat, including surface-to-air missiles (SAMs). In 1969, American and British manufacturers produced the Harrier Jump Jet, a jet-powered subsonic aircraft with the capacity to take off and land on short runways, such as car parks and aircraft carriers.

In addition to air travel, the Cold War triggered a Space Race that expanded the horizons of aviation. The Soviet Union took an early lead in the Space Race with Sputnik 1 (1957), a satellite launched into low orbit, and sending the first man, Yuri Gagarin, into space (1967). However, the United States ultimately won the Space Race when Apollo 11 successfully landed on the moon under the leadership of Neil Armstrong and Buzz Aldrin. The Space Race had a lasting impact on aviation history for a number of reasons, including the development of rockets, advancements in computing power, and use of satellites for digital navigation.

Contemporary developments in aviation have centered on digital tools. In the present day, airplanes are equipped with advanced avionic software that automates many aspects of flying. Because glitches in the autopilot software can result in deadly consequences, countries have extensive regulations intended to increase reliability and safety. For example, the Federal Aviation Administration (FAA) heavily regulates avionics software through the enforcement of Federal Aviation Regulations (FARs). Most regulatory agencies also require planes to have a flight recorder to preserve data in the event of an accident.

Unmanned aerial vehicles (drones) have been extensively deployed throughout the War on Terror (2001–present). Drones typically include some combination of autopilot software and remote control. General Atomics' MQ-1 Predator is one of the most lethal drones in the world. This drone is capable of following targets for fourteen hours and firing laser-guided Hellfire missiles. In addition to combat, drones can handle a wide variety of civilian and military tasks, ranging from aerial surveillance to product deliveries. The rapidly rising popularity of drones presents a major challenge to the regulation of airspace. The FAA has promulgated numerous regulations and restrictions on drones as the number of civilian drones has soared.

In recent years, the United States has invested significant resources to develop the Lockheed Martin F-35 Lightning II. The F-35 is classified as a stealth multirole fighter jet, but it also has the capability to perform reconnaissance missions and conduct electronic warfare. Despite its enormous potential, the F-35 has come under scrutiny for costing taxpayers more than $400 billion.

Nautical Terminology and Procedures

Nautical History

The U.S. Navy was founded in the fall of 1775 with a focus on establishing and maintaining peace, safety, and a democratic way of life. The Navy has also been a key player in humanitarian efforts, combatting international aggression and coming to the aid of nations in times of crisis. Although rarely used, the Navy's official motto is *Semper Constans—always constant, always trustworthy.*

1700s–1800s
Although the first American Navy was established in June of 1775 as the Rhode Island Navy, the Continental Navy was established by the Continental Congress just four months later. From that point on, October 13, 1775 has been recognized as the official beginning of the U.S. Navy.

New to his presidency, Thomas Jefferson ordered the U.S. Navy to combat Tripolian pirates in the Mediterranean. The Navy's resilience, coupled with President Jefferson's negotiation skills, resulted in the successful reopening of safe shipping lanes.

In 1807, the British HMS Leopard was triumphant in capturing the USS Chesapeake in its attempt to locate British Navy deserters, but the Chesapeake reemerged and fought again during the War of 1812.

1900s
In 1900, the Navy received the USS Holland—the first commissioned Navy submarine—and seven years later, the Navy welcomed sixteen battleships known as the **Great White Fleet**. In 1915, The Navy Reserve was born and by August of 1916, the first U.S. Navy reservists were sent to find and destroy German U-boats. In 1917, the USS Fanning and the USS Nicholson were the first to successfully sink the German U-boat known as U-58, and in 1918, the U.S. Navy was successful in sinking yet another U-boat. By September of that same year, the war had ended.

Although the United States had not officially entered World War II until the surprise attack on Pearl Harbor on December 7, 1941, Navy Reservists were readying themselves for battle. Immediately following the attack, the Navy was deployed. Fighting tirelessly against German and Japanese forces of aggression, the Navy was well equipped, fully trained, and focused on its mission. One of the most significant battles was fought on the seas near Midway Island. Due in large part to the Pacific Fleet cryptanalysts who were instrumental in intercepting hundreds of Japanese messages every day and who correctly translated approximately a quarter of these messages, the U.S. Navy was able to ready themselves for the planned attack and in so doing, ultimately succeeded against the Japanese. By June 6, 1944, Operation Overlord (D-Day) was successfully carried out on the shores of Northern France. With the aid of allied forces from both Britain and Canada, the United States forced the surrender of German Nazis. The war was finally over.

During the 1950s, the U.S. Navy was involved in significant operations, from the destruction of Korean torpedo boats in the Battle of Chumonchin Chan, to the launching of the USS Nautilus in 1954—its first nuclear submarine. The U.S. Navy now boasts a submarine fleet with full nuclear power capabilities.

By the early 1960s, the U.S. Navy added the USS Enterprise to its fleet, which was the world's first nuclear-powered aircraft carrier that paved the way for the Navy's present-day super carriers. From 1963 to 1972, the Navy SEALS (Sea, Air, and Land), known as the United States' special operators, played

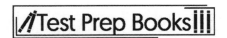

a significant role in the conflict with North Vietnam, earning countless recognitions and awards for their many acts of honor and heroism.

The 1980s saw the invasion of the Gulf of Sidra against the Libyan dictator, Colonel Muammar Gaddafi, as well as the 1988 Operation Praying Mantis, in which the Navy, the SEALS, and the Marines entered into the largest U.S. Naval battle since WWII. This combat mission was also the first to use ship-to-ship missiles. With the invasion of Iraq in the 1990s, the Navy proved invaluable with its Airborne Warning and Control System (AWACS), its Grumman E-2 Hawkeyes, and its satellite communication systems. In 1995, in a response to Bosnian Serb aggression, the Navy employed Tomahawk missiles and fighter bombers, and in the 1999 Kosovo War, the Navy challenged Yugoslavia to heroically combat ethnic cleansing.

On September 11, 2001, the United States endured the worst attack on its civilians in its history. After the attacks on the World Trade Center and the Pentagon, Operation Enduring Freedom led the invasion of Afghanistan with the Navy SEALS as the first ground troops. In 2003, the Navy invaded Iraq and by December of that same year, a joint special operations team captured Saddam Hussein, who was executed in 2006. In 2009, The MV Maersk Alabama, along with its captain, Richard Phillips, was overtaken by Somali pirates. SEAL snipers quickly positioned themselves with the full authority to use deadly force. Three successful targets were hit and killed, and Captain Phillips was rescued.

On the humanitarian front, from 2005 to 2013, the world saw devastating tsunamis, hurricanes, earthquakes, and typhoons. The USNS Mercy and the USNS Comfort set off on countless medical deployments to bring medical personnel and supplies to devastated areas.

Common Nautical Terms

The following terms and accompanying definitions are some of the most commonly used in the U.S. Navy:

- Airedale: Any sailors who work in the air wing
- All Hands: Officers and enlisted personnel in the ship's company
- Barracks: A building where Sailors live when not on active duty on water
- Bomb Farm: Specific location on a ship where bombs are stored
- Bubble Head: Submariners
- Cadillac: A bucket containing wheels and a ringer
- Carry On: An order allowing for one to resume duties
- Chit: Form required when requesting a leave of absence
- Crank: Mess deck worker
- Cumshaw: An exchange of goods or services outside of official procedures and usually void of monetary payment
- First Lieutenant: The officer responsible for the Deck Department and/or Division on the ship
- Galley: The kitchen
- Ground Tackle: Necessary equipment when anchoring a ship
- Head: Bathroom
- Knee-Knockers: Bottom portion of a door's frame
- Leave: Authorized leave of absence
- Lifeline: Safety lines placed around the decks of a ship in order to help prevent personnel from falling over the side

- Marlinspike: A life-sized model ship used for recruits to practice some skills of basic seamanship
- Mess Deck: Dining area for the crew
- Muster: A meeting
- Navy Reserve: A component of the U.S. Navy in which sailors and officers are brought into active duty as needed
- Officers: The Navy's and Navy Reserve's management team
- P-Days: Processing days when recruits arrive at boot camp and are issued equipment, uniforms, and supplies
- Ricky: A recruit
- Scullery: An area to wash dishes
- Scuttlebutt: Water fountain
- Sick Bay: Medical facility
- Snipe: Those who work in the engineering department
- Taps: Time for sleep

Ship Directions, Lights, and Parts of a Vessel

The following section provides an overview of some common terms in the Navy regarding ship directions, vessel lights, and parts of a vessel:

- Aboard: On a ship
- Above: A higher level or deck on a ship
- Ashore: Toward the shore
- Athwartships: Toward a ship's sides
- Below: The ship's lower deck
- Bottom: The lowest portion of a ship's hull
- Bow (Stem): The ship's front
- Port: The left side of the ship
- Starboard: The right side of the ship
- Stern: The rear of the ship
- Underdeck: A ship's lower deck
- Waterline: Where the water surface meets the hull of the ship

Lights

With advanced technology, the Navy now employs the use of signal lights, especially if there is a need to silence radio communications. With sophisticated lighting designed to operate in the infrared spectrum, the Navy is fully capable of nighttime travel. Infrared lighting has the added advantage of being difficult to detect.

Air traffic control towers still use signal lamps; however, these lights are rarely used for any other purpose other than as a backup source of light for instances when an aircraft's radio experiences a complete loss of power. The three dominant colors for lighting are white, red, and green, and although some messages may still be conveyed using lighting, these messages are limited to basic instructions rather than Morse code.

There are four main common navigation lights, namely:

- Sidelights: Red and green lights that are visible to another vessel approaching from the side or head on. Red indicates a vessel's portside and the green indicates its starboard side.

- Stern Lights: Strictly white in color, they are only seen from behind or nearly behind the vessel.

- Masthead Lights: Also white, masthead lights not only shine on both sides of a ship, but they shine forward as well. All power-driven vessels are required to have masthead lights.

- All-Round White Lights: Acting as an anchor light when sidelights are out, all-round white lights are generally used for vessels less than 39.4 feet long. They combine a masthead light and a stern light to form a single white light visible by other vessels from any direction.

Parts of a Vessel

Below the main outside deck, the main body of the ship is referred to as the **hull**. It is comprised of an outside covering known as the **skin**, as well as an inside framework to which the skin is securely fastened. These two parts are generally made of steel and securely welded.

The **keel**, the main centerline of the hull and known as the *backbone* of the ship, runs from the stem at the bow directly to the sternpost. Frames are fastened to the keel and act as the ship's *ribs*, giving the hull a specific shape and strength. To support the decks, deck beams and bulkheads provide additional strength that works to resist water pressure on the hull's sides.

Hull Construction Diagram

Labels (clockwise from top right):
Deck plating
Bulkhead
Transverse frame
Sheer strake
Deck beam
Stanchion
Bilge strake
Strakes A, B, C and so on
Keel
Longitudinal frame
Outer plating
Inner bottom plating

Bulkheads and Decks

Bulkhead and Deck diagram

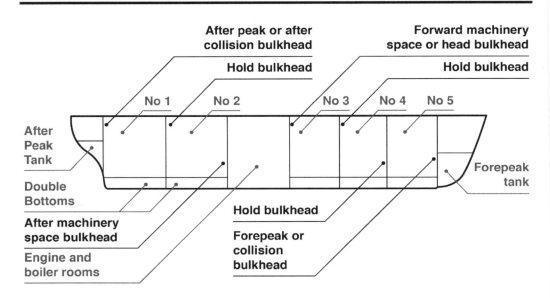

External Parts of a Hull

External parts of a hull

126

Weather Decks

Types of Vessels

The U.S. Navy is arguably one of the most powerful and modern navies in the world. From aircraft carriers and submarines, to multi-mission ships including cruisers, destroyers, frigates, amphibious crafts and more, the U.S. Navy is ready to go at a moment's notice.

- Amphibious War Crafts: These vessels are admired for their swift travel in water and over land, delivering troops and assisting in crisis response, humanitarian operations, and disaster relief.

- Carriers: The largest warships in history, the U.S. Navy's carriers are considered the best in the world, operating in international waters and each acting as a sovereign U.S. territory.

- Cruisers: Known as seaborne platforms with modern guided-missile systems, cruisers are capable of eliminating targets in the air, shore, sea, and beneath the surface of the sea.

- Destroyers: Multi-mission vessels equipped to operate in battle groups or on their own with guided-missiles.

- Hospital Ships: Hospital ships that provide invaluable humanitarian relief and medical care at home and abroad to deployed troops as well as to civilians throughout the globe following a crisis or tragedy.

- Littoral Combat Ships: Littoral Combat Ships meaning *near shore*, operate close to land, and work to detect mines, quiet diesel submarines, as well as fast-surface crafts

- Submarines: Watercrafts capable of independent underwater operation

- Types: Attack, Ballistic Missile, Guided Missile, and Deep Submergence Rescue Vehicles.

- USS New York: An amphibious transport dock intended to bring home Marine Landing Forces

- Vessels: With a primary purpose of retrieving troops, equipment, and supplies, each vessel also provides unique capabilities, and all are equipped with tracked and wheeled, all-terrain vehicles with other amphibious craft and assault vehicles

Instrument History

Early tools and instrumentation by ocean navigators consisted largely of maps, nautical charts, the mariner's compass, astrolabes, sextants, chip logs, and calipers. With significant advancements in naval instrumentation, the modern era has largely replaced these tools with electronic and technological instrumentation such as the following:

- ARPA: An acronym for Automatic Radar Plotting Aid. ARPAs display the position of a ship and other vessels nearby.

- Automatic Tracking Aid: Automatic Tracking Aids display information on tracked targets in order to create a planned layout for a safer, collision-free course.

- Echo Sounder: This measures the water's depth below a ship using sound waves.

- GPS: Introduced in the late 1990s, the global positioning system (GPS) employs the same basic principles of time difference from separate signals as did the LORAN, but its signals come from satellites instead.

- Gyroscopic Compass: Introduced in 1907, the gyroscopic compass has one significant advantage over the magnetic compass—it is not affected by the Earth's (or even the ship's) magnetic field and will always point to the true north.

- Long Range Tracking and Identification System (LRIT): The LRIT is a thorough tracking system for ships around the world.

- Long Range Navigation – LORAN: LORAN was a U.S. navigation system developed in the early 1940s. It employed pulsed radio transmissions in order to determine a ship's position but was decommissioned in 2010.

- Radio Detection and Ranging (RADAR): Radar sends out radio waves and detects any reflections made from distant objects. Installed on ships, radar is still very useful in helping ships locate other ships as well as land when visibility proves difficult.

Weather and Sea Conditions

The United States Naval Meteorology and Oceanography Command (NMOC) provides the military, the scientific community, and civilians with essential information regarding weather and sea conditions, from the depths of the ocean to the far reaches of space.

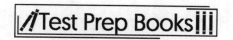
The various components of the NMOC provide critical weather and sea condition information to the Navy:

- The Naval Oceanography Operations command (NOOC): Known as the *operational arm* of the NMOC, the NOOC advises the U.S. Navy with regard to the impact of ocean and atmospheric conditions that impact U.S. naval operations.

- The U.S. Naval Observatory (USNO): As one of the country's first federal agencies for scientific research, the USNO specializes in the areas of producing, positioning, timing, and navigating. NOOC reports their findings directly to the U.S. Navy and the United States Department of Defense.

- The Joint Typhoon Warning Center (JTWC): Located in Pearl Harbor, Hawaii, the JTWC works in cooperation with the U.S. Navy, as well as with the United States Air Force. Charged with the responsibility of issuing tropical cyclone warnings in the Indian Ocean and the North-West and South Pacific Ocean, the JTWC has been in operation since 1959.

- The Fleet Numerical Meteorology and Oceanography Center (FNMOC): Located in Monterey, California, the FNMOC shares with the U.S. and coalition forces the most current and most reliable global meteorology and oceanographic support.

- The Naval Oceanographic Office (NAVO): Works to share relevant oceanographic knowledge to support U.S. National security and maximize sea power.

Navigation and Travel Controls

Navigation refers to studying, monitoring, and controlling movement from one place to another by way of land, water, sky, or space. To determine as exact a positioning as possible, it is critical that operators of any vessel pay strict attention to a number of indicators:

- Longitude: An angle on the Earth's surface that ranges from 0 degrees at the Equator to 90 degrees at either the North or South Pole.

- Latitude: The imaginary lines that run vertically around the Earth called meridians whose purpose is to measure how far east or west any given object is located.

- Loxodrome (Rhumb Line): An imaginary line that cuts through all meridians at the same angle and is the path taken by a ship or plane that maintains a constant compass direction.

- Dead Reckoning (DR): The method of navigation used by ships and aircraft using the vessel's last known position—the fix.

- Celestial Navigation: Although largely replaced by GPS, this ancient science of position fixing with the use of angular measurements taken between the Sun, Moon, a planet, or a star, is making a comeback in the U.S. Navy with a growing concern that the Navy is relying too heavily on GPS systems, which can be hacked and blocked.

- Radio Navigation: The application of radio frequencies to determine the exact position of an object on the Earth's surface

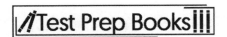

- Radar Navigation: Transmits microwave signals intended to locate other vessels and objects or to help determine the distance between objects and/or vessels

- Satellite Navigation: The system can determine the exact location of objects by using orbiting satellite signals.

Boating Right of Ways

General Boat-Passing Rules

A vessel trailing behind another is referred to as the **give-way vessel**, as it is charged with the greater burden of responsibility should it decide to pass. The vessel in front is referred to as the *stand-on* vessel, with the advantage over the latter. This vessel's skipper can deny the latter passage if he or she feels the passage would be too dangerous.

Sounding two short sounds from a vessel's horn is the universal signal that a vessel would like to pass another vessel from its portside. If the vessel receives two short sounds in return, this indicates permission to pass. However, if the stand-on vessel sends 5 horn sounds, permission is denied.

If two vessels are on a path that could result in a collision, the stand-on vessel has the right of way, with the privilege to pass in front of the give-way vessel on its portside.

If two vessels are head-on, both vessels should immediately steer to the right in order to safely pass one another portside to portside.

International Regulations

The International Regulations for the Prevention of Collisions at Sea (COLREGS) governs the rules on the oceans. COLREGS also helps to establish the political line dividing inland waterways, which adhere to unique navigation rules as well as coastal waterways that follow international navigation rules. The primary purpose of COLREGS is to help to prevent collision on open waters.

Although the term *right of way* is not used by COLREGS, there are nonetheless specific rules to follow. All COLREG rules are clearly laid out into three main sections:

- Conduct of Vessels in Any Condition of Visibility: This section primarily mainly deals with lookout, safe speed, risk of collision, collision avoidance, narrow channels, and traffic separation schemes.

- Conduct of Vessels in Sight of One Another: Section Two focuses on sailing vessels, overtaking, head-on and crossing situations, actions by give-way and stand-on vessels, and the responsibility between vessels.

- Conduct of Vessels in Restricted Visibility: The final section focuses on lights, shapes, sound and light signals, and exemptions.

Docks

From 1842 to 1966, the Bureau of Yards and Docks was a unique branch of the U.S. Navy charged with building and maintaining the Navy's yards, dry docks, and any other facility directly related to ship construction, maintenance, and repair. As part of the Department of Defense's reorganization efforts, the Bureau was abolished in 1966 and replaced by the Naval Facilities Engineering Command (NAVFAC).

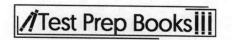

Docks can refer to dry docks, dock landing ships, and landing platform docks, all of which are critical to the Navy's ability to load and unload military personnel, civilians, equipment, and cargo.

Dry docks can refer to either a narrow basin or a vessel that has the capability of being flooded in order to allow a load to be safely floated in. The dock is then drained to allow that same load to be safely secured on the dock floor. Dry docks are also a beneficial platform to construct, maintain, and repair a variety of waterborne vessels.

Dock Landing Ships, also called Landing Ships, Docks, or LSDs for short, are the smallest of the amphibious warships, even though they are the fourth largest ship in the Navy, measuring over 600 feet in length. They carry landing craft and amphibious vehicles and can also carry helicopters. LSDs have well decks that are almost the length of the ship itself. With a helicopter pad above the well deck, LSDs have limited space for troops and equipment. Its main purpose is to serve as a mobile deck for landing craft.

With a shorter well deck, **Landing Platform Docks (LPDs)** are amphibious warfare vessels that embark, transport, and land elements of a landing force, such as troops, for expeditionary warfare missions. LPDs have the capability of carrying amphibious tractors, but the deck is not used for housing landing craft, although some can be carried. LPDs have the capability of housing hundreds of troops as well as crew members.

Nautical Units and Maps

With unique nautical measurement systems, the U.S. Navy can better determine speed, depth, and wind force of their vessels. The following is a general list of common nautical measurement terms along with their definitions:

- Fathom: The equivalent of 6 six feet which is almost exactly one-thousandth of a nautical mile (6,080 feet).

- Fathom Curves (Bathymetric Lines): A grouping of fathoms—e.g., 20 fathoms (120 feet), 50 fathoms (300 feet), 100 fathoms (600 feet), and so on.

- Nautical Mile: 10 cable lengths or the equivalent of 1.1508 miles. The distance of one nautical mile corresponds to one minute of latitude on a chart.

- Cable Length: The length of a ship's cable—approximately 600 feet

- Knot: The measure of speed on water. 1 knot is equivalent to 1 nautical mile per hour

- Beaufort Scale: Although not used as often any more, the following gives a few of the Beaufort Scale measurements:

    0 knots: calm
    22 – 27 knots: strong breeze
    48 – 55 knots: storm
    64 knots and above: hurricane

- Cardinal Directions: Directions are measured on a compass in degrees starting at the North and traveling clockwise. North represents zero degrees, East is 90 degrees, South is 180 degrees, and West is 270 degrees.

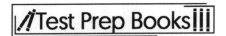

Safety

Several years ago, the U.S. Navy recognized the need for centralized management of all safety efforts. Gradually, a single command emerged to deal with all Navy safety concerns both on and off land. Additionally, with the introduction to the Occupational Safety and Health Act (OSHA), the need for increased awareness for safety became a centralized concern for the Navy.

Today, the Commander of the Naval Safety Center is charged with advising and assisting the Chief Naval Operations (CNO) in promoting, monitoring, and evaluating the Department of the Navy safety programs.

Some of the most significant safety concerns for the Navy are listed below:

Personal
IMSAFE (Illness, Medication, Stress, Alcohol, Fatigue, and Emotion) is a personal checklist used as a daily reminder to check for the wellbeing of all those Enlisted.

Electrical
The U.S. Navy offers training for all those who work near electrical systems. All personnel should receive training in basic electrical safety, the requirements for using personal protective equipment (PPE), how to recognize symptoms of electrical shock and electrical shock trauma, and emergency first-aid responder techniques.

Hazards
Hazards are a part of life in virtually every living space, and the U.S. Navy is no exception. After receiving mandatory training, Navy personnel will be expected to:

- Adhere to all safety precautions related to work or duties
- Report unsafe conditions
- Wear issued, protective equipment and clothing
- Wear eye and/or full-face protection
- Report all injuries or illnesses

Remain alert and look for any possibilities of danger.

Aviation Concepts

Weight and Balance

In discussing the forces acting upon the aircraft, it's important to expand upon weight—perhaps the most important force to consider when flying—and how weight relates to another concept: balance.

Weight
The basic concept of weight has already been discussed earlier as it exists principally as the opposing force to lift. This section will focus on the more technical aspects of weight and how weight pertains to aircraft. The heavier something is, the more difficult that object is to move, thus the greater the lift required to get off the ground. Even if the aircraft is theoretically capable of generating the lift needed to do so, the strain of an overloaded aircraft can cause structural damage to the airframe.

 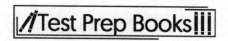
When talking about aircraft, there are several terms that are often used when discussing weight: basic empty weight, maximum gross weight, and weight limitations.

Basic Empty Weight

Basic empty weight, as the name suggests, is the weight of the aircraft once everything directly unattached to the aircraft is removed. More technically, the basic empty weight solely includes the weight of the aircraft itself, any optional equipment, and all the fluids contained within the components themselves, including unusable fuel, transmission oil, hydraulic fluid, etc. As a general rule of thumb, if the aircraft could still function properly without something, that something isn't included in the basic empty weight.

Some aircraft may also have a different value listed called the **licensed empty weight**, which is the basic empty weight with the engine and transmission oil excluded. If this is the case, the oil's weight will need to be accounted for and added manually when determining the actual weight of the aircraft.

Maximum Gross Weight

The **maximum gross weight** is the maximum weight that an aircraft can bear safely. This weight is often broken up into an internal maximum gross weight and external maximum gross weight.

Internal maximum gross weight is the maximum weight within the interior of the aircraft, including the pilot, passengers, and any gear or baggage.

External maximum gross weight is the weight that can be supported externally by the aircraft, including external winches. When properly balanced, the external maximum gross weight can reach tremendous levels.

Weight Limitations

It is very important for a pilot to understand the **weight limitations** on the aircraft. As weight increases, the power required to produce the lift needed to compensate for the additional weight must also increase. By reducing weight, the helicopter is able to safely takeoff or land at a location that would not be possible for heavier aircraft. If sufficient takeoff power is questionable, the takeoff should be delayed until the aircraft is lighter or the density altitude has decreased. If airborne, a landing zone that favors better conditions, or that does not require landing to a hover, would be a safer choice. Also, aircraft operating at higher gross weights are required to produce more torque. The additional torque requires more tail rotor thrust to compensate for the main rotor torque effect. Some helicopters may experience loss of tail rotor thrust during high altitude operations.

If the helicopter is packed too lightly, it can easily become unbalanced with the sole addition of the pilot, which can, in turn, make controlling the helicopter more difficult. This is easily remediated by adding extra weight in the rear of the helicopter to act as ballast. The goal is ultimately to balance the weight, using the center of the rotor disk (for single rotor helicopters) or some space between them (for multi-rotor helicopters). This need for balance connects to the concept of the center of gravity.

Center of Gravity

The **center of gravity** is the point at which the entire weight of the aircraft, including both internal and external attachments, is averaged. It's helpful to visualize an unweighted seesaw to understand how this works.

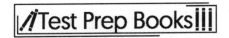
With no other forces acting on it, the seesaw will be perfectly balanced, and the center of gravity is on the pivot point or the fulcrum. When a ten-pound weight is added to one side, there will be more weight on one side of the pivot; the center of gravity is no longer on the pivot, and the seesaw begins to tip. Putting a second, identical weight opposite of the first would cancel the two out. The weight can also be canceled with a larger weight placed closer to the fulcrum or a smaller weight placed further away.

Seesaw with weight

A helicopter acts similarly to a seesaw, with the rotor disk acting as the pivot point. Too much weight on one side will cause the helicopter to tip. Unlike a seesaw, however, a helicopter can adjust the angle of its rotor disk in order to stabilize, but doing so comes at the cost of some lift. This lost lift, in turn, results in reduced performance, and reduced performance makes every other task that much more difficult. Therefore, knowing how to spot and solve center of gravity problems is crucial.

While lateral center of balance problems can occur, they are less frequently a problem when compared to longitudinal center of gravity issues. This is primarily due to the shape of helicopters, which are generally longer than they are wide, so more weight is required to disrupt the helicopter's stable flight. Laterally-imbalanced centers of gravity are occasionally created as some helicopters might dictate which seat to use when flying solo. When using a side mounted winch, or something similar, the weight can quickly place the helicopter outside of the center of gravity limits. However, a front-loaded or aft-loaded center of gravity is much more common.

Front-Loaded Center of Gravity
A **front-loaded center of gravity** can be identified by the fuselage tipping forward, with the nose pointing down towards the ground. This will cause the helicopter to pull forward when hovering and makes slowing down from forward movement more difficult.

This is most often the result of having a heavy pilot at the front, with little-to-no cargo in the rear. A front-loaded center of gravity can also occur midflight, if the fuel tank is located in the rear. As the fuel is consumed, the weight in the rear decreases, and the front begins to tip.

A common solution to a front-loaded center of gravity is to add weight to the back of the helicopter, until the fuselage is once again level. If a longer flight is expected, it may be beneficial to add weight to the rear of the helicopter in anticipation of the fuel tank decreasing in weight.

134

Aft-Loaded Center of Gravity

An **aft-loaded center of gravity** can be identified by the fuselage tipping backwards, with the nose pointing up towards the sky. This will cause the helicopter to pull backwards when in a neutral hover position and will make accelerating forward more difficult.

An aft-loaded center of gravity, in conjunction with strong winds, can even potentially tilt the helicopter sufficiently that the tail boom is forced into the rotor disk when attempting to move forwards. This is a fringe case, requiring both a significantly aft-loaded center of gravity and a compromising factor, such as strong winds or poor technique. Pilots should be cognizant of the risk of this condition, even if two of the three conditions are met. An aft-loaded center of gravity is most often the result of having a light pilot with a large amount of cargo in the rear, possibly including a full fuel reserve.

A common solution to an aft-loaded center of gravity is to remove weight from the back of the helicopter and add weight to the front until the fuselage is once again level. Some helicopters have a forward tilt built into the mast to compensate for an aft-loaded center of gravity.

Recognizing a front- or aft-loaded center of gravity is much easier when doing so outside the craft than doing so while within the helicopter. For this reason, using ground personnel to observe the helicopter to spot a displaced center of gravity can be very beneficial, but if that's not possible, the signs of poor center of balance can still be observed from within. If there are no strong winds, a front- or aft-loaded center of gravity can be identified by the helicopter's tendency to pull forward or backwards, respectively. If strong winds are present, separating idle movements caused by the winds and those caused by the center of gravity can be exceedingly difficult. If that is the case, the horizon will need to be used as a level guide as the helicopter lifts off.

Helicopter Flight Controls

Now that the principles of flight have been covered, the next step is to understand the controls of flight. There are four primary controls that are used to control the helicopter: the collective pitch control, the throttle, the cyclic pitch control, and the anti-torque pedals. Each has a specific function in moving the helicopter through the air, except for the throttle, whose purpose is to control the engine's power output.

Flight controls

The Collective Pitch Control

The **collective pitch control**, often simply called the *collective*, is primarily used to create lift and control vertical movement. The collective is typically located to the left of the pilot's seat and can be raised or lowered to increase or decrease lift, respectively.

Mechanically, the collective achieves this by altering the pitch of the rotor blades simultaneously (collectively). By increasing the pitch of the blades, the angle of incidence is also increased, and more lift is generated. Conversely, decreasing the pitch of the blades results in a lower angle of incidence and less lift. However, increasing or decreasing lift will also have an identical effect on the drag on the blades. This drag will slow down the rotations per minute (RPM) of the helicopter, unless compensated for by increasing the power to the engine using the throttle.

The Throttle

The **throttle** is used to control the power to the engine. Rotor RPM needs to stay within a certain range to operate the helicopter safely; the throttle is used whenever the RPM drops or rises beyond that value. Using the throttle is much like a motorcycle throttle, with a clockwise turn decreasing power and a counterclockwise turn increasing power.

Since sudden and drastic changes can quickly lead to a destabilized flight, slower and smoother adjustments to the throttle are ideal for maintaining control of the helicopter. Making large, sudden adjustments often leads to over-controlling, where the desired position is passed, and an opposite adjustment is needed to correct the mistake. This is actually excellent advice for all the controls, but is particularly true for the throttle, because the throttle controls the all-important RPM.

Although every helicopter has a throttle, not every helicopter requires manual use of the throttle. Some helicopters are equipped with either a correlator or a governor, which is a tool designed to simplify throttle control. Both are designed to maintain RPM so the pilot does not need to, although they do so in different ways.

A **correlator** is a mechanical tool that links the collective to the throttle, automatically increasing and decreasing the throttle as the collective is used. While effective, the correlator does not account for any other factor that could decrease RPM, so some manual control is still occasionally required.

The **governor** includes an electronic sensor that tracks the current RPM directly, rather than using the position of the collective to guess. If the governor detects that the RPM is out of the desired range, it will automatically adjust the throttle as needed. Since the governor measures the RPM directly, it can account for any variable that might impact RPM. In a properly set up governor system, the pilot rarely needs to touch the throttle at all.

The Cyclic Pitch Control

The **cyclic pitch control**, or the *cyclic*, is primarily used to generate thrust and control horizontal movement. The cyclic can be pushed in any direction, and is normally situated either between the pilot's legs or the two pilot seats.

Like the collective, the cyclic functions by altering the pitch of the rotor blades. However, unlike the collective, the cyclic does not increase the pitch of all the blades at the same rate, but rather cyclically. In other words, the cyclic alters the pitch of the blade based on where that blade is in the disk. The cyclic might decrease the pitch of the blades as they approach the aft, only to increase the pitch again as the blade nears the front. This results in the lift being generated unequally, which, in turn, causes the disk to tilt. Since generated lift is always perpendicular to the rotor disk, tipping the disk in this way results in a small, horizontal component to the lift, which creates the thrust needed to move.

For example, if forward movement is desired, the pilot pushes the cyclic forward. In a counterclockwise-spinning rotor blade, this causes the blades' pitch to swivel as they rotate, keeping a low pitch as the blade moves over on the right and increasing to a higher pitch as the blade moves by the left. In a clockwise-spinning rotor blade, the pitch is reversed. This results in the rotor blade tipping forward, converting a small portion of the generated lift into forward thrust.

The Anti-Torque Pedals

The **anti-torque pedals** are located at the feet of the pilot, much like the gas and brake pedals of a car. The purpose of this flight control mechanism is to control the pitch of the tail rotor blades.

As the main rotor spins, the rotor creates torque that spins the helicopter in the opposite direction to counteract. The tail rotor does this by creating thrust at the tail of the helicopter. Since this thrust pushes so far away from the center of gravity, rather than simply pushing the helicopter to the side, the anti-torque pedals instead create torque in the opposite direction than that of the main rotor.

The anti-torque pedals themselves allow the pilot to alter the pitch of the tail rotor, which, in turn, increases or decreases the torque the rotor creates. This has two purposes.

The first purpose is to counteract the torque of the main rotor. As the main rotor's pitch increases or decreases, its torque does as well, so the tail rotor must also be able to increase or decrease its opposing torque in order to keep the helicopter's heading constant. The second purpose is by willfully allowing the tail rotor's torque to increase or decrease past the main rotor's torque, a pilot can create a controlled rotation that allows the helicopter to change to a new heading.

The anti-torque pedals are designed so that pushing the left pedal creates more torque in a counterclockwise direction, and pushing the right pedal creates torque in a clockwise direction. In a counterclockwise rotor helicopter, this means that the left pedal increases the pitch of the tail rotor, while the right pedal decreases the pitch. This is because the torque generated by the main rotor is clockwise, so the tail rotor must generate counterclockwise torque to counter the main rotor, and the pitch determines the strength of that counterclockwise torque.

It may help to remember that no net torque is not the same as no torque at all. Even when flying perfectly straight, there are two torques acting on the helicopter: one from the main rotor and one from the tail rotor.

This scenario is not that different from the example used when discussing lift—the block between two springs. The only difference is that now, rather than having one compressed spring and one stretched spring, there are two compressed springs, both attempting to push the block. The anti-torque pedals effectively control the compression of one of the springs. By reducing the compression, the other spring can push the block one way, and by increasing the compression, the controlled spring can overpower the other spring, moving the other way instead, like a game of reverse tug-of-war. Replace compression with torque, and one has the anti-torque pedals.

Some helicopters, rather than having a tail rotor, have multiple main rotors that spin in opposing directions. This allows the counter-rotating main rotor systems' torques to cancel each other out, removing the need for the tail rotor. Such helicopters do still have anti-torque pedals, but they alter the pitch of the main rotors, rather than altering the pitch of tail rotors. Specifically, the right anti-torque pedal increases the pitch of all counterclockwise rotor blades, which increases the clockwise torque, and the left pedal increases the torque of all the clockwise rotor blades, which increases the counterclockwise torque. In this way, the pedals can serve the same function, despite not having a tail rotor.

Trim Control

In-flight variable trim control along the three axes is used to level an aircraft in pitch and roll while eliminating yaw. The trim system serves to counter the aerodynamic forces that affect the balance of the aircraft in flight. The control pressures on an aircraft change as conditions change during a flight. Trim control systems can compensate for the change in weight and center of gravity that occurs in flight as the aircraft burns fuel, as well as compensating for change in wind and atmospheric pressure. Trim can relieve all possible control pressures held after the desired attitude has been reached. Larger and more sophisticated aircraft tend to have a more sophisticated trim system in the pitch, roll, and yaw axes. Smaller aircraft tend to have only pitch control.

The primary flight controls are positioned in-line with the aircraft surfaces during straight-and-level flight. When the flight is not balanced, one or more flight control surfaces will need to be adjusted by continuous control input. This input can be performed through the use of trim tabs; therefore, avoiding the need for constant adjustments by the pilot. The trim systems also prevent the pilot from having to exert strong control force for an extended amount of time—essentially easing the physical workload required to control the aircraft.

Angle of Attack

The angle of attack (AOA) is the angle between the relative wind and the chord line (line between the leading and trailing edge of the airfoil). The AOA can be used to affect the amount of lift on an aircraft. The greater the AOA, the greater the lift generated until the AOA reaches the critical angle of attack. The critical angle of attack induces a stall because the induced drag exceeds the lift. During a stall, the wing is no longer able to create sufficient lift to oppose gravity. Stall angle is usually around 20°. Thus, once it's been reached, any subsequent increase in the AOA hurts aerodynamics.

Fixed-Wing Flight Controls

Fixed-wing aircraft controls rotate flight control surfaces about the three axes—lateral, longitudinal, and vertical. It is important to maintain light contact with the controls to be able to feel feedback. A tight grip and leaden foot reduce sensitivity to slight resistances in the controls, so it is important to get a comfortable position with legs relaxed and heels on the ground, with balls of the feet on the rudder pedals, and only fingers on the pitch and roll controls.

Elevator Controls

The elevators are flight control surfaces that rotate about the lateral axis, producing a difference in lift between the front and aft ends of the plane, causing it to pitch. The elevators are usually located on the horizontal stabilizer, and are deflected using the elevator pitch control. To pitch down, the elevator control must be pushed forward using smooth pressure, or in the aft direction to pitch up.

Aileron Controls

Ailerons are flight control surfaces located on the outer aft edge of the wings. They rotate about the lateral axis in opposition to each other to create more lift on one side of the airplane, causing it to roll. The aileron control is usually on the same control as elevator control.

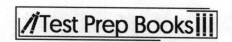

Rudder Controls
The rudder controls yaw in fixed-wing aircraft and are used in adjusting for adverse yaw from rolling maneuvers. The rudder controls are a pair of counter-sprung pedals located at the pilot's feet; control pressure on one is reversed in the other.

Throttle and Prop Controls
The throttle and prop controls are the primary controls for thrust on a constant-speed propeller plane. The throttle is controlled by the throttle lever or knob, which is positioned to set the engine

Prop controls may be found on planes with variable-pitch propellers, to change the pitch of the blades mid-flight. Fixed-pitch propeller planes have middling performance in takeoff, descent, and cruise, while variable-pitch propellers adjust the angle to maximize thrust in a wider range of airspeeds.

Basic Maneuvers

The Four Fundamentals
There are many different maneuvers, but all can ultimately be broken down into what are known as the four fundamentals of flight—straight-and-level flight, turns, climbs, and descents. Learning any maneuver is just a matter of learning the specific combination required by that maneuver.

Straight-And-Level Flight
Straight-and-level flight is perhaps the simplest maneuver as once an aircraft has reached the desired speed, only minimal control is required to keep moving. Most of the pilot's effort will be directed towards keeping the aircraft level, which means using the various controls to make sure that the heading, airspeed, and altitude remain constant and that the aircraft's course relative to the ground remains in a straight line. An exception is when this fundamental maneuver is combined with another, such as a climb or descent. Even then, care should be taken to ensure that any adjustments that are made to the flight path are done slowly and smoothly.

Turns
Turns are unique among the fundamentals for helicopters as they have two methods depending its speed. If the helicopter is flying at low speeds (or even just hovering), turns are performed using the anti-torque pedals, while at higher speeds, the cyclic is used to bank the helicopter. In either case, the goal of the turn is to change the helicopter's heading. A perfect turn would result in no altitude or airspeed change, and the rate of turning would remain constant, aside from the initial acceleration and final deceleration.

The reason for this difference is due to the *laws of motion*, which state that an object in motion will remain in motion. The anti-torque pedals change only the heading of the helicopter, not the velocity, so while in motion, attempting to turn using only the anti-torque pedals will result in the helicopter flying in the same direction, only sideways.

To actually change the direction of flight, the helicopter must change the direction of the generated thrust through banking. where banking comes in. By tilting the rotor disk to the side, the helicopter creates sideways thrust, which accelerates the helicopter in the new desired direction.

Similar to helicopters, changing heading with only yaw from the rudder will turn a plane without immediately changing its direction, while also creating unnecessary drag, so most turns are carried out using the ailerons to roll. Pressure on the aileron control will cause the corresponding wing to lower and

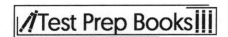

raise the opposite, rolling the plane. When the plane is then banked, the lift from the wings is no longer purely vertical, but partly horizontal, pulling the plane towards a new heading. The lower wing will experience a lower airspeed due to being on the outside of the turn, decreasing its lift, so maintaining sufficient airspeed is also necessary to prevent stalling. While banked, the overall vertical lift from the wings is decreased, so additional engine power or pitching with the elevators is needed to counteract the loss of vertical lift to maintain altitude during level turns. The higher airspeed on the outer wing also increases its drag, creating adverse yaw towards the outside of the turn, which needs to be compensated for using the rudder.

Climbs and Descents

Ascent and **descent** are two sides of the same coin and follow similar procedures. In helicopters, during both, the collective will be used to alter the pitch of the main rotor blades, which, in turn, will change altitude either up or down. When the collective is increased in counter-clockwise rotating helicopters, the nose of the helicopter tends to pitch up, and the pilot is required to apply forward cyclic to maintain the same airspeed. In addition, when power is increased, the nose of the helicopter will turn right, due to the torque increase, and the pilot is required to increase left pedal input to maintain the desired heading and trim. When the collective is reduced, the opposite occurs. The nose pitches down and to the left. The pilot has to apply aft cyclic and the right pedal to compensate for these aerodynamic changes.

The procedure for fixed-wing aircraft differs from rotorcraft. To enter a climb, the elevators must be raised using back pressure on the elevator control and increased airspeed is required to create the additional lift to counteract gravity. The maximum climb rate is limited by how much more thrust is available. Levelling off a climb or descent should begin at the last 10% of an altitude change, gradually decreasing pitch while letting airspeed increase. Descent is effectively the reverse, reducing power just to maintain airspeed when pitched down to reduce altitude. During normal cruise, the rate of descent is recommended to be 500 feet per minute, maintaining constant airspeed, pitch, and engine power during descent.

The same principals in level turns also apply during ascending and descending turns. The pilot must be aware of both the effects from a turn on the plane and the climb or descent, including the tendency of the plane to stabilize or bank on its own depending on the roll angle, adverse yaw from drag on the outer wing, and the need for increased power to maintain vertical lift.

Helicopter Maneuvers

Hovering

Hovering is perhaps the most common technique employed by helicopter pilots, and the ability to do so is what distinguishes helicopters from many other aircraft. The goal of a hover is to position the helicopter so that the helicopter remains a set distance off the ground (typically just a couple of feet) and then remains stationary. This is, unfortunately, not as easy as it sounds, as a helicopter is anything but stable. The helicopter cannot simply be brought up to a desired height, then parked in the air like a car might be parked in a driveway. Instead, the controls must be constantly fined-tuned to keep the helicopter at a stationary hover.

The collective is usually the easiest to adjust, as the collective acts as a position control. A **position control** is any control that controls position, rather than velocity or acceleration. The handles on a foosball table are an excellent example of a position control, with the figure moving at a rate proportionate to the handles. Due to a phenomenon called ground effect, this is similar to how the collective works, in that raising the collective will cause the helicopter to rise a proportionate amount and then stop.

This also makes the collective less susceptible to over-control, as the collective must be raised significantly before the helicopter overcomes the ground effect and begins rising freely. Since the goal of hovering is to get to a certain altitude and then stop, this is ideal behavior, and once the desired altitude is reached, the collective is not likely to need much adjustment.

Ground effect refers to the reduced drag and increased lift that is experienced by an aircraft flying in close proximity to the ground. For a fixed-wing aircraft, it is considered in ground effect when the wing is in close proximity to the ground. A helicopter is considered to be in ground effect when it is within one rotor diameter of the ground. For example, if the rotor diameter of the helicopter is 50 feet, then 50 feet and below is considered to be in ground effect.

The anti-torque pedals, meanwhile, are a **rate control**, which means that the pedals control the rate of change. An example of a rate control is the gas pedal on a car, with the car accelerating faster the harder its pedal is pushed and the car slowing down when the pedal is released. Similarly, pushing the anti-torque pedal causes the helicopter to begin rotating in that direction at a rate determined by the pressure on the pedal. Releasing the pedal causes the rotation to slow to a stop.

It is ideal in a hover to use only minimal pressure on the pedals to keep the helicopter's bearing constant. Otherwise, there is the chance that the pedals might be over-controlled, with the helicopter unable to stop rotating before reaching the desire point. On calm days, the anti-torque pedals might not even be needed to maintain a hover, but on windy days, the thrust generated by the tail rotor can become inconsistent, requiring far more manipulation to steady.

By far the most difficult, however, is the cyclic. Whereas the collective is position-controlled and the anti-torque pedals are rate-controlled, the cyclic is **acceleration-controlled**. Manipulation of the collective results in movement to a particular position, while pressing the anti-torque pedals to continue to spin the helicopter until released. In comparison, use of the cyclic causes the helicopter to speed up as long as the cyclic is held, but upon release, the helicopter will continue to move in that direction at a similar velocity until the cyclic is pushed in the opposite direction to create a negative acceleration and decrease the velocity to zero.

For example, if a horizontal drift is noticed, the cyclic must be pushed gently in the desired direction of movement for a brief moment, released, and then reapplied in the opposite direction as the destination is reached. If the cyclic is only pushed once, the helicopter will continue to move in that direction until drag eventually slows the helicopter to a stop. This makes the cyclic doubly-easy to over-control as there are twice as many opportunities to do so, and acceleration is more difficult to perceive than position or speed. This also means that the helicopter is almost always moving slightly, and controlling the cyclic in such a way that the helicopter's velocity is truly zero is nearly impossible. Even if the helicopter did reach zero velocity, it would only take the slightest of breezes to shift the helicopter slightly and begin the process anew.

Vertical Takeoff to Hover

In a **vertical takeoff to hover**, the objective is to start from a landed position and end with the helicopter hovering just a few feet off the ground. Before beginning this maneuver, there are a few steps that must be done outside the helicopter.

The first task is to make sure that the helicopter has the necessary clearance to take off. The next step is to make sure that the area around the helicopter, particularly above and to the left and right of the aircraft, is free of any obstructions. Once that has been done, takeoff can proceed.

With the collective fully down, the cyclic should be placed in a neutral position, and the collective should be increased smoothly. Pedals should be applied to maintain heading, and the cyclic should be coordinated for a vertical ascent. As the aircraft leaves the ground, the proper control response and aircraft center of gravity (COG) should be checked.

Hovering Turn

In a **hovering turn**, the object is to change the heading of the helicopter while maintaining a constant position relative to the ground. Neither a horizontal nor a vertical position should shift during the maneuver. The anti-torque pedals are the primary controls needed for this maneuver.

To perform the hovering turn, light pressure should be applied on the anti-torque pedals in the direction desired. The helicopter should begin to rotate in that direction. Just like a hover, keeping the helicopter otherwise stationary is important, which means the cyclic and collective may need to be used to prevent the helicopter from drifting. However, doing so should be no more difficult than before.

When the helicopter nears the desired heading, the pedals should be released, and the helicopter's rate of turn should begin to slow and eventually stop. If the pedals have been used lightly, this should take very little time, and the pedals can be released moments before reaching the target heading without fear of overshooting the target heading. If the pedals are pushed with more pressure and the helicopter is allowed to rotate at a faster rate, considerably more space will be required. This is because the helicopter will not only turn further in a set amount of time, but also require more time to stop. Therefore, a slower, steady rate of turn is preferable.

The above all assume a relatively windless day, as strong winds can greatly impact a hovering turn. While turning away from the direction of the wind, the tail turns into the wind, which is more difficult due to the increased drag, so it requires more pressure to maintain turning speed.

When the helicopter reaches a parallel position, the tail tends to **weathervane** and may even be pulled with the wind. If this happens, it may be necessary to switch the pedals to keep the helicopter from turning too swiftly. This switching-over is possibly the hardest part about a hovering turn, as the sudden shift requires an equally swift shift in the pedals.

In addition to the difficulty from trying to find the proper pedal position to keep the helicopter from spinning too quickly, the sudden change in forces often upsets the balance of the other controls, requiring smaller, but still significant, adjustments simultaneously. The graphic below shows a theoretical 360-degree turn and the necessary adjustments to keep the helicopter moving consistently throughout every 90° increment.

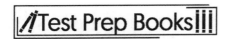

Hovering to Forward Flight

In a **hovering to forward flight** maneuver, the helicopter will be leaving a hovering position to move forward. This maneuver is not designed to be a quick flight maneuver and is not to be used for long travel distances. Instead, the purpose of this maneuver is to reposition the helicopter or to travel short distances. Ideally, the helicopter should not exceed the speed of a brisk walk during its execution.

Starting from a hovering position, the first step is to make sure that the intended path is cleared and that the helicopter is properly lined up with the desired target. If not, the pilot can perform a hovering turn to align the helicopter correctly. Once that is done, two points directly between the helicopter and the destination should be mentally identified. These are the **reference points** and will be used to ensure the helicopter does not drift during the maneuver.

To begin, the pilot should apply slight pressure to the cyclic. As previously mentioned, the cyclic is acceleration-controlled, so there is no need for the pressure to be sustained. Continuing to hold the cyclic forward will just cause the helicopter to continuously get faster, while the helicopter will continue to move forward, even if the cyclic is released. Because the cyclic functions by tipping the rotor disk and redirecting some lift to create thrust, the altitude may drop slightly while the cyclic is applied, but as long as the pressure applied to the cyclic is light, the lost altitude should be negligible and return once the cyclic is put back into the neutral position.

Once the helicopter has begun to move, it will continue to do so for quite some time. During this time, the reference points should be frequently checked to make sure that the two points—the destination and the helicopter—still form a straight line. If not, that means that the helicopter has drifted, and use of the cyclic may be necessary to correct the drift. Heading will also need to be maintained; although, barring crosswind conditions, the only time a heading is at risk of changing is whenever the cyclic is applied.

As the target is reached, rearward cyclic pressure should be applied to slow the helicopter down. Releasing and reapplying pressure may be necessary to control the helicopter's airspeed during the approach, with the goal being to slow down to a hover just as the position is reached. The cyclic may be used to increase speed or reverse it, if the destination is under-shot or over-shot respectively, but when making this sort of minor adjustment, the cyclic should be used sparingly in order to maintain control of the helicopter's motion.

Note that even though this is called **forward flight**, the same technique is used when performing *sideward* or *rearward* flight, with only a few modifications. Rather than applying forward cyclic pressure, a sideward or rearward flight requires a sideward or rearward pressure, respectively. Reference points will still be used to watch for signs that the helicopter is drifting from its path, but because of the reduced visibility of the helicopter's side and rear arcs, clearing the area first is especially important, and using ground personnel to assist is highly recommended whenever possible.

Lastly, a problem unique to sideward flight is that the aircraft will attempt to **weathervane**. This is when the helicopter begins to turn due to the helicopter's tail striking the air. In this instance, use of the anti-torque pedals is necessary to counteract the weathervane effect.

Takeoff from Hover

In a normal **takeoff from hover**, the goal is to bring the helicopter from a hovering position to straight and level flight in the air. While similar in principle to forward flight, takeoff differs primarily in the altitude and speed of flight. For safety reasons, certain combinations of velocity and altitude are

144

prohibited, and although the exact range varies depending on the helicopter, a higher velocity generally requires a higher altitude and vice versa. What this means is that while the helicopter is accelerating, it will also need to climb in order to stay within those parameters. Thus, the collective and cyclic must be used in unison. Typically, this maneuver is broken up into five transitional phases, as seen below, starting with a hovering position at phase one and ending with straight and level flight at phase five.

Takeoff from Hover

In **phase one**, the helicopter is in hover. Before moving forward with the rest of the maneuver, a **performance check** is advisable—checking the power required to hover against performance planning data. A performance check is used to determine if the aircraft is within the maximum gross weight and if sufficient power is available to perform the mission.

The pilot must ensure that all the controls move freely, that they do not get stuck at any point during their full rotation of movement, and that there is sufficient power available to continue. Just as with forward flight, two reference points should be obtained in between the helicopter and its intended direction of flight, which will be used to ensure the helicopter is kept laterally stable.

The **second phase** begins by applying forward pressure on the cyclic. Because a higher speed is desired, more pressure can be applied to the cyclic than that used when performing forward flight, although the increase should be steady rather than rapid, to ensure the helicopter remains in controlled flight. This greater pressure on the cyclic results in a greater portion of lift being used to create thrust, and while this amount is negligible in forward flight, that is not be the case here.

The collective will need to be raised to keep the helicopter from losing altitude. Raising the collective requires a proportionate increase in power to keep RPM constant, and the increased power from the throttle will create more torque, which needs to be accounted for with the anti-torque pedals. This means that during this phase, *all four controls need to be used simultaneously*. This is the reason why the cyclic should be increased slowly during this phase, to give ample time to adjust the other controls as needed.

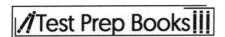

In **phase three**, the helicopter has gained enough speed to reach **effective translational lift (ETL)**. This typically occurs around speeds of 16 to 24 knots; it is easily recognizable by the helicopter beginning to climb and the nose beginning to rise. At this point, the collective should be increased to begin climbing, and the cyclic must be pushed forward enough to counteract the nose's inclination to rise during this phase.

Again, because the collective is being raised, the pilot should expect to increase the throttle and use the anti-torque pedals to counteract the increased torque and maintain the RPM and heading.

In **phase four**, the helicopter is climbing and accelerating forward simultaneously. Care must be taken to control both, so that the helicopter does not end up in the shaded area of the height-velocity diagram, but otherwise this phase is mostly about maintenance.

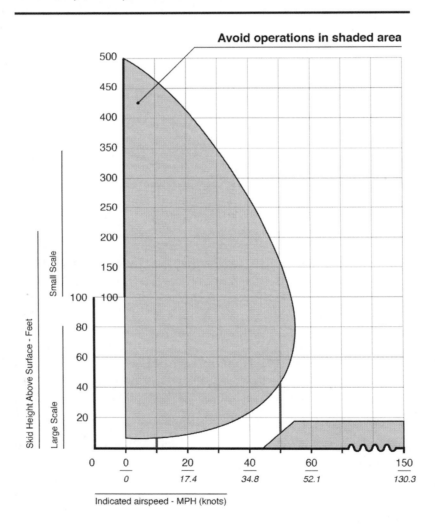

A Sample Height Velocity Diagram for Smooth, Level, Firm Surfaces

In **phase five**, the helicopter has escaped the curved section of the height-velocity diagram, and the helicopter can now climb or accelerate, mostly at will. The shaded areas must still be avoided, but typically by this phase, enough distance has been put between the shaded areas and the helicopter's height/velocity that such concerns should only be an afterthought—something to be remembered if airspeed or altitude decreases significantly, but otherwise, it's not likely to be relevant in normal flight. At this point, the helicopter has entered straight and level flight.

Takeoff from Surface

A **takeoff from the surface**, sometimes called a **running takeoff**, is similar in many ways to a takeoff from a hover—both involve increasing altitude and airspeed significantly, and both end up in straight and level flight. In fact, after a certain point, the technique for both become identical. However, there are enough differences, particularly early in the maneuver, to warrant a brief discussion.

Typically, this maneuver is used in preference to a takeoff from a hover only when the helicopter lacks sufficient power to hover. This is usually because the helicopter is overweight, but is also sometimes due to environmental conditions, such as high-density altitude.

As the name implies, a takeoff from the surface involves starting from a landed position and ending in a straight and level flight. This maneuver involves sliding across the surface as speed is picked up, so wheeled helicopters perform better than skidded ones. However, special "skid shoes" can be equipped to the helicopter to help.

The maneuver begins with the helicopter on the surface, with the collective and throttle at their lowest respective settings. Since this maneuver involves the helicopter riding across the ground for some distance, it is especially important to clear the area that will be servicing as the runway. The throttle should be increased until the proper RPM is achieved; then, the collective should be raised. The goal is to reach the point where the helicopter is light on its skids. The anti-torque pedals and cyclic are used as needed to ensure that the helicopter is properly turned towards the intended flight path; then, the pilot should begin with slight forward pressure on the cyclic.

The helicopter will begin to slide forward on the ground. As it does so, use of the anti-torque pedals should continue to keep the helicopter's heading constant, and left or right cyclic should be applied if the helicopter starts to drift laterally. As the helicopter accelerates, the rotor will become more effective, and the helicopter will start to become progressively lighter. This will reduce the friction between the wheels (or skids) and the ground, causing the helicopter to accelerate even faster.

Eventually, the helicopter will become light enough to lift off the ground. As it does, the pilot should increase the collective to assist and prepare to increase the cyclic when the helicopter's nose begins to rise due to translational lift. From this point, the technique to finish takeoff is identical to a takeoff from hover (starting from phase three) and the same procedure can be used.

Straight and Level Flight

In **straight and level flight**, the goal is to keep a helicopter in cruising flight on a straight flightpath and prevent any change in altitude, velocity, or heading that the pilot doesn't initiate. A helicopter is anything but stable, so this is often easier said than done. Fortunately, the helicopter is very controllable, so an experienced pilot can often make corrections before the helicopter has even begun to move, relying more on feel than sight.

The airspeed of a helicopter depends primarily on its attitude (or pitch up or down relative to the horizon), which, in turn, is controlled by the cyclic. Increasing the pressure to the cyclic increases the rate at which the attitude changes, but in most cases, there's little need for rapid acceleration. Instead, the cyclic should be applied slowly and in moderation. Although drag dampens the helicopter's acceleration somewhat, the cyclic is still an acceleration control, and too much forward pressure can make maintaining a constant rate difficult.

Additionally, there is a bit of control lag with the cyclic, in that there is a short delay between input through the cyclic and output through the helicopter. One all too common mistake is for a pilot to adjust the cyclic too far. This results in the helicopter moving much faster than intended, a loss of altitude, and many other potential complications that could easily be avoided simply by remembering the delay between input and output.

The same procedure also works in reverse, should the speed need to be decreased. Applying aft pressure to the cyclic raises the helicopter's nose and levels out its attitude. With less thrust being generated, the drag created by the helicopter's movements eventually slows the helicopter down until the thrust and the drag are once again opposite. Additional care must be taken while slowing down, however, so that the helicopter does not end in the shaded area of the velocity-height diagram.

Whenever the cyclic is used, the collective almost certainly needs to be adjusted as well. As mentioned previously, the cyclic functions by changing the angle of the rotor disk, which changes the direction of lift and repurposes some of the lift as thrust. In order to keep the same altitude, lift must remain the same. This can be achieved by increasing or decreasing the collective, while simultaneously adjusting the cyclic, so that the lift lost to thrust is immediately regained by raising the collective. Of course, increasing the collective requires more power, so the throttle also needs to be rotated to keep RPM. More power creates more torque, so the anti-torque pedals need to be used as well.

Banking Turns

There are many parallels between hovering forward flight and straight and level flight. Though each has their own nuances, many of the same principles from one apply to the other as both use a similar mechanism to create and control airspeed. The same cannot be said for hovering turns and banking turns, which share only one commonality—the goal to change the heading of the helicopter.

In a hovering turn, the primary control used to make the turn is the anti-torque pedals. However, when attempting to perform a **banking turn**, the cyclic is used instead. Specifically, the cyclic is pushed laterally to bank the helicopter, which allows the generated thrust to rotate the helicopter in an arc.

The final banking angle, and the rate at which it banks, depends on the duration and force applied to the cyclic. Like always, the control should be applied slowly so that control of the helicopter's turn can be maintained. When the desired turn angle is reached, releasing the cyclic to its neutral position will keep the helicopter banking at that angle.

The greater the angle, the sharper the turn, but this sharpness comes at the cost of the lift generated. Thus, the greater the angle, the more the collective needs to be raised to keep altitude throughout the maneuver and the more power that is needed to keep up the RPM. Care should be taken to ensure that sufficient power is available to complete the turn at the desired angle or else the helicopter will lose altitude.

The anti-torque pedals are still needed during this maneuver, but since the heading is supposed to change during the maneuver, using the helicopter's facing as a guideline for when to apply the pedals will not work. Instead, the pilot should look for signs of slipping or skidding and react appropriately. Both involve a failure of the helicopter's heading and actual direction of movement to match, which result in inefficient flight.

Slipping occurs when the helicopter's banking angle is too great for the rate of turn. In this case, the helicopter's nose will be pointing outwards from the direction of the turn. This results in the helicopter sliding laterally into the turn. This can be corrected by increasing the pressure on the pedal in the direction of the turn or decreasing the pressure on the pedal away from the turn.

Skidding occurs when the helicopter's rate of turn is too great for the angle of bank. In this case, the helicopter's nose will be pointing inwards from the direction of the turn. This results in the helicopter sliding laterally away from the turn. This can be corrected by increasing the pressure on the pedal away from the turn or by decreasing the pressure on the pedal in the direction of the turn.

Once the turn nears the finish, cyclic pressure should be applied in the opposite direction of the turn to level out the helicopter, and the helicopter will stop turning. Reducing the banking angle will restore the lift, so the collective and throttle will need to be decreased. Otherwise, the helicopter might climb. Also, if the cyclic is not applied until the turn is actually reached, the helicopter will end up turning too far as the helicopter requires time to level out. To prevent this, the pilot should begin to apply counter cyclic pressure shortly before arriving at the desired angle.

Normal Climb and Descent

Although technically two separate maneuvers, climbing and descending are very similar in execution, with one being basically the opposite of the other. Both primarily use the collective and the throttle, although both allow for cyclic adjustments to influence the rate of climb and descent at the expense of airspeed.

To perform a climb, the collective must be raised to generate additional thrust. The throttle needs to be raised in tandem to keep RPM consistent, which requires additional application of the anti-torque pedals to keep the helicopter's heading constant. Since this application increases the total thrust generated (irrespective of the angle of the rotor disk), it will also increase the airspeed of the helicopter, if the helicopter has any forward attitude. Minor aft pressure should be applied to the cyclic to raise the helicopter's attitude slightly. This change in attitude will decrease the amount of thrust derived from the lift, but the lost thrust should be replaced as the net lift is increased.

If a faster climb is desired, more aft pressure can be applied to the cyclic, further reducing the amount of generated thrust to increase the amount of generated lift. This results in decreased airspeed, however, so caution must be taken to ensure that the helicopter continues to maintain enough airspeed to stay out of the shaded areas of the velocity-height diagram. However, as altitude increases, the shaded area gets smaller and smaller, allowing progressively lower speeds.

When leveling off a climb, the helicopter's momentum will carry it beyond the desired altitude, so the pilot should begin leveling off a bit before reaching the desired height. Typically, 10% of the helicopter's rate of ascent is ideal, so a 100 FPM climb would only need 10 feet to stop in time, while climbing at 700 FPM would need 70 feet.

The collective should be lowered slowly, adjusting the throttle and anti-torque pedals as needed to keep the RPM and heading consistent throughout the process. As the lift decreases, the thrust decreases. The

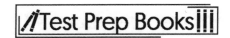

pilot should apply forward pressure on the cyclic as well to keep airspeed and assist with reducing lift. As the intended height is reached, cyclic pressure should be applied to return to the desired attitude, and any final adjustments to the collective and throttle should be made to stabilize the helicopter's altitude.

A descent functions very much the same, just in reverse. To descend, thrust must be decreased, to allow gravity to pull the helicopter down. To do this, the collective must be lowered, and the throttle must be dialed back. With less lift being generated, thrust and airspeed will also decrease. If a constant airspeed is desired, the cyclic will need to be pushed forward slightly to increase the thrust component of the lift. Since the greater thrust component comes at the cost of the lift, this also results in the helicopter descending faster.

By applying the same method, the descent can be sped up by increasing the forward pressure on the cyclic further and increasing airspeed, causing the helicopter to descend more rapidly. Just as with a climb, the helicopter must not be allowed to reach the shaded area of the velocity-height diagram.

When leveling off a descent, just as with a climb, a pilot should expect forward momentum to carry the helicopter some distance after beginning to slow down. The same 10% rule applies here. To begin leveling off from a descent, the collective should be raised slowly, controlling throttle and the anti-torque pedals to maintain RPM and heading, just as was done when climbing.

Also, like climbing, leveling off will influence airspeed; in this case, the increasing lift will increase thrust, and aft pressure to the cyclic is needed to keep airspeed constant. Adjustments should continue to be made to the collective and cyclic, until the helicopter has leveled out at the desired airspeed.

Taxiing

Taxiing is less a maneuver and more of a combination of other maneuvers performed with additional limitations. Taxiing is primarily used to move a helicopter a short distance, either to ferry passengers or cargo or simply to reposition the aircraft for some other purpose, such as a cleared runway to allow the helicopter to take off. Taxiing is also unique in that it often involves the use of taxiways or other prescribed routes to follow ahead of time, not unlike a road. There are three types of taxiing for helicopters, each with its own uses. The three types are hover, air, and surface taxiing.

Hover Taxiing

Hover Taxiing involves moving about in a hovering helicopter and employs hovering, forward flight, and hovering turns to move about. Although the exact height of flight varies by taxiway, it is virtually always no more than 25 feet above the ground. Because of the low speed of hover taxiing, this is most often used to reposition a helicopter rather than as a form of transportation.

Air Taxiing

Air taxiing involves higher speeds and altitudes, although generally it does not exceed heights of 100 feet. Since the helicopter is flying both higher and faster, straight and level flight and banking turns are used instead, as well as climbing and descending when necessary.

Additionally, a takeoff is always required to enter an air taxi, whether from a hover or the surface. Otherwise, there is little difference between free flight and a taxiway, though in the latter, the helicopter pilot is expected to avoid flying directly above other vehicles or personnel, whether on the ground or in the sky.

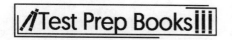

Surface Taxiing

Surface taxiing is the only one that requires any technique that hasn't already been discussed. In a surface taxi, the helicopter is kept on the ground the entire time. To accomplish this, the collective is raised until the helicopter is light on its wheels (or skids), just as if preparing for a surface takeoff. Also, like a surface takeoff, the collective is then used to create forward movement. That, however, is where the similarities end.

When performing a surface taxi, the helicopter should never move faster than a brisk walk, to prevent the lift from having any chance of taking the helicopter off the ground. Additionally, although some cyclic is needed to start the forward movement, the speed of the helicopter is controlled through the collective instead.

Although the friction between the wheels (or skids) and the ground makes the helicopter far more stable than when it is in the sky, yawing still occurs, requiring some anti-torque pedal application to negate. Likewise, any strong winds capable of pushing the helicopter need to be countered by applying cyclic pressure in the direction of the incoming wind.

Fixed-Wing Maneuvers

Takeoffs and Departure Climbs

Although one maneuver, takeoffs can be separated into three parts for ease of explanation. The FAA terms them takeoff roll, lift-off, and the initial climb.

Takeoff Roll

There are several things to note during the takeoff roll. To achieve sufficient airspeed during takeoff, normal takeoffs preferentially head into the wind. Throttle should be applied gradually during the takeoff roll, to prevent sudden torque turning the plane in single-engine planes or multi-engine planes without counter-rotating propellers. The rudder and aileron controls should be moved right to counteract the clockwise spin of propeller (or reverse in craft with counterclockwise single propellers). During the takeoff roll the elevator should be used minimally to keep the plane steady, but ideally kept in a neutral position if the plane is properly trimmed.

To start the takeoff roll, the throttle should be applied gently and the plane steered to the runway primarily with the rudder and some brake use and then aligned with the centerline on the runway. Once on the runway, throttle can be gradually increased. Note that in a crosswind, ailerons should be used to roll into the crosswind to keep the plane centered on the runway. As the speed increases, fewer rudder and elevator adjustments will be necessary as they will move towards a neutral position. Once the plane has accelerated enough, it's time for lift-off.

Lift-off

During takeoff roll, the plane's pitch was kept level with the runway. Once the plane reaches a speed where all of the flight controls become effective, the elevator controls can be pulled back gently to pitch the plane up and raise the nose wheel slightly off the ground. This is the lift-off pitch attitude, which should then be maintained by adjusting the trim to reduce elevator control pressures. This pitch should be held until the plane lifts off. Applying excessive back pressure on the elevator control should be avoided, because raising the pitch will create an excessive angle of attack, which can cause it to lower back to the ground or stall. Conversely, too little back pressure on the elevators or not maintaining elevator control through lift-off will allow the nose to lower, reducing the angle of attack and lift, allowing the plane to settle back to the ground.

Initial Climb

Once the plane lifts off, it should be at the pitch attitude to accelerate to the best rate of climb (V_Y). If trimmed correctly during lift-off, some back pressure on the elevators may be needed to maintain this pitch attitude. This should be held until reaching the climb speed and into a positive rate of climb, at which point flaps and landing gear should be retracted.

Engine power should be kept at takeoff power until at least 500 feet above any surrounding obstacles. To control airspeed during takeoff, minor pitch adjustments must be made while scanning outside the plane to adjust in relation to the horizon. For pitch adjustments during climb, wait a few moments to allow plane to accelerate or decelerate from the change in pitch.

Approaches and Landings

For every takeoff there's a landing. A normal landing involves flying directly into a light wind, with engine power to spare, and landing along flat, rigid ground with no obstacles and plenty of room to stop. These are ideal conditions, but conditions are not always ideal, though the plane *will* reach the ground again, one way or another. Therefore, it's imperative to be versed on how to land in many conditions. Like with takeoffs, an approach and landing can be split into segments to explain the changes needed during different stages of approach and landing.

Base Leg

This step of approach requires finding the best height and distance for the plane to enter the final approach smoothly and then descending towards that point with reduced speed and power. The airspeed of the plane in the base leg should be approximately 1.4 times the aircraft's landing configuration stall speed (V_{S_0}), which is the stall speed if the engine was powered off with the landing gear and flaps down. The approach in this stage should be perpendicular to the runway until a slight-to-medium banked turn—the base-to-final approach turn—can bring the aircraft parallel to the runway at the desired final approach point. If landing with a headwind, the base leg will have a crosswind, so turning partly into the wind during the base leg may be necessary to avoid drifting off track.

Final Approach

After the turn to final approach in an ideal headwind, the plane should be aligned longitudinally with the centerline of the runway. After the plane is aligned, the flaps and pitch can be adjusted to set the rate of descent onto the runway. A plane's recommended airspeed for final approach should be found in the manufacturer's documents, but otherwise 1.3 times the V_{S_0} is recommended. Airspeed can be maintained at this stage with power and pitch adjustments, but it should be noted to avoid pitching up excessively without appropriate power increase, due to the increased stall speed. The goal during the final approach stage is to descend at an airspeed that will allow the plane to touchdown just above stall speed and minimize floating above the runway. Executing a proper final approach makes the following landing steps easier to perform.

Round Out

The round out during landing is the gradual transition from an approach attitude to a landing attitude and bringing the plane to fly parallel to the runway. This stage begins between 10 and 20 feet above the runway. Airspeed is decreased steadily during this stage When the plane slows down its descent, the pitch attitude needs to be raised slowly as well. During this stage, the elevators should not be lowered. If the pitch attitude is too high, loss of lift should instead be compensated for using the throttle.

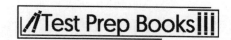
Touchdown

Touchdown is the stage of landing where the plane is supposed to make contact with the runway. If the airspeed has been properly slowed, the plane can touchdown near its stalling speed. This is also ideal for nose-wheel planes since it allows touchdown primarily on the main wheels with the plane at the appropriate landing attitude. Once the plane has touched down, elevator back-pressure is used to maintain a positive angle of attack to slow the plane. Once the plane has lost some speed, the elevators are gradually brought closer to neutral to reduce lift and bring the front landing gear down to allow the plane to roll on the runway. In a crosswind landing the plane faces partially into the wind, but in all cases the plane's facing must be parallel with the direction it's moving to avoid placing side stress on the landing gear.

After-Landing Roll

The last step of landing is decelerating the plane to taxi speed after touchdown while keeping the plane under control. While on the ground it remains critical to limit sideways forces on the landing gear. Sharp turns without appropriate aileron control can cause the outer wing to drop and damage the landing gear. As the plane slows down the effectiveness of the rudder will also decrease, since its ability to yaw the plane depends on airspeed, so the nose wheel steering takes over for steering at low speeds. During the landing roll the pilot should ideally place as much weight on the wheels as possible to increase the effectiveness of the brakes, which should be applied gradually and firmly, and not feathered. As with the rudder, the aileron controls still control the roll of the plane, depending on their speed, and can be used to stabilize the plane through ground turns and in crosswinds. The flaps may be retracted once the plane has slowed and has moved onto the taxiway.

Taxiing

Taxiing is moving the plane, on the ground, with its own power (as opposed to moving them with a tractor or tug). The first step when taxiing is to test the brakes. Throttle should be applied gently to slowly move forwards, then slowly returning throttle to neutral and lightly applying one brake then the other to ensure they are functioning.

Steering on ground is done with the rudder controls and landing gear brakes. Initiating a turn and to start moving may require higher throttle than to maintain the maneuver, similar to overcoming static friction. The rudder should be turned in the direction of the turn until shortly before reaching the correct heading, and then set to neutral or the opposite position to straighten or counteract any continued rotation. At low speeds, planes with steerable nose wheels will steer largely by the front wheel.

Fixed-Wing Aircraft

A fixed-wing aircraft is one in which movement of the wings in relation to the aircraft is not used to generate lift, even though technically they flex in flight, as do all wings. In contrast, helicopters generate lift through rotating airfoils.

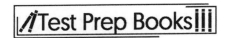

Fixed-wing aircraft have the following items in common: wings, flight controls, tail assembly, landing gear, fuselage, and an engine or powerplant. Here's an illustration of the parts of a plane:

Wings

An airfoil is a surface such as a wing, elevator, or aileron that is designed to help create lift and control of an aircraft by using and manipulating air flow. The standard wing, or airfoil, is mounted to the sides of the fuselage. The outline or cross section of the airfoil is referred to as the "airfoil profile." The standard wing has an upper surface that is curved while the lower surface is relatively flat. The air moves over the curved surface of the wing at a higher speed than it moves under the flat surface. The difference in airflow on the surfaces of the wing creates lift due to the aircraft's forward airspeed, which enables flight.

Many modern aircraft structures use full cantilever wings, meaning no external bracing is required. The strength in this design is from the internal structural members and the fuselage. Semi-cantilever wings use some form of external bracing, whether it be wires or struts.

Aircraft wing designs vary based on the characteristics and type of performance needed for the aircraft. Changing the wing design changes the amount of lift that can be created and the amount of stability and control the aircraft will have at different speeds. Some aircraft have wings that are designed to tilt, sweep, or fold. So long as they do not generate lift, they are still considered fixed-wing aircraft. Wing geometry is related to the shape of the aircraft wings when viewed from the front of the aircraft, or from above.

Flight Controls

Flight controls, like the name implies, are used to direct the forces on an aircraft in flight for the purpose of directional and attitude control. Flight controls vary from simple mechanical (manually operated)

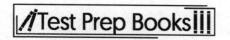

systems, to hydro-mechanical systems, to fly-by-wire systems. Fly-by-wire systems send signal via wire to control the plane.

When discussing flight controls, it's important to understand the terms **leading edge** and **trailing edge**. Leading edge refers to the front part of the wing that separates air, forcing it to go above or below the wing. Trailing edge is the back part of the wing and where the air comes back together.

The flight controls typically are divided into primary and secondary systems.

The primary flight controls are responsible for the movement of the aircraft along its three axes of flight. Primary flight controls on an aircraft are the **elevators**, **ailerons**, and **rudder**. Elevators are mounted on the trailing edges of horizontal stabilizers and are used for controlling aircraft pitch about the lateral axis. The ailerons are mounted on the trailing edges of the wings and are used for controlling aircraft roll about the longitudinal axis. The rudder is mounted on the trailing edge of the vertical fin and is used for controlling rotation (yaw) around the vertical axis. Here's an illustration of pitch, roll, and yaw along the three axes.

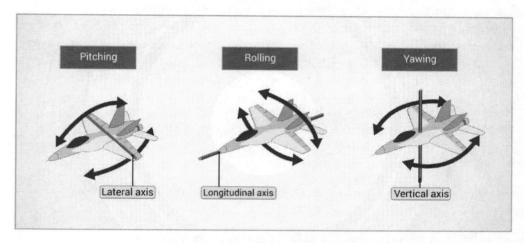

Secondary, or auxiliary, flight controls include (but are not limited to): flaps, slats, spoilers, speed brakes, and the trim system. Flaps are the hinged portion of the wing trailing edge between the ailerons and the fuselage, and sometimes may be located on the leading edge of a wing as well. If used during takeoff, flaps reduce the amount of runway and time needed to takeoff. During landings, flaps increase the drag on the wings slowing the plane down and allowing it to go slower right before it lands, which then reduces the amount of runway needed. Essentially, flaps allow the aircraft to produce more lift at slower airspeeds. Flaps are also utilized on some planes to increase maneuverability. The amount of flap extension and the angle can be adjusted by the flap levers located in the cockpit.

Spoilers are located on the upper, or trailing edge, of the wing and are used to decrease lift. They allow the nose of the aircraft to be pitched down without increasing the airspeed, allowing for a safe landing speed. Slats are located on the middle to outboard portion of the leading edge of the wing. They are used to create additional lift and slower flight by extending the shape of the wing. Flaps and slats are hidden inside the wing and are extended during takeoff and landing.

The trim system is an inexpensive autopilot that eliminates the need for the pilot to constantly maintain pressure on the controls. Most aircraft trim systems contain trim, balance, anti-balance, and servo tabs. These tabs are found on the trailing edge of primary flight control surfaces and are used to counteract hydro-mechanical and aerodynamic forces acting on the aircraft.

Tail Assembly

The tail assembly of an aircraft is commonly referred to as the empennage. The empennage structure typically includes a tail cone, fixed stabilizers (horizontal and vertical), and moveable surfaces to assist in directional control. The moveable surfaces are the rudder, which is attached to the vertical stabilizer, and the elevators attached to the horizontal stabilizers.

Landing Gear

Aircraft require landing gear not only for takeoffs and landings but also to support the aircraft while it is on the ground. The landing gear must be designed to support the entire weight of the aircraft and handle the loads placed on it during landing, as well as be as light as possible. Small aircraft that fly at low-speeds usually have fixed landing gear, which means it is stationary and does not have the ability to retract in flight. Aircraft that fly at higher speeds require retractable landing gear so that the gear is not damaged in the airstream. Retractable landing gear makes the aircraft more aerodynamic by reducing drag, but usually at the cost of additional weight when compared to the fixed landing gear. Also, the landing gear should only be operated (extended or retracted) when the airspeed indicator is at or below the aircraft's maximum landing-gear operating speed, or V_{LO}. Airspeeds above V_{LO} can damage the landing gear operating mechanism. When the gear is down and locked, the aircraft should not be operated above the aircraft's maximum landing-gear extended speed, or V_{LE}. Since landing gear is more stable when all the way down than when being moved, V_{LE} will be higher for an aircraft than V_{LO}. A switch or lever that resembles the shape of a wheel is used to raise and lower the landing gear.

Landing gear is made from a variety of materials, such as magnesium, steel, and aluminum. Most landing gear has some type of shock absorbers and braking system. Not all landing gear uses wheels. Depending on what the aircraft is used for, it may have skis, skids, pontoons, or floats instead of tires for landing on snow, ice, or water.

Landing gear is typically found in two configurations: tricycle gear and conventional gear (also known as tail wheel gear).

Tricycle gear is the most common configuration. Tricycle gear has a single wheel in the front (usually under the nose) and two wheels side-by-side at the center of gravity of the aircraft. Large, heavy aircraft may contain extra wheels in this configuration. Small aircraft equipped with nose landing gear can typically be steered with rudder pedals.

Conventional tail wheel aircraft or "tail draggers" were more common in the early days of aviation. The two main wheels supported the heaviest portion of the aircraft, with the third smaller wheel was near the tail. Having the smaller wheel in the tail allowed the aircraft to rest at an incline on the ground, which provided more clearance for the nose propeller. In some conventional gear, the tail wheel could be steered mechanically with the rudder pedals.

Fuselage

The fuselage is the main structure, or airframe, of an aircraft. The fuselage is where the cockpit, or cabin, of the aircraft is, and where passengers or cargo may be located. It provides attachment points for the main components of the aircraft such as the wings, engines, and empennage. If an aircraft is a single-engine, the fuselage houses the powerplant as well. If the powerplant is a reciprocating engine, it is mounted in the front of the aircraft, while a turbine engine would be mounted in the rear of the aircraft. **Cowling** is the term for the covering of an airplane's engine which is streamlined to maximize aerodynamics.

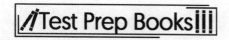
Aircraft contain a battery that is charged by an alternator or generator. Wiring takes the electric current to where it's needed throughout the plane. Some type of warning system will be in place to warn of inadequate current output. This could be a warning light or an ammeter. If the number showing on an ammeter is positive, it means the battery is charging. If the number is negative, it means that the alternator or generator cannot keep up with the amount of current being used. Some aircraft have a load meter, which shows the amount of current being drawn from the battery.

Fuselage structures are usually classified as truss, monocoque, and semi-monocoque. The truss fuselage is typically made of steel tubing welded together, which enables the structure to handle tension and compression loads. In lighter aircraft, an aluminum alloy may be used along with cross-bracing. A single shell fuselage is referred to as monocoque, which uses a stronger skin to handle the tension and compression loads. There is also a semi-monocoque fuselage, which is basically a combination of the truss and monocoque fuselage, and is the most commonly used.

Powerplant

The powerplant of an aircraft is its engine, which is a component of the propulsion system that generates mechanical power and thrust. Most modern aircraft engines are typically either turbine or piston engines.

Flight Envelope

The flight envelope (also known as the performance envelope or service envelope) refers to the capabilities of an aircraft based on its design in terms of altitude, airspeed, loading factors, and maneuverability. When an aircraft is pushed to the point where it exceeds design limitations for that specific aircraft, it is considered to be operating outside the envelope, which is considered dangerous.

All aircraft have approved flight manuals that contain the flight limitations or parameters. To ensure an aircraft is being operated properly, a pilot needs to be familiar with the aircraft's flight envelope prior to flight. The flight parameters are based on the engine and wing design and include the following: maximum and minimum speed, stall speed, climb rate, glide ratio, maximum altitude, and the maximum amount of gravity forces (g-forces) the aircraft can withstand.

- The **maximum speed** of an aircraft is based on air resistance getting lower at higher altitudes, to a point where increased altitude no longer increases maximum speed due to lack of oxygen to "feed" the engine.

- The **stalling speed** is the minimum speed at which an aircraft can maintain level flight. As the aircraft gains altitude, the stall speed increases (since the aircraft's weight can be better supported through speed).

- The **climb rate** is the vertical speed of an aircraft, which is the increase in altitude in respect to time.

- The **climb gradient** is the ratio of the increase in altitude to the horizontal air distance.

- The **glide ratio** is the ratio of horizontal distance traveled per rate of fall.

- The **maximum altitude** of an aircraft is also referred to as the service ceiling. The ceiling is usually determined by the aircraft performance and the wings, and is where an altitude at a given speed can no longer be increased at level flight.

- The **maximum g-forces** each aircraft can withstand varies but is based on its design and structural strength.

Commercial aircraft are considered to have a small flight envelope, since the range of speed and maneuverability is rather limited, and they are designed to operate efficiently under moderate conditions. The Federal Aviation Administration (FAA) is the controlling body in the United States pertaining to authorized flight envelopes and restrictions for commercial and civilian aircraft. The FAA may reduce a flight envelope for added safety as needed.

Military aircraft, especially fighter jets, have extremely large flight envelopes. By design, these aircraft are very maneuverable and can operate at high speeds as their purpose requires. The term "pushing the envelope" originally referred to military pilots taking an aircraft to the extreme limits of their capabilities, mostly during combat, but also during aircraft flight testing. The term "outside the envelope" is when the aircraft is pushed outside the design specifications and is considered very dangerous. Operating outside the limits of the aircraft can severely degrade the life of components, or even lead to mechanical failure.

Some of the modern fly-by-wire aircraft have built-in flight envelope protection. This protection is built into the control system and helps prevent a pilot from forcing an aircraft into a situation that exceeds its structural and aerodynamic operational limits. This system is beneficial in emergency situations because it prevents the pilots from endangering the aircraft while making split-second decisions.

Helicopters

Helicopters, a type of rotary-wing or rotorcraft, are extremely versatile aircraft that may be used for a wide array of situations where a typical aircraft could not perform. A helicopter differs from other types of aircraft that derive lift from their wings, as it gets its lift and thrust from the rotors. The rotors are basically rotating airfoils; hence the name rotorcraft. The "rotating wing," or main rotor, may have two or more blades whose profiles resemble that of aircraft wings.

Although rotorcraft come in many shapes and sizes, they mostly have the same major components in common. There is a cabin, an airframe, landing gear, a powerplant, a transmission, and an anti-torque system. The cabin of the rotorcraft houses the crew and cargo. The airframe is the fuselage where components are mounted and attached. The landing gear may be made up of wheels, skis, skids, or floats.

Due to its operating characteristics, a helicopter is able to:

- Take off and land vertically (in almost any small, clear area)
- Fly forward, backward, and laterally
- Operate at lower speeds
- Hover for extended periods of time

Common uses for the helicopter include military operations, search and rescue, law enforcement, firefighting, medical transport, news reporting, and tourism.

Helicopters are subjected to the same forces as other aircraft: lift, weight, thrust, and drag. In addition, helicopters also have some unique forces they are subjected to: torque, centrifugal and centripetal force, gyroscopic precession, dissymmetry of lift, effective translational lift, transverse flow effect, and Coriolis effect.

Here are some examples of different helicopter designs:

Torque

Torque from the engine turning the main rotor forces the body of the helicopter in the opposite direction. Most helicopters use a tail rotor, which counters this torque force by pushing or pulling against the tail.

Centrifugal and Centripetal Force

Centrifugal force is the apparent force that causes rotating bodies to move away from the center of rotation. Centripetal force is the force that keeps an object a certain distance from the center of rotation.

Gyroscopic Precession

Gyroscopic precession is when the applied force to a rotating object is shown 90° later than where the force was applied.

Dissymmetry of Lift

Dissymmetry of lift is the difference in lift between the advancing and retreating blades of the rotor system. The difference in lift is due to directional flight. The rotor system compensates for dissymmetry of lift with blade flapping, which allows the blades to twist and lift in order to balance the advancing and retreating blades. The pilot also compensates by cyclic feathering. Together, blade flapping and cyclic feathering eliminate dissymmetry of lift.

Effective Translational Lift

Effective translational lift (ETL) is the improved efficiency that results from directional flight. Efficiency is gained when the helicopter moves forward, as opposed to hovering. The incoming airflow essentially pushes the turbulent air behind the helicopter, which provides a more horizontal airflow for the airfoil to move through. This typically occurs between 16 and 24 knots.

Transverse Flow Effect

Transverse flow effect is the difference in airflow between the forward and aft portions of the rotor disk. During forward flight, there is more downwash in the rear portion of the rotor disk. The downward flow on the rear portion of the disk results in a reduced AOA and produces less lift. The front half of the rotor produces more lift due to an increased AOA. Transverse flow occurs between 10 and 20 knots and can be easily recognized by the increased vibrations during take-off and landing.

Coriolis Effect

The Coriolis Effect is when an object moving in a rotating system experiences an inertial force (Coriolis) acting perpendicular to the direction of motion and the axis of rotation. In a clockwise rotation, the force acts to the left of the motion of an object. If the rotation is counterclockwise, the force acts to the right of the motion of an object.

A typical helicopter is controlled through use of the cyclic control stick, the collective controls lever, and the anti-torque pedals.

Cyclic Control

The cyclic is the control stick that is used to control the movement of the helicopter forward, backward, or sideways. Simply stated, the cyclic changes the pitch of the rotor blades cyclically in any of 360°. The cyclic stick also contains several buttons that control the trim, intercom, and radio. These will differ slightly depending on each model helicopter.

Collective Controls

The collective control is used to increase the pitch of the main rotor simultaneously at all points of the rotor blade rotation. The collective increases or decreases total rotor thrust; the cyclic changes the direction of rotor thrust. In forward flight, the collective pitch changes the amount of thrust, which in turn can change the speed or altitude based on the use of the cyclic. During hovering, the collective control is used to adjust the altitude of hover.

Anti-Torque Pedals

The anti-torque pedals are used to control yaw on a helicopter. These pedals are located in the same place, and serve a similar purpose, as rudder pedals on an airplane. Application of pressure on a pedal changes the pitch of the tail rotor blade, which will increase or reduce the tail rotor thrust and cause the nose of the helicopter to yaw in the desired direction.

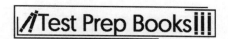

Aerodynamic Principles

The Nature of Flight

Flight is not a natural state. All objects are affected by gravity, which constantly pulls things downwards—unless something else is providing support. A person sitting in a chair is certainly off the ground and, despite the constant pull of gravity, as long as he or she is supported by the chair, that's not likely to change. Even as gravity pulls down on the person, he or she collides with the chair, which then pushes the person up. It may seem rather confusing that an inanimate object has the ability to push up, but that is exactly what the chair does. If it didn't, then the chair would simply collapse under the person's weight, and the person would fall to the ground. Instead, the chair's rigidity keeps the chair intact, and the chair pushes upwards with enough force to maintain its shape and form. The ultimate takeaway message here is that in order to overcome the downward force of gravity, there needs to be some source of upward force to cancel it out.

Overcoming the force of gravity presents a unique challenge for an aircraft, as there isn't any chair equivalent that can conveniently lift a helicopter off the ground. Even if there were, this hypothetical object would also be affected by gravity and would, in turn, need to be supported by the ground. Obviously, this force has to come from somewhere. In the case of a helicopter, the force comes in the form of lift generated by an airfoil.

Lift

An **airfoil** (used in virtually all aspects of flight) is a blade or wing; it cuts through the air so that air passes above and below it. Moreover, the air is not treated equally by the airfoil's design. The top of the airfoil is *cambered*, or curved, allowing the air to quickly get past the airfoil and create a low pressure. The air that goes below the airfoil has a shorter distance to travel and is slower, which results in high pressure. **Lift** is the upward force created by the difference in air pressure above and below the airfoil. It is what allows aircraft to fly. A good way to visualize why this works is to consider a block between two springs:

When the block is directly between the two springs, the block doesn't move because the pressure from the springs is equal and opposite, canceling each other out. However, if one spring were to be compressed while the other was stretched, the compressed spring would suddenly exert more force, while the stretched spring would exert less. The block would be pushed until the springs are once equal and opposite. Likewise, the reduced pressure above the airfoil pushes *downward* with less force than the increased pressure below pushes *upward*, and lift is created.

The amount of lift created depends on several things, from the material and shape of the airfoil to the density of the air in the vicinity. A pilot can directly influence only two—the angle of incidence (pitch angle) and the angle of attack (AOA).

Pitch Angle
The **pitch angle** is the angle between the *chord line* (a line drawn between the leading edge and the trailing edge of the airfoil) and the direction of the rotor's spin. The angle can be controlled by adjusting pitch with the elevators on an airplane or directly controlled using the collective on a helicopter (to be discussed in further detail, below).

AOA
The **angle of attack (AOA)** is the angle between the chord line and the direction of the incoming air. On a windless day, AOA and pitch angle can potentially be the same when hovering as the only relative wind will be that created by the rotation, but knowing the difference is important.

Typically, in order to create lift, a *positive AOA* is needed—the *front* of the airfoil needs to be raised above the *back*, relative to the wind. If the angle is *zero* (when the two are actually at the same height, relative to the wind), no lift will be generated. *Negative lift* is technically possible by flying at a *negative AOA*. There are exceptions; however, some airfoils (specifically those that are either *cambered* or *nonsymmetrical*) can be designed to generate lift with a zero, or even negative, AOA, though increasing the AOA will still result in more lift.

Weight
It's not enough to simply create lift. **Weight** is the force acting on a body due to gravity, and **gravity** is the acceleration acting on a body due to the Earth's mass. The average acceleration upwards must be larger than the average gravity acting on the body, and the total generated lift needs be a larger force than the loaded weight. The **weight of the aircraft** refers to the weight of the helicopter itself, all of its passengers, cargo, fuel, and anything else that would fall to the ground, if they were not supported by the helicopter. The heavier the aircraft, the greater the force needed to move it, thus requiring more lift to get off the ground. Of course, gravity does not stop because the helicopter is off the ground, and the helicopter must continue maintaining at least as much lift or it risks losing altitude.

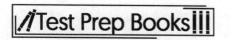

There are several factors that can potentially increase the weight and ultimately increase the amount of lift needed to stay aloft. To say that the aircraft's *weight* has increased, however, is a bit of a misnomer as the mass of the helicopter does not generally change significantly midflight (other than the burning of fuel). Rather, some factors can either decrease the effectiveness of lift or increase the potency of weight. Either change requires that additional lift is created to compensate as if its weight had actually increased. Strong winds and other adverse weather conditions can cause this, but a more frequently observable example is the simple act of banking the helicopter.

When **banking** the helicopter, the lift is no longer generated directly downwards; rather, some of the vertical lift is redirected into horizontal movement. This results in a descent, unless the total airfoil is increased to produce the appropriate amount of vertical lift once more. While, at small angles, the effect is quite tame, the effect gets exponentially stronger for each increase in banking angle. For example, a bank of 25° would result in a 10% increase in required lift, but increasing the angle by just nine more degrees, to an angle of 34°, the helicopter will have already reached a 20% increase. By the time an angle of 48° is reached, the lift will have increased by half again of what an upright helicopter requires. Were a helicopter to bank all the way to 90°, the airfoils would be generating only horizontal lift, with no vertical lift, and so the helicopter would essentially be free falling.

The added strain created by this effect is often called the **load factor** (or the **G load**) because the strain increases the load, or weight, on the airfoil. The value of the load factor does not give an exact value for this additional weight, but rather is expressed as a percentage of the helicopter's resting weight. This value can be calculated using the following equation:

$$G = \frac{L_1}{L_0}$$

Here, G is the load factor, L_1 is the actual load on the rotor blades, and L_0 is the resting, or normal, load. So, a 1-ton helicopter with a load factor of 3 experiences the same force as a 3-ton helicopter hovering at rest. If the helicopter is not able to generate sufficient lift to offset this increase, the helicopter will begin to lose altitude unless the pilot can adjust for the weight in other ways, such as reducing the banking angle. For that reason, knowing how much lift the helicopter can produce is crucial. Otherwise, the helicopter may become overloaded, which will cause the rotor to droop, and the aircraft will descend.

Thrust

Lift and weight are perhaps the most important forces involved in the helicopter's movement, but if they were the only two, the helicopter would be little more than a glorified elevator capable only of rising and falling. Just as force is needed to lift the helicopter vertically from the ground, force is also needed to move the helicopter horizontally. This force, called **thrust**, can be in any direction, but is almost always measured in horizontal motion. Thrust is primarily created by converting lift via alterations of the pitch angle and AOA. Since horizontal movement does not have to contend with gravity, less effort is required to shift the helicopter horizontally compared to that required vertically. This means that only a small portion of lift needs to be sacrificed to achieve some movement, although more can be sacrificed if faster horizontal movement is desired.

Drag

Just as lift contends with the weight of gravity, thrust also has an opposing force to overcome, called drag. **Drag** is actually a composite force, usually broken up into three subcategories known as profile, parasitic, and induced. All three forces change in varying amounts with the speed of the helicopter and, in most cases, with increasing, comes increasing drag. The faster the helicopter travels, the more thrust force is required to overcome the increased drag. However, there is a narrow but important exception, which will be discussed in more detail below.

Anyone who has ever ridden a bike or stood outside on a windy day has experienced drag. Drag is simply the sensation of the wind exerting force on objects that the wind passes through. The strength of that drag depends only on the relative speed of the wind, such that standing still in 20 MPH winds creates just as much drag as moving 20 MPH in still winds, or even moving 10 MPH into a 10 MPH wind. Regardless of the exact combination, the result is the same—both the object and the air attempt to occupy the same space, and the object must exert force to displace the air, even as the air tries to do the same to the object. The faster the wind is moving relative to the object, the more air that object has to push out of the way and the more air that pushes back on the object. This explains why increasing velocity also increases drag.

Parasitic Drag
Parasitic drag is the simplest of the three subtypes of drag and functions exactly as explained above. It is caused by the non-lifting portions of the helicopter, such as the fuselage, engine cowlings, hub, mast, landing gear, and external loads. Specifically, parasitic drag increases with airspeed and is the dominant type of drag at high airspeeds.

Profile Drag
Profile drag is similar to parasitic drag, but with one critical difference—it only concerns the drag created by the frictional resistance of spinning airfoils. Since the airfoils are much smaller than the rest of the helicopter and designed to be as aerodynamic as possible, profile drag is a lot smaller than the high speeds of the rotor blades might suggest, although the drag is still significant at lower speeds. Drag does increase as velocity increases, but only by a small margin, because relative to the speed at which the rotor blades are spinning, the velocity added by a moving helicopter only represents a small percent increase to its effective speed. Going from 5 MPH to 10 MPH will quadruple parasitic drag, but the rotor's speed is changing from approximately 605 MPH to 610 MPH, which would only increase the rotor's drag by less than one percent. This is not entirely accurate; since the airfoil is rotating, the actual speed of the rotor blade relative to the air changes, based on how far down the blade contact occurs and what direction the blade is currently spinning. However, this example should at least explain why profile drag increases so slowly relative to parasitic drag. When compared to the other two types of drag, profile drag remains midway throughout—neither dominating nor negligible.

Induced Drag
Induced drag is a byproduct of the lift created by the rotor, and its very existence is unique. As the blades spin, they briefly leave a small gap of empty space behind them where they once were, which is quickly filled by the air above and below the blade. Since the air is at a different pressure above and below, the air creates a spiral directly behind the blade, which pushes air in the opposite direction of lift. When the lift the helicopter creates is at an angle (such as is the case while banking), the induced drag is too, which causes some of the normally-downward directed force to instead face rearwards. This rearwards force pushes the helicopter back as the helicopter tries to move forward. The greater the AOA is, the greater the portion of the force that is directed rearwards. Since the angle of attack is usually greatest at lower airspeeds and reduced at higher airspeeds, this is the only drag that typically decreases as airspeed increases. When compared to the other two types of drag, induced drag is the primary force at low speeds, but at higher speeds becomes barely meaningful.

The **total drag** on the helicopter is simply the sum of the three subtypes. The graphic below shows how the individual components of drag add up at different speeds:

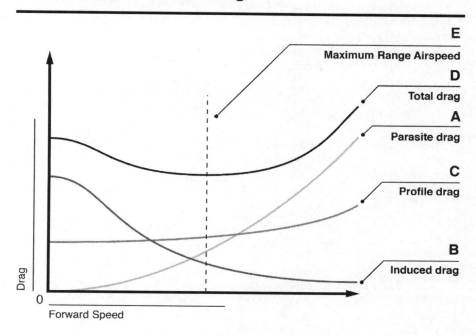

The Components of Drag

Induced drag generally contributes the most at lower speeds, while parasitic drag dominates at higher velocities. This unique behavior means that most helicopters have an optimal velocity, wherein induced drag has decreased significantly, but parasitic drag has not yet taken over. This speed is important because this value is the point at which the lift to drag ratio is highest, and is often used to determine a helicopter's best rate of climb and other numerical figures. This point is called the **maximum lift/drag ratio**, or $\frac{L}{D_{max}}$. Point E on the drag/airspeed relationship diagram represents the maximum range airspeed. This airspeed will allow the helicopter to fly the furthest distance on a tank of gas.

Airport Information

Airports come in all shapes and sizes, from tiny dirt strips to enormous concrete runways. Pilots are required to know the procedures and rules of the specific airports being used and understand pavement markings, lights, and signs that provide takeoff, landing, and taxiway information.

Procedures have been developed for airport traffic patterns and traffic control. These procedures include specific routes or specific runways for takeoffs and landings. Each airport traffic pattern depends on a number of factors, including obstructions and wind conditions.

Terms

- Clearway: A specified area after the runway that is clear of obstacles, at the same or nearly the same altitude as the runway, and specifically for planes to fly over in their initial ascent.

- Decision height (DH): The lowest height (in feet) in which if a pilot cannot see specified visual references, they must stop landing.

- Holding/Flying a Hold: Refers to a plane flying in an oval flight path near the airport while waiting for clearance to land.

- Runway visual range (RVR): The distance away from the airport in which a pilot should be able to see runway markings and/or lights.

- Threshold: The start or end of a runway.

- Taxiway: The paved area that planes travel on between the terminal and runway. The path a plane should follow on a taxiway is marked by a yellow line.

- Taxiway intersections: Where two taxiway routes intersect.

Signs
Here are some common taxiway signs:

Name	Sign Color	Letter Color	Function
no entry	red	white	indicates an area planes should not go into
runway location	black	yellow	displays current runway name
taxiway location	black	yellow	displays current taxiway name
direction/runway exit	yellow	black	displays name of upcoming taxiway that airplane is about to intersect with
runway	red	white	displays name of runway that airplane is about to intersect with

Lighting
These lights are visible to about 3 miles in the daytime and up to 20 miles at night.

- Approach Lighting Systems (ALS): A series of light bars leading up to a runway that assist the pilot in lining up with the runway.

- Runway centerline lights: these are used to aid aircraft when landing in darkness or other difficult visibility conditions. These lights are embedded into the runway. They begin as white, then alternate between red and white, and then are completely red at the end of the runway.

- Obstructions/aircraft warning lights: *Red* or *white* lights used to mark obstructions (like building and cell towers) both in airports and outside of them.

- Runway edge lights: These are *white* and highlight the boundaries of the runway. These are referred to a high, medium, or low intensity depending on the maximum intensity they can produce.

166

- Runway end identifier lights (REIL): Many airport runways have these two flashing *red* lights. They provide a warning that the runway is ending.

- Taxiway centerline lights: *Green* lights indicating the middle of a taxiway.

- Taxiway edge lights: *Blue* lights denoting the edge of a taxiway.

- Threshold lights: *Green* lights that indicate the start of the runway

Visual Approach Slope Indicators (VASI)

The visual approach slope indicator (VASI) is a light system of two sets of lights designed to provide visual guidance during approach of a runway. The light indicators are visible 3 to 5 miles away during daylight hours and up to 20 miles away in darkness. The indicators are designed to be used once the aircraft is already visually aligned with the runway. Both sets of lights can appear as white or red. When the front lights appear white and the back lights appear red, it indicates that the plane is at the proper angle. If both lights appear white, it means the pilot is too high, and if both appear red, it means the pilot is too low.

Precision Instrument Runways

Precision instrument runways have operational visual and electronic aids that provide directional guidance. These aides may be the ILS, Precision Approach Radar (PAR), or Microwave Landing System (MLS). Instrument runways have visual aids with a decision height greater than 200 feet and a runway visual range of 2,600 feet. These runways have **runway end lights**, which consist of eight lights (four on each side of the runway) that can appear as green or red—green to approaching planes and red to planes on the runway.

Non-Precision Instrument Runways

Non-precision instrument runways provide horizontal guidance only when there is an approved procedure for a straight-in non-precision instrument approach. The non-precision runways do not have full Instrument Landing System (ILS) capabilities, but they have approved procedures for localizer, Global Positioning System (GPS), Automatic Direction Finder (ADF), and Very High Frequency Omni-Directional Range (VOR) instrument approaches.

Visual Flight Rules Runways (VFR)

Visual flight rules (VFR) runways, also known as visual runways, operate completely under visual approach procedures. The pilot must be able to see the runway to land safely. There are no instrument approach procedures for this type of runway. They are typically found at small airports. Visual runways have centerline, designators, and threshold markings, as well as hold position markings for taxiway intersections.

Localizer Type Directional Aid (LDA)

Directional runways use a Localizer Type Directional Aid (LDA). The LDA provides a localizer-based instrument approach to an airport where, usually due to terrain, the localizer antenna is not in alignment with the runway. The LDA is more of a directional tool to enable the pilot to get close enough to where the runway can be seen.

Flight Rules and Regulations

Governments typically enjoy sovereign control over the airspace in the area above and surrounding their territories, and to optimize safety and efficiency, they promulgate and enforce regulations. Some of these rules and regulations are related to broad concepts, whereas others are hyper-focused on minute details or exceptions. In the United States, the Federal Aviation Administration (FAA) holds sweeping regulatory authority over general matters related to aviation, including nearly all matters related to civilian and commercial air travel.

The FAA publishes its rules and regulations for domestic air travel in Federal Aviation Regulations (FARs) Part 91, "General Operating and Flight Rules." The FARs are compulsory for all pilots operating within the jurisdiction of the FAA, although there are some limited exceptions for military aircraft under certain circumstances.

Some of the most prominent exceptions are expounded upon in the US Navy's NATOPS (Naval Air Training and Operating Procedures Standardization) General Flight and Operating Instructions Manuals (NATOPS manuals). The most important NATOPS manual is Commander, Naval Air Forces (CNAF) M-3710.7, which contains all of the rules applicable to US Navy aircraft. CNAF M-3710.7 orders all navy pilots to abide by the rules and regulations contained in FAR Part 91 except in situations explicitly described in the military manual. In other words, all departures from requirements contained in Part 91 need to be explicitly waived in the relevant NATOPS manual. Some military aircraft also have their own specific NATOPS manual (e.g., T-6 NATOPS), which override general NATOPS manuals and the FARs when there's conflict.

In addition to the FARs, the FAA publishes its regulations and best practices in Aeronautical Information Manuals (AIMs). The AIMs are published semi-regularly and contain glossaries and layman explanations, making them more approachable for readers lacking subject matter expertise. Despite the differences in style and format, the rules and regulations contained in the AIMs are entirely consistent with the FARs. Furthermore, the AIMs often have articles detailing how certain factors can affect flight, including the pilot's health, medicines, and substance abuse as well as weather patterns.

Although a broad and detailed regulatory framework governs flight in the United States, nothing in the FARs, NATOPS manuals, or other American flight regulations prevents pilots from breaking with standard operating procedures, as necessary, under exigent circumstances. Examples of exigent circumstances include an extreme weather event, a mechanical issue with the plane, or a health issue affecting a critical member of the flight crew.

One of the most important guiding principles in aviation holds that the pilot is the final decision maker and therefore is directly and fully responsible for the aircraft. For example, when facing an emergency or other exigent circumstances, FAR Part 91.3 grants pilots the authority to violate rules and regulations contained elsewhere in FAR Part 91 when such action is deemed necessary for safety. Pilots must provide a written explanation from the deviation in an after-action report under FAR Part 91.3(c). In addition to these emergency scenarios, pilots must heed the advice and adhere to the directives issued by air traffic controllers.

Air traffic control (ATC) agencies enforce the FAA's regulatory authority as provided in FAR Part 91. ATC is the sole source of clearances for a wide variety of flight activities, and FAR PART 91.123 states that pilots must comply with clearances except in the event of an emergency, traffic alert, collision system advisory, or amended clearance. If a pilot deviates from the clearance, the pilot must immediately notify ATC and later file emergency reports as requested by ATC.

ATC consists of four subsidiary facilities: Flight Service Station (FSS), Control Tower, Approach & Departure Control, and Air Route Traffic Control Center (ARTCC).

The FSS functions as a clearinghouse for information and, among other responsibilities, issues pilot briefings, handles en route communication, assists in emergencies, disseminates ATC clearances, and processes flight plans. Furthermore, some FSSs issue En Route Flight Advisory Service (Flight Watch), advise Customs and Immigration on international flights, and conduct limited search-and-rescue services. The military counterpart to the FSS is commonly referred to as **Base Operations**.

Control Tower is responsible for air traffic and seeks to optimize traffic for safety as well as orderly and speedy travel. Most Control Towers have three components: Clearance Delivery, Ground, and Tower. Clearance Delivery disseminates ATC clearances to aircraft prior to departure. Ground is responsible for aircraft travel on the ground at the airport and is primarily tasked with providing clearance to taxi. However, Ground cannot issue clearance for aircraft to enter active runways. Tower is responsible for maximizing the efficiency and ensuring the safety of airport traffic within a designated area. Most importantly, Tower provides clearance for aircraft to enter a runway, cross runways, take off, and land.

Approach Control (APC) is responsible for monitoring and controlling Instrument Flight Rules (IFR) traffic within the terminal area, meaning the entire area in which APC is capable of providing traffic control services. The terminal area is usually divided into numerous sections, and a designated air traffic controller and radarscope monitor each section. APC operates two frequencies to separate information related to Approach and Departure traffic.

The ARTCC is responsible for controlling IFR traffic between terminal areas. As a result, each ARTCC enjoys authority over a vast airspace that typically stretches across several states. In addition to its IFR services, some ARTCCs can provide limited services to visual flight rules (VFR) aircraft.

Airspace is categorized as either controlled or uncontrolled based on several factors, including the safety of the airspace, type of operations regularly being conducted in the area, and complexity of aircraft movement. Controlled airspace is governed by an air traffic controller with the authority and ability to exercise control over the entire area and is classified as either Class A, B, C, D, or E. Air traffic controllers have limited authority over uncontrolled authority due to either a lack of regularity authority or ability to enforce that authority. Uncontrolled airspace is either classified as Class G or left unclassified. Airspace designations can be found on aeronautical charts, and pilots must know the type of airspace and abide by all relevant restrictions.

Class A airspace includes most airspace between 18,000 feet above mean sea level (MSL) and FL600 (pressure altitude of 60,000 feet) over the continental United States and extending over 12 nautical miles of the coastline. ATC will not authorize VFRs in Class A airspace, and the FAA requires pilots and aircraft to be instrument certified and have a transponder with Mode C. Additionally, pilots need to obtain IFR clearance from ATC before entering the airspace and establish two-way communication with ATC.

Class B airspace is most common in the immediate area surrounding busy airports and extends from the surface to 10,000 feet MSL. Most Class B airspace contains multiple layers for safety purposes. The FAA requires all pilots to have a Private Pilot Certificate, an operable very high frequency (VHF) omnidirectional range (VOR) or Tactical Air Navigation (TACAN) system receiver, a transponder with Mode C, ATC clearance, and two-way radio communication.

Class C airspace extends from the surface to 4000 feet above ground level (AGL) in the immediate area surrounding airports with radar approach control, an operational control tower, and a specified number of IFR operations. The size of the Class C airspace can be tailored to the needs of the airport, but it usually has a radius core area of 5 nautical miles and a radius shelf area of 10 nautical miles. To operate in Class C airspace, aircraft must have a transponder with Mode C and pilots must establish and maintain two-way radio communication with ATC. For Class C airspace, communication is considered to have begun once ATC responds to the aircraft with its designated call sign.

Class D airspace is also most commonly found around airports and extends from the surface to 2500 feet AGL horizontal limits depending on the airport, but Class D airspace typically has a core radius of 4 nautical miles with some extensions for instrument approaches. Two-way communication needs to be established before entering a Class D airspace and maintained throughout that airspace.

Class E airspace generally has no vertical limit and extends to the adjoining controlled airspace. In general, Class E airspace is located above 14,500 feet MSL, with areas in the western United States being closer to the lower limit due to less air traffic. Although Class E airspace is controlled airspace, there are no pilot, equipment, or travel requirements. There are several different uses of Class E airspace, including extensions to other classes of airspace, transitions from takeoff to en route, and federal airways.

Class G airspace is the only classified type of uncontrolled airspace in the United States. There's relatively limited Class G airspace above the United States except for some areas with unreliable radar or extremely minimal traffic. Given its rarity and relative lack of hazards, the FAA provides limited guidance for aircraft operating in a Class G airspace.

In addition to controlled and uncontrolled classifications, some airspace is designated as "special use." Special use airspace restricts operations and/or imposes limitations on aircraft traveling through the airspace. In general, special use airspace is designated to serve the public interest, increase safety, or facilitate a governmental or military operation.

There are six different types of special use airspace: prohibited areas, restricted areas, warning areas, military operation areas (MOAs), alert areas, and controlled firing areas (CFAs). Prohibited areas have specifically defined boundaries in which no flights are allowed, typically for security reasons. For example, the airspace above the White House and nuclear test sites are prohibited areas. Restricted areas are designated due to the existence of a hazard and require permission from the authority in control of the airspace. Warning areas have potential hazards and are generally located in international airspace, so the FAA typically doesn't have jurisdiction over these areas. MOAs are most often designated to safely facilitate military training and have both vertical and lateral boundaries. Air traffic controllers will reroute or restrict aircraft around the MOA unless the aircraft can safely pass through. Alert areas are marked on aeronautical charts to notify pilots about uncommon and potentially hazardous aerial activity, such as high-volume pilot training activities, hot-air ballooning, or glider plane activities. CFAs designate areas in which a military training operation is firing weapons, but the firing ceases when an aircraft is spotted approaching the CFA.

The United States also has specific airway and route systems. These systems mostly connect airports, functioning like the interstate highway system. Multiple radio navigational stations, such as VOR/Tactical

Aircraft Control (VORTAC), typically define the routes, and the airway is a controlled space. One of the most extensive and prominent route systems is VOR Airways ("Victor Airways"). These federal highways are classified as Class E airspace and run between 12,000 feet AGL and 17,999 feet above MSL; the width of the airways is usually 8 nautical miles. Routes can be identified by the letter "V" followed by a number, and the numbering system is identical to the national highway system.

Light signals play a critical role in communication between aircraft and ATC. In general, most of the light signals have different meanings depending on whether the aircraft is on the ground or in the air. Steady green lights mean cleared for takeoff on the ground and cleared for landing in the air. Flashing green means cleared to taxi on the ground and return for landing in the air. Steady red means stop on the ground and give way to another aircraft and keep circling when in the air. Flashing red means the runway is in use, so aircraft cannot taxi or land. Flashing white means to return to gate on the ground and nothing in the air. Alternating red and green lights always means to exercise extreme caution.

Aircraft must also have a lighting system. Over recent years, the importance of lighting has become more magnified due to significantly increased air traffic, airway closures, and visibility issues. FAR Part 91.209 mandates that aircraft operate with lighted position lights from sunset to sunrise. Additionally, aircraft cannot be moved, taxied, or parked unless the aircraft has lighted position lights, the area is clearly illuminated, or the area is surrounded by obstruction lights.

When operating near another aircraft, pilots must do everything they can to create separation and mitigate the risk of a collision. As such, the FAA prohibits formation flight with planes carrying commercial passengers and only otherwise permits formations through an arrangement with a pilot in command of the constituent aircraft.

To mitigate the risk of collisions, aircraft must obey right-of-way rules while operating in airspace. Whenever an aircraft enjoys the right-of-way, all of the other aircraft in that airspace must not pass or approach unless they are well clear of the aircraft with the right-of-way. FAR Part 91.113 provides the right-of-way rules for all aircraft operations except those occurring over water. When flying over land, aircraft in distress have right-of-way over all other aircraft. If two aircraft of the same type are converging, the aircraft on the right has the right-of-way. If the aircraft are not of the same type, the aircraft with the least maneuverability has the right-of-way. When aircraft are approaching head-on, both aircraft should move to the right. Any aircraft that's being overtaken has the right-of-way over the aircraft that's overtaking it. Landing aircraft have the right-of-way, and if there are two or more landing aircraft, the aircraft at the lower altitude has the right-of-way.

The right-of-way rules for flying over water are provided in FAR Part 91.115. When aircraft and vessels are on crossing courses, the aircraft or vessel on the right has the right-of-way. As with flying over land, all of the involved aircraft and vessels in a head-on approach must move to the right, and aircraft or vessels that are being overtaken have the right-of-way. Finally, when there's a risk of collision, the aircraft and/or vessel must pay more attention to special circumstances, including the limited maneuverability of the other aircraft or vessel.

Speed and altitude are two of the most critical factors in flight, so the FAA promulgates and enforces several regulations to optimize for safety. According to FAR Part 91.117, aircraft are prohibited from flying faster than 250 knots (288 mph) below 10,000 feet above MSL. Aircraft are also prohibited from flying faster than 200 knots (230 mph), at or below 2500 feet above surface, within 4 nautical miles of a Class C or Class D primary airport. Likewise, aircraft are prohibited from flying faster than 200 knots (230

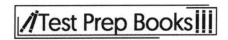

mph) within 4 nautical miles of a Class B airport. However, FAR Part 91.117 also expressly allows pilots to exceed speed limit whenever the minimum safe speed is higher than the limit.

FAR Part 91.119 defines general altitude regulations. When flying over a congested and highly populated area, aircraft must fly 1000 feet above the highest obstacle within 2000 feet of aircraft. Helicopters, powered parachutes, and weight-shift-control aircraft may fly below 1000 feet above the highest obstacle in a congested area under certain conditions, such as when flying a route designated by the FAA. In uncongested areas, aircraft must remain 500 feet above the surface unless they are flying over water or in sparsely populated areas, in which case the aircraft only need to fly 500 feet above any vessels or obstacles. FAR Part 91.121 mandates that every aircraft sets its cruising altitude or flight level by using an altimeter, and the regulation provides formulas for setting altimeters at a variety of specific settings.

Under FAR Part 91.143, the FAA may issue a Notice to Airmen (NOTAM) to prohibit the operation of aircraft within a designated airspace except as authorized by ATC. The FAA most commonly issues a NOTAM in the immediate aftermath of a natural disaster or hazardous conditions for the purpose of protecting people, property, the environment, or the public interest. All restrictions are typically temporary and lifted when the threat subsides. NOTAMs can also be issued under FAR Part 91.141 whenever the president, vice president, or any public figure deemed important to the national interest is flying through the airspace.

The FAA enforces numerous rules related to the protection of flight crews, aircraft passengers, and the general public. FAR Part 91.17 prohibits crewmembers from working under the influence of alcohol and drugs. Additionally, crewmembers cannot work within eight hours of consuming an alcoholic beverage. If a crewmember is suspected of violating FAR Part 91.17, they must submit to a test for banned substances and permit the FAA to evaluate the results.

Both the FAA and military air forces also have strict rules that restrict the scheduling of crewmembers because accident rates increase dramatically when people are awake for more than sixteen hours. In FAR Part 91.061, the FAA caps a crewmember's total flight time at 500 hours per quarter, 800 hours in consecutive quarters, and 1400 hours per calendar year. Furthermore, the FAA bars crewmembers from working more than eight hours of flight deck duty within a twenty-four-hour period. Similarly, the US Navy requires crewmembers to have an opportunity for eight hours of uninterrupted sleep within a twenty-four-hour period and prohibits continuous flight duty in excess of eighteen hours.

All civil aircraft must have a number of certifications to be in compliance with FAR Part 91.203, including both an airworthiness certificate and an active US registration certificate for the specific aircraft. Specialized and military aircraft typically must submit additional certifications to ATC. Other safety requirements involve using and maintaining the airworthiness of instruments and equipment. FAR Part 91.205 provides exhaustive lists of instruments and equipment rules to satisfy VFRs and IFRs, including the different requirements for night and day operations. The FAA also has an extensive framework for determining whether and how an aircraft can fly with inoperative equipment or instruments. Among other requirements, FAR Part 91.213 mandates that an aircraft can only take off with inoperative equipment or instruments when it has all of the items included in its aircraft-specific Minimum Equipment List.

Practice Quiz

1. When generating lift, what should the pressure below the airfoil be in relation to the pressure above the airfoil?
   a. Greater than it
   b. Less than it
   c. Equal to it
   d. The opposite of it

2. What is the load factor of a 2000-pound helicopter that is currently experiencing an effective load of 4000 pounds?
   a. 0.25
   b. 0.5
   c. 1
   d. 2

3. Which of the following type or types of drag increase as the speed increases?

   I. Parasitic drag

   II. Induced drag

   III. Profile drag

   a. I only
   b. II and III
   c. I and II
   d. I and III

4. Which of the following decreases upon an increase to the collective pitch controller?
   a. RPM
   b. Altitude
   c. Drag
   d. Lift

5. Which of the following is FALSE about the governor?
   a. It adjusts the throttle as needed.
   b. It uses an electronic sensor.
   c. It controls the pitch of the rotors.
   d. It regulates the power to maintain RPM.

See answers on next page

Answer Explanations

1. A: The pressure below the airfoil needs to be greater to push upwards on the airfoil. If the pressures are equal, there will be no lift generated at all, and if the pressure above is greater, the pressure from above would actually push down on the airfoil, generating negative lift.

2. D: Since the effective load is double its normal weight, the load factor is 2. In this case, simple eyeballing of the numbers is likely enough to solve this problem. If the numbers were less convenient, the problem could still be solved by using the equation, $G=L_1/L_0$. Using 4000 as L_1 and 2000 as L_0, the result would be $G=4000/2000$, which equals 2.

3. D: Parasitic drag and profile drag both increase as airspeed increases. As airspeed increases, induced drag decreases. Both parasitic drag and profile drag are created by air resistance, which increases the faster the helicopter is going. However, induced drag is created by backwash from the main rotor and thus, it depends only on the angle of attack of the helicopter, which is typically lower in higher speed flight.

4. A: Raising the collective pitch control increases the pitch of the blades, which increases the angle of incidence. This generates lift, which results in increased altitude and drag, which then reduces the RPM, if the throttle is not simultaneously increased to compensate.

5. C: The governor utilizes an electronic sensor, which is fully-automated to maintain the RPM of the rotor blades. The governor does not, however, control the pitch of the rotors. That function is reserved for the collective pitch control and cyclic pitch control.

Naval Aviation Trait Facet Inventory (NATFI)

The Naval Aviation Trait Facet Inventory (NATFI) section is akin to a personality test. It is designed with the goal of specifically assessing a candidate's behavioral and personality suitability for success in an aviation program and service at the various career stages he or she will encounter.

On the NATFI section of the exam, test takers will encounter 88 statements presented in 44 pairs. Test takers must select the one statement from the pair that most accurately reflects the way they think, feel, or act, depending on the parameters provided in the possible responses. The statements in each pair are provided as complete sentences written in first-person perspective. Some of the 44 pairs will present two positive statements, addressing favorable personality traits. The following pair is an example of this type:

☐ I firmly believe that I am capable of being a strong leader.

☐ I am confident that I can excel in a wide variety of situations.

Other pairs will include two unflattering statements, such as the following:

☐ I tend to act impulsively.

☐ I am often disorganized.

Because the NATFI is a personality inventory, there are no "right" or "wrong" answers. Accordingly, it is unnecessary to study for this section. However, test takers can practice or prepare by reviewing the format of the section to ensure they understand what the NATFI entails.

A candidate's responses are evaluated for the specific personality traits the items are designed to measure. The evaluated traits are confidence, work motivation, warmth, unrestrained behavior, aggressiveness, and adaptability. The 88 statements address these aforementioned different personality traits that are then paired up in various combinations (and using different wording), so that the aggregate of the candidate's answers establishes a pattern for each of the traits. This pattern, determined by the set of all responses rather than by one single answer from the 44 pairs, helps to form a picture of the candidate's personality, behaviors, and ways of thinking and feeling. Admissions officers and administrators use this picture to determine what the candidate is like and if he or she is a good fit for the aviation program and career, based on prior research and consideration of what types of traits the most successful candidates embody. The personality picture painted can also help screen out candidates who lack the desired traits for program attrition and career success.

Performance Based Measures Battery (PBM)

The Performance Based Measures Battery (PBM) section of the ASTB-E measures a test taker's processing speed, divided-attention and multitasking ability, and manual dexterity through a variety of tracking tasks and dichotic listening exercises. The battery of exercises in this section evaluates the candidate's ability to accurately complete tracking tasks using a provided stick-and-throttle set, as well as their spatial orientation and dichotic listening aptitudes. The PBM exercises assess these skills in isolation as well as in simultaneous usage.

To minimize proctor involvement, the administration of the PBM employs picture screens accompanied by automated instructions. There are seven exercises in the PBM, the first of which evaluates the candidate's situational awareness. The remaining six items are intended to simultaneously measure elements of one's multitasking ability and dexterity in various forms. The candidate's multitasking aptitude is considered the strongest predictor of success in the aviation field. The following descriptions provide basic information about the seven exercises included in PBM:

1. Unmanned Aerial Vehicle (UAV) Test: evaluates spatial orientation and reasoning. The left side of the computer screen presents a North-up oriented tracker map with an aircraft symbol denoting the direction and position in which it is facing. The right side of the screen will show a map with a building and pictures of four adjacent parking lots (shown as gray blocks) that is intended to indicate the camera view relative solely to the aircraft heading. The panel will also include an aircraft symbol and a moveable crosshair. Using the map as a guide, the test taker's first task is to identify each parking lot's cardinal direction. Test takers are then instructed to move the crosshairs by using the joystick to target one of the specified parking lots. It is important to remember that the right panel, in which the test taker is guiding the aircraft, is shown relative to the aircraft heading. Test takers must mentally orient themselves as if they are positioned as the pilot in the aircraft so that they correctly move the crosshairs relative to the aircraft's heading.

It should be noted that test takers are afforded the option to practice this exercise in an unscored trial run prior to attempting it during the scored administration. It is recommended that test takers take advantage of this opportunity for a mock run, to familiarize themselves with the problem constraints as well as the provided equipment: a headset, joystick, and throttle.

2. Dichotic Listening Test (DLT): an audio test in which test takers will hear a series of numbers and letters in groupings through their headset, in one ear or the other. Test takers must listen carefully and will be directed to press one or two buttons on the joystick or throttle in response to the numbers, corresponding to whether an odd or even number (or particular letter sequence) is heard. For example, test takers may hear the following instructions: "Whenever you hear an odd number in your left ear, press the thumb button on the right throttle, and whenever you hear an even number in your left ear, depress the trigger on the joystick." Each audio series, called a string, will consist of seven numbers and/or letters.

The DLT contains 40 strings. Speed and accuracy of responses are assessed; incorrect actions will penalize the test taker's score. This type of dichotic multitasking listening skill closely models the management of the many different radios coming into a cockpit. Research has demonstrated that people tend to process audio cues in the right ear faster than the left because the right ear is tied to left brain functions (which include language and speech processing). Audio cues that are isolated in the left ear are processed by the right side of the brain, which lacks the ability to completely process spoken

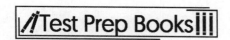

language. Consequently, the information then has to get rerouted to the left side of the brain, causing the slower response time. It can be beneficial for test takers to dedicate additional practice time to left-ear listening.

3. Airplane Tracking Test (ATT): utilizes the right screen panel and the joystick in an exercise that involves tracking and guiding a moving image of a yellow-colored aircraft from the rear perspective. This aircraft moves in two-dimensions (horizontal and vertical) and test takers move red crosshairs in such a way that demonstrates their ability to follow and anticipate the aircraft's movement. The crosshairs interact with the aircraft like magnets of the same polarity, such that moving the crosshairs toward the aircraft will repel or push the aircraft away. Because of this relationship, the test taker should anticipate the aircraft's movement in their tracking, as they attempt to move the aircraft to the desired target. It is important that test takers use finesse when using the throttle. Full-throttle deflections will aggressively intercept and repel the aircraft, which is often undesirable for the exercise. Test takers are informed if they have correctly locked onto the aircraft's trajectory and have leveled up by an information panel at the bottom of the screen. As the level of the exercise advances, the reactiveness of the aircraft increases.

4. Vertical Tracking Test (VTT): like the ATT, the VTT requires test takers to anticipate the aircraft's motion and attempt to "push" it with the crosshairs to the intended targets. The VTT uses the left throttle to control the airplane image presented on the narrower left panel of the screen.

5. Airplane Tracking and Horizontal Tracking Test (AHTT): a simultaneous combination of the ATT and VTT that assesses the test taker's ability to multitask and track both aircrafts at once. It is recommended that test takers practice with video games that incorporate targeting in at least two-dimensions.

6. Airplane Tracking, Vertical Tracking, and Dichotic Listening Test (AVDLT): assesses the candidate's speed, accuracy, and tracking skill when multitasking, combining the DLT and AHTT, utilizing both the right and left screen panels.

7. Emergency Scenario Test (EST): builds on the AHTT exercise by adding three light indicators representing potential emergency scenarios—engine, fire, and propeller—which appear at the bottom of the screen. These emergency indicators will illuminate red and an audio tone will sound to alert that action must be taken. Actions that manipulate the controls for power, fuel, and a reset must be memorized by the test taker because the required emergency procedure differ for each of the three potential dangers. The actions can be a series of buttons or sliders to engage on the throttle and/or joystick, which necessitate memorization skills, multitasking ability, and sustained concentration. The dichotic listening and two-panel tracking tests do enter a distress mode when an emergency sounds, which temporarily allows the speed and accuracy performance of those tasks to be suspended until the test taker has addressed the emergency situation. Instead, scoring during emergency procedures is based on the test taker's speed and accuracy in identifying and completing the appropriate actions, and their ability to prioritize this procedure while already multitasking. While this task may sound outrageously complicated, it's a realistic situation for aircraft officers, who often need to multitask, prioritize, and compartmentalize while on a mission. Successful officers must not only develop these multitasking skills cognitively but must also learn emotional control during stressful in-flight situations.

The PBM is the most hands-on, and in many ways, most practical section of the ASTB-E. As such, it provides valuable information to the test administrators and aviation program admissions officers about the candidate's potential understanding and skills related to the duties of a flight officer. Obtaining a high score on the PBM is important for overall ASTB-E exam success. While many test takers find this the most "fun" section of the ASTB-E, the included tasks are often some of the most unfamiliar or newest-learned. For this reason, test takers are encouraged to prepare for the Performance Based Measures Battery by practicing mental rotation problems (such as encountered in the first exercise with the parking lots) and familiarizing themselves with flight simulator software that uses a stick-and-throttle set, if possible.

Biographical Inventory with Response Verification (BI-RV)

The Biographical Inventory with Response Verification (BI-RV) is a self-paced, untimed section of the ASTB-E that gathers information about the candidate's relevant background experiences. These are applicable and potentially predictable of their success in the demanding and fast-paced aviation program and future career. Questions address factors such as high school and collegiate academic achievements and participation in extracurricular activities. The ASTB-E test developers believe that the BI-RV is a useful predictor of program attrition and aviation service success.

There are 110 questions on the BI-RV and it usually takes test takers between forty-five minutes and two hours and forty-five minutes to complete. Because the BI-RV section is untimed and addresses personal experiences with no universal "right" or "wrong" answers, test takers may complete it on any web-enabled computer, including the candidate's home computer, once an ASTB-E Examiner has provided them with a username and password. It can be completed either before or after any of the other ASTB-E sections and does not necessarily need to be completed in one sitting. Questions do not need to be answered in order, though test takers must address all unanswered questions to satisfactorily complete the section. Test takers who wish to take the BI-RV section prior to sitting for the remainder of the ASTB-E can contact their recruiter to receive the required credentials and instructions. Test takers have ninety days after receiving their login information to complete the BI-RV. It is generally recommended that test takers complete the BI-RV prior to attempting the written sections of the exam, because doing so will permit ASTB-E score release immediately after the scores for the remaining sections.

Some questions on the BI-RV will prompt test takers to provide further details and verification of their responses during the administration of the section. For example, if a test taker lists a leadership position for their collegiate newspaper, he or she will need to enter further details about this involvement including school name, position title, years of participation, and other salient information in the provided blank lines. It should be noted that the truthfulness of responses on the BI-RV (or any other section on the ASTB-E) is mandatory. Even if the test taker has already started or completed aviation training, any falsification of provided information is deemed sufficient grounds to disqualify and reject their candidacy and eligibility for the aviation program and service.

Because the BI-RV is simply a personal questionnaire addressing the test taker's academic, extracurricular, and aviation-related experiences and accomplishments, there is no way to study for the section. Honesty is the sole requirement. Candidates can prepare by reviewing their potentially-relevant experiences and making a list of positions held and accolades obtained so that this information is readily available when the questions prompt the test taker to verify their response with further detai

Practice Test #1

Math Skills

1. A company invests $50,000 in a building where they can produce saws. If the cost of producing one saw is $40, then which function expresses the amount of money the company pays? The variable y is the money paid and x is the number of saws produced.
    a. $y = 50,000x + 40$
    b. $y + 40 = x - 50,000$
    c. $y = 40x - 50,000$
    d. $y = 40x + 50,000$

2. How could the following function be rewritten to identify the zeros?

$$y = 3x^3 + 3x^2 - 18x$$

    a. $y = 3x(x + 3)(x - 2)$
    b. $y = x(x - 2)(x + 3)$
    c. $y = 3x(x - 3)(x + 2)$
    d. $y = (x + 3)(x - 2)$

3. A rectangle has a length that is 5 feet longer than three times its width. If the perimeter is 90 feet, what is the length in feet?
    a. 10
    b. 20
    c. 25
    d. 35

4. An accounting firm charted its income on the following pie graph. If the total income for the year was $500,000, how much income was received from Audit Services and Taxation Services?

Income

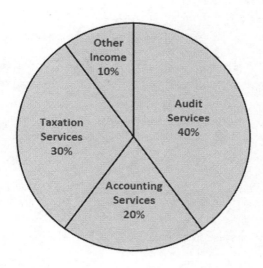

a. $200,000
b. $350,000
c. $150,000
d. $300,000

5. What is the value of the expression: $7^2 - 3 \times (4 + 2) + 15 \div 5$?
   a. 12.2
   b. 40.2
   c. 34
   d. 58.2

6. On a map, $\frac{1}{8}$ inches represent 75 miles. If two cities on the map are $4\frac{1}{2}$ inches apart, how far apart are they in real life?
   a. 3,100 miles
   b. 2,900 miles
   c. 2,400 miles
   d. 2,700 miles

7. In feet per second, the velocity of an object dropped off a building is $v(t) = -32t - 8$. If the object was dropped from 500 feet, what equation describes its height in feet as a function of time in seconds?
   a. $h(t) = -32t - 8 - 500$
   b. $h(t) = -32t^2 - 8t + 500$
   c. $h(t) = -16t + 500$
   d. $h(t) = -16t^2 - 8t + 500$

8. Mo needs to buy enough material to cover the walls around the stage for a theater performance. If he needs 79 feet of wall covering, what is the minimum number of yards of material he should purchase if the material is sold only by whole yards?

    a. 23 yards
    b. 25 yards
    c. 26 yards
    d. 27 yards

9. Before a race of four horses, you make a random guess of which horse will get first place and which will get second place. What is the probability that both your guesses will be correct?

    a. $\frac{1}{4}$

    b. $\frac{1}{2}$

    c. $\frac{1}{16}$

    d. $\frac{1}{12}$

10. Greg buys a $10 lunch with 5% sales tax. He leaves a $2 tip after his bill. How much money does he spend?

    a. $12.50
    b. $12
    c. $13
    d. $11.50

11. There are $4x + 1$ treats in each party favor bag. If a total of $60x + 15$ treats are distributed, how many bags are given out?

    a. 15
    b. 16
    c. 20
    d. 22

12. Is the following function even, odd, neither, or both?

$$y = \frac{1}{2}x^4 + 2x^2 - 6$$

    a. Even
    b. Odd
    c. Neither
    d. Both

13. What is the volume of a pyramid, with a square base whose side is 6 inches, and the height is 9 inches?

    a. $324\ in^3$
    b. $72\ in^3$
    c. $108\ in^3$
    d. $18\ in^3$

14. Five of six numbers have a sum of 25. The average of all six numbers is 6. What is the sixth number?
   a. 8
   b. 10
   c. 11
   d. 12

15. In 2015, it was estimated that there were 7,350,000,000 people living on Earth. Express this value in scientific notation.
   a. 7.35×10^7
   b. 7.35×10^9
   c. 73.5×10^8
   d. 73.5×10^9

16. Simplify: $(5x^2 - 3x + 4) - (2x^2 - 7)$
   a. x^5
   b. $3x^2 - 3x + 11$
   c. $3x^2 - 3x - 3$
   d. $x - 3$

17. A ball is thrown from the top of a high hill, so that the height of the ball as a function of time is $h(t) = -16t^2 + 4t + 6$, in feet. What is the maximum height of the ball in feet?
   a. 6
   b. 6.25
   c. 6.5
   d. 6.75

18. For the following similar triangles, what are the values of x and y (rounded to one decimal place)?

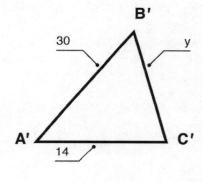

   a. $x = 16.5, y = 25.1$
   b. $x = 19.5, y = 24.1$
   c. $x = 17.1, y = 26.3$
   d. $x = 26.3, y = 17.1$

19. A ball is drawn at random from a ball pit containing 8 red balls, 7 yellow balls, 6 green balls, and 5 purple balls. What is the probability that the ball drawn is yellow?

a. $\frac{1}{26}$

b. $\frac{19}{26}$

c. $\frac{7}{26}$

d. 1

20. Write the following number in standard form:

$$(1 \times 10^4) + (3 \times 10^3) + (7 \times 10^1) + (8 \times 10^0)$$

a. 137
b. 13,078
c. 1,378
d. 8,731

21. A line goes through the point $(-4, 0)$ and the point $(0, 2)$. What is the slope of the line?

a. 2

b. 4

c. $\frac{3}{2}$

d. $\frac{1}{2}$

22. A line that travels from the lower left of a graph to the upper right of the graph indicates what kind of relationship between an independent and a dependent variable?

a. Positive
b. Negative
c. Exponential
d. Logarithmic

23. What is the value of the following expression?

$$\sqrt{8^2 + 6^2}$$

a. 14
b. 10
c. 9
d. 100

24. What is the measurement of angle *f* in the following picture? Assume the lines are parallel.

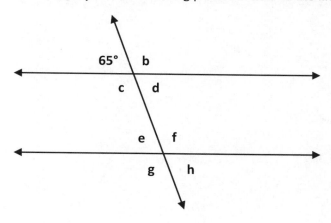

    a. 68 degrees
    b. 112 degrees
    c. 128 degrees
    d. 52 degrees

25. The following graph compares the various test scores of the top three students in each of these teacher's classes. Based on the graph, which teacher's students had the smallest range of test scores?

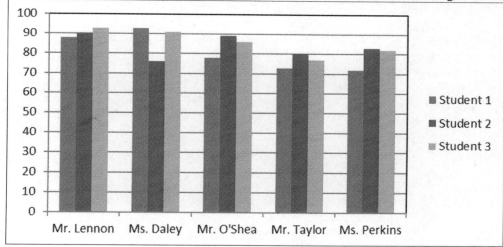

    a. Mr. Lennon
    b. Mr. O'Shea
    c. Mr. Taylor
    d. Ms. Daley

26. Kimberley earns $10 an hour babysitting, and after 10 p.m., she earns $12 an hour. The time she works is rounded to the nearest hour for pay purposes. On her last job, she worked from 5:30 p.m. to 11 p.m. In total, how much did Kimberley earn on her last job?
    a. $45
    b. $57
    c. $62
    d. $42

27. What value of x would solve the following equation?

$$9x + x - 7 = 16 + 2x$$

    a. $x = -4$

    b. $x = 3$

    c. $x = \frac{9}{8}$

    d. $x = \frac{23}{8}$

28. What is the y-intercept for $y = x^2 + 3x - 4$?
    a. $y = 1$
    b. $y = -4$
    c. $y = 3$
    d. $y = 4$

29. An equilateral triangle has a perimeter of 18 feet. The sides of a square have the same length as the triangle's sides. What is the area of the square?
    a.   6 square feet
    b.   36 square feet
    c.   256 square feet
    d.   1,000 square feet

30. Ten students take a test. Five students get a 50. Four students get a 70. If the average score is 55, what was the last student's score?
    a.   20
    b.   40
    c.   50
    d.   60

Reading Comprehension

Directions: Assume each passage below to be true. Then, pick the answer choice that best answers the question.

1. Aircraft propulsion must achieve two objectives: It has to balance the thrust and drag of a craft in cruising flight, and thrust must exceed drag to accelerate movement. Balancing the thrust and drag of a craft in cruising mode follows Sir Isaac Newton's first law of motion. This law states that an object in motion will remain in motion, in a straight line, with the absence of a net force to effect a change. In other words, if all external forces cancel each other, an object remains at a constant velocity. This is necessary to understand the idea of flight at a constant altitude. However, if a pilot effects a change to a craft's thrust, the balance between that thrust and the drag of a craft is disrupted. The net forces have been changed in a manner that will affect acceleration and propel the aircraft until there is a new balance between thrust and drag in velocity.

Which answer choice is true based on the passage?
   a.   None of Sir Isaac Newton's other scientific theories are relevant to the study of thrust and drag.
   b.   Sir Isaac Newton's first law of motion is relevant to aircraft propulsion.
   c.   Only thrust and drag have an effect on the balance of net forces.
   d.   Acceleration is more difficult to achieve than cruising.

2. As summer approaches, drowning incidents will increase. Drowning happens very quickly and silently. Most people assume that drowning is easy to spot, but a person who is drowning doesn't make noise or wave his arms. Instead, he will have his head back and his mouth open, with just his face out of the water. A person who is truly in danger of drowning is not able to wave his arms in the air or move much at all. Recognizing these signs of drowning can prevent tragedy.

What is the main purpose of this passage?
   a.   To explain the dangers of swimming
   b.   To show how to identify the signs of drowning
   c.   To explain how to be a lifeguard
   d.   To compare the signs of drowning

3. Although ecosystems are often broken down into two primary categories (terrestrial and aquatic), terrestrial ecosystems are further divided into forest, desert, grassland, and tundra. Similarly, aquatic ecosystems can be divided by fresh water and salt water. However, that doesn't mean that ecosystems falling into these categories are identical. In fact, abiotic elements, such as temperature, altitude, and sunlight, have a significant impact on the type and variety of flora and fauna, or biotics, in any specific ecosystem.

Based on the passage, which of the following components would also be abiotic?
   a.   Grasses
   b.   Insects
   c.   Soil
   d.   Wind

4. The names of lava flows come from the Polynesian culture. Lava flows on land are called either a'a (pronounced "ah-ah") or pahoehoe ("paw-hoy-hoy"). A'a lava flows are often from composite volcanoes, loaded with earthen debris and rock. In contrast, pahoehoe lava flows are smooth and fast running and come from shield volcanoes.

What is the primary danger of a'a lava flows on land?
    a.   That cannot be determined from this passage.
    b.   The speed and low viscosity of the lava flow
    c.   Debris and rock in the lava flow
    d.   The distance it can travel given its makeup

5. Don't attempt to fly through thunderstorms. Try to circumnavigate them safely and wisely. Know your personal skills and limitations regarding weather flight before you gather forecast information. Keep in mind that a variety of conditions in-flight can change quickly. Don't fly into areas of rain where the air temperature is at or close to freezing. Always allow more margin of error for weather at night, and do not attempt to navigate through cloud "holes."

Based on the passage, which of the following answer choices is true?
    a.   Pilots commonly lack a strong understanding of their personal skills and limitations.
    b.   Thunderstorms are the most dangerous aspect of flying at night in cold weather.
    c.   Circumnavigating thunderstorms is a relatively safe course of action.
    d.   Cloud holes are impenetrable under certain atmospheric conditions.

6. Koko the gorilla, who passed in 2018 at the age of forty-six, knew more than 2000 words and could sign at least 1000 of those. Although this was a feat unto itself, even more interesting was the belief that Koko, in addition to learning words, was actually communicating with the researchers she worked with. Perhaps even more interesting, in terms of language acquisition and learning, is that Koko created her own word combinations for words she didn't know. For example, she coined "eye hats" to mean a mask and, more famously, "finger watches" to mean rings.

Why was Koko's communication so interesting?
    a.   She had a vocabulary of 2000 words.
    b.   She created new words.
    c.   She could sign 1000 words.
    d.   She had the ability to acquire vocabulary.

7. Raul is going to Egypt next month. He has been looking forward to this vacation all year. Since childhood, Raul has been fascinated with pyramids, especially the Great Pyramid of Giza, which is the oldest of the Seven Wonders of the Ancient World. According to religious custom, Egyptian royalty is buried in the tombs located within the pyramid's great labyrinths. Since it has been many years since Raul read about the pyramid's history, he wants to read a book describing how and why the Egyptians built the Great Pyramid thousands of years ago.

How long has Raul been excited about his vacation to Egypt?
    a.   Since childhood
    b.   All month
    c.   All year
    d.   Many years

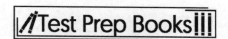

8. Piloting is a consummate skill to obtain, and for many, it's a skill that remains unattainable. A potential pilot must be so well-versed in flight instruction that studying the requirements can seem overwhelming. In addition, thousands of flight hours must be logged in practice before a pilot can begin a career. The physical and mental demands on many potential students can be prohibitive. It takes a dedicated person to persevere and become successful in the flight industry.

According to the passage, which of the following answer choices is true?
   a. Perseverance is the most important attribute for potential students to have.
   b. Pilots face physical and mental demands during their career.
   c. Some potential students don't become successful pilots.
   d. All consummate skills require a significant amount of work to obtain.

9. After many failed attempts, Julio made a solemn promise to his mother to clean his room. When she came home from a long day of work, she found her son playing video games, his room still a disaster. Her fists clenched, her eyebrows knitted, she stared down her son and delivered an angry speech that made him hang his head regretfully.

What did Julio break?
   a. His video game
   b. Nothing
   c. Everything in his room
   d. His promise

10. A chain of events often defines incidents that lead to an accident. In aviation, this chain of events is often referred to as the error chain. This term purports that it isn't one single event that leads to an air disaster but a chain of separate events. In other words, an accident is caused by more than one problem and most likely has more than one root cause. These events can be caused by human error or mechanical issues. A recent study indicates that pilot error is more likely to contribute to air disasters than mechanical problems.

According to the passage, which of the following answer choices is true?
   a. Problems with more than one root cause are the most difficult to remedy.
   b. Error chains always involve more than one event.
   c. Pilot errors are easier to correct than mechanical problems.
   d. Isolated problems with single root causes never cause air disasters.

11. It's expected that climate change will have the largest impact on the loss of biodiversity because of the drastic effects on climate zones. More specifically, tropical zones now known for their hot and wet climates, such as the Amazon rainforest, may see significant decreases in rain, drastically impacting both animal and plant life.

What are tropical zones best known for?
   a. Their climate
   b. Their biodiversity
   c. Their geography
   d. Their elevation

12. Although it can be dangerous, turbulence during flight is common and manageable. Turbulence is a disruption in airflow. Think of it as a bump on the road while driving to work. It happens all the time, and, when managed effectively, it's fairly benign. One type of turbulence is clear air turbulence (CAT). It cannot be seen, and one way to avoid it is to fly at a higher, and likely smoother, altitude. Severe turbulence, a disturbance that results in an altitude deviation of 100 feet, is uncomfortable but not dangerous.

According to the passage, which of the following answer choices is true?
   a.   Flying at higher altitudes can limit disruptions in airflow.
   b.   Some types of turbulence cannot be managed effectively.
   c.   Severe turbulence is common and manageable.
   d.   Aircraft experience less turbulence while taxiing.

13. Following the Civil War, Congress passed the Fifteenth Amendment (1870) to prohibit denying the vote based on "race, color, or previous condition of servitude." During the early twentieth century, the Seventeenth Amendment (1913) expanded political participation by establishing the popular election of U.S. Senators. Prior to the Seventeenth Amendment, state legislatures selected the U.S. Senators.

According to the passage, how does the Fifteenth Amendment compare to the Seventeenth *Amendment in regard to the expansion of democracy in the United States?*
   a.   The Fifteenth Amendment increased the number of eligible voters, and the Seventeenth Amendment allowed more input from the public.
   b.   The Fifteenth Amendment guaranteed the right to vote for people regardless of sex, and the Seventeenth Amendment established the popular election of U.S. Senators.
   c.   The Fifteenth Amendment prohibited discrimination based on race, and the Seventeenth Amendment limited political corruption by prohibiting the sale of alcohol.
   d.   The Fifteenth Amendment lowered the eligible voting age, and the Seventeenth Amendment created the Electoral College.

14. Asbestos was an insidious yet popular product, mass produced for over one hundred years. Due to its durability and fire resistance, it was used in a wide range of products, such as houses, cars, and ships. As with tobacco, evidence was presented early on that asbestos was dangerous and had cumulative adverse effects, but production didn't decline until the 1970s.

When did production of asbestos decrease?
   a.   One hundred years ago
   b.   When evidence was presented that it was dangerous
   c.   When it was no longer durable
   d.   In the 1970s

15. A helicopter pilot maneuvers many controls to maintain equilibrium in flight. These controls include the cyclic stick, anti-torque pedals, and the collective lever. The cyclic stick maintains the pitch angle of the craft's rotating blades. The anti-torque pedals control the nose of the helicopter. The collective lever controls the pitch angle of the rotating blades together or independently as needed. All three controls help the pilot stay stable in flight.

According to the passage, which of the following answer choices is true?
    a. The nose of the helicopter is controlled by the aircraft's equilibrium.
    b. A helicopter's pitch angle affects its equilibrium.
    c. Anti-torque pedals are related to the pitch angle.
    d. More than three factors impact equilibrium in flight.

16. The majority of records that are taken as part of court proceedings are considered part of the public domain, and are therefore available to anyone who requests access. These documents can be used to conduct background checks, revealing information such as age, marital status, military status, and whether a person has ever been convicted of a crime. In some cases, the records can be obtained through a quick search of a state or county database, but others will require a request of the appropriate department.

Which is true about records from court proceedings?
    a. They are all part of the public domain.
    b. These records can only be used to conduct background checks.
    c. They can be used for background checks.
    d. The majority can be found on the internet.

17. Asteroids and comets are thought to be remnants from the same giant cloud of gas and dust that condensed to create the Sun, planets, and moons about 4.5 billion years ago during the Big Bang. Some people even theorize that the main asteroids, which lie in a tight belt between Mars and Jupiter, may all be fragments from another planet that was forming there that suffered some sort of major collision and broke into thousands of little pieces.

Which of the following are theorized to be a result of a major collision that caused a planet to break into thousands of pieces?
    a. The Sun, planets, and moons
    b. Mars and Jupiter
    c. The main asteroids that are found between Mars and Jupiter
    d. Comets

18. Osteoporosis is a medical condition that occurs when the body loses bone or makes too little bone tissue. This can lead to brittle, fragile bones that easily break. Bones are already porous, and when osteoporosis sets in, the spaces in bones become much larger, causing them to weaken. Both men and women can develop osteoporosis, though it is most common in women over age 50. Loss of bone can be silent and progressive, so it is important to be proactive in prevention of the disease.

What is the main purpose of this passage?
    a. To discuss some of the ways people contract osteoporosis
    b. To describe different treatment options for those with osteoporosis
    c. To explain how to prevent osteoporosis
    d. To define osteoporosis

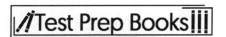

19. The synchropter arrangement was first designed for use in Germany's anti-submarine war craft. Often referred to as intermeshing rotor configuration, this design sets two oppositional rotors at a slight angle from each other in a transverse manner so that they actually intermesh. The configuration allows a helicopter to function without a tail rotor to save power.

According to the passage which of the following answer choices is true?
 a. Helicopters require the most power when using an intermeshing rotor configuration.
 b. Helicopters rely on the tail rotor for power.
 c. The synchropter arrangement has one oppositional rotor.
 d. The synchropter arrangement helps helicopters save power.

20. Jason had never been the best student. He had flunked three math tests and turned in only half of his homework. Worrying about his graduation, Jason's mother signed him up for tutoring. Even after several sessions, it was unclear whether he would pass. In the last week of math class, Jason buckled down and passed. Jason's math teacher marveled at his improvement.

When did Jason begin to show improvement?
 a. After half of his tutoring sessions.
 b. After his last tutoring session.
 c. This cannot be determined.
 d. During the last week of class.

Mechanical Comprehension

1. A car is traveling at a constant velocity of 25 m/s. How long does it take the car to travel 45 kilometers in a straight line?
 a. 1 hour
 b. 3,600 seconds
 c. 1,800 seconds
 d. 900 seconds

2. A spaceship with a mass of 100,000 kilograms is far away from any planet. To accelerate the craft at the rate of 0.5 m/sec^2 , what is the rocket thrust?
 a. 98.1 N
 b. 25,000 N
 c. 50,000 N
 d. 75,000 N

3. A football is kicked so that it leaves the punter's toe at a horizontal angle of 45 degrees. Ignoring any spin or tumbling, at what point is the upward vertical velocity of the football at a maximum?

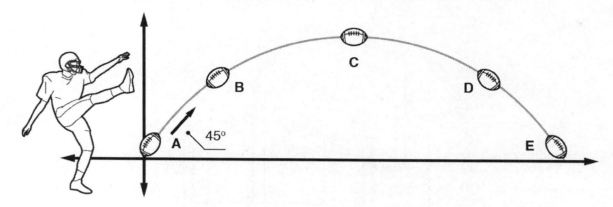

a.   At Point A
b.   At Point C
c.   At Points B and D
d.   At Points A and E

4. Which statement is true of the total energy of the pendulum?

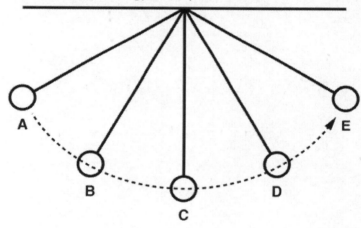

a.   Its total energy is at a maximum and equal at Points A and E.
b.   Its total energy is at a maximum at Point C.
c.   Its total energy is the same at Points A, B, C, D, and E.
d.   The total energy can't be determined without knowing the pendulum's mass.

5. How do you calculate the useful work performed in lifting a 10-kilogram weight from the ground to the top of a 2-meter ladder?
a. $10 \text{ kg} \times 2 \text{ m} \times 32 \text{ m/s}^2$
b. $10 \text{ kg} \times 2 \text{ m}^2 \times 9.81 \text{ m/s}$
c. $10 \text{ kg} \times 2 \text{ m} \times 9.81 \text{ m/s}^2$

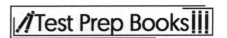

6. The master cylinder (F_1) of a hydraulic jack has a cross-sectional area of 0.1 m^2, and a force of 50 N is applied. What must the area of the drive cylinder (F_2) be to support a weight of 800 N?

a. 0.4 m^2
b. 0.8 m^2
c. 1.6 m^2
d. 3.2 m^2

7. The driver gear (Gear A) turns clockwise at a rate of 60 RPM. In what direction does Gear B turn and at what rotational speed?

a. Clockwise at 120 RPM
b. Counterclockwise at 120 RPM
c. Counterclockwise at 30 RPM
d. Clockwise at 30 RPM

8. Considering a gas in a closed system, at a constant volume, what will happen to the temperature if the pressure is increased?
a. The temperature will stay the same.
b. The temperature will decrease.
c. The temperature will increase.
d. It cannot be determined with the information given.

9. Which of the following is the minimum requirements of what must be present in order for current to flow?
a. A closed path for electrons
b. A battery and an open circuit
c. A closed path for electrons and a voltage
d. A battery or generator

10. Circular motion occurs around what?
a. The center of mass
b. The center of matter
c. An elliptical
d. An axis

11. A syringe is full of air. If a person holds the opening closed and pulls back the plunger, the air's - _____ will increase and the _____ will decrease.
a. Temperature; density
b. Pressure; density
c. Volume; pressure
d. Pressure; volume

12. A snowboarder begins at the top of a mountain and rides down the slope to the bottom; at which point is their potential energy the greatest?
    a. Standing still on top of the mountain
    b. Halfway down the slope
    c. At maximum speed reaching the bottom of the slope
    d. Just after starting down the slope at the top of the mountain

13. Water is flowing in a rectangular canal 10 meters wide by 2 meters deep at a velocity of 3 m/s. The canal is half full. What is the flow rate?
    a. $30 \text{ m}^3/\text{s}$
    b. $60 \text{ m}^3/\text{s}$
    c. $90 \text{ m}^3/\text{s}$
    d. $120 \frac{\text{m}^3}{\text{s}}$

14. What is the total mechanical energy of a system?
    a. The total potential energy
    b. The total kinetic energy
    c. Kinetic energy plus potential energy
    d. Kinetic energy minus potential energy

15. Which of the following is a vector quantity?
    a. Mass
    b. Length
    c. Velocity
    d. Speed

16. In a shipping warehouse, there is a block and tackle pulley system with two ropes connecting the moving block to the fixed block. How much force is required to lift each 20-kg pallet of garden mulch?
    a. 5 kg
    b. 10 kg
    c. 20 kg
    d. 40 kg

17. How is the mechanical advantage of a system, such as a simple machine, calculated?
    a. Output force times input force
    b. Input force minus output force
    c. Output force divided by input force
    d. Input force divided by output force

196

Use the graphic below for questions 18–20:

18. What is the total resistance in the circuit above?
    a. 85 ohms
    b. 510 ohms
    c. 320 ohms
    d. 260 ohms

19. What is the total current leaving the battery?
    a. 25,600 amps
    b. 0.25 amps
    c. 510 amps
    d. 80 amps

20. What is the voltage drop across the 100-ohm resistor?
    a. 6 volts
    b. 9 volts
    c. 15 volts
    d. 25 volts

21. Which of the following on the electromagnetic spectrum possesses the highest energy?
    a. Infrared waves
    b. Visible light
    c. Ultraviolet rays
    d. Gamma rays

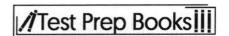

22. Which statement is true regarding electrostatic charges?
    a. Like charges attract.
    b. Like charges repel.
    c. Like charges are neutral.
    d. Like charges neither attract nor repel.

23. A rectangular fish tank measuring 1 ft x 4 ft holds 10 gallons of water. If a gallon of water weighs approximately 8 pounds, what is the pressure exerted on the bottom of the tank when full?
    a. 10 lb/ft^2
    b. 20 lb/ft^2
    c. 300 lb/ft^2
    d. 320 lb/ft^2

24. Which is NOT a form of energy?
    a. Sound
    b. Heat
    c. Mass
    d. Microwaves

25. Which of the following equations is not an accurate representation of Ohm's Law?
    a. $V = I \times R$
    b. $R = \dfrac{V}{I}$
    c. $I = \dfrac{V}{R}$
    d. $V = \dfrac{R}{I}$

26. A wheelbarrow is an example of a Class __ lever.
    a. I
    b. II
    c. III
    d. IV

27. Jerome ran out of gas and is pushing his car to the gas station down the road. Ignoring friction and air resistance, at what rate is his car accelerating?
    a. 2.6 meters per second
    b. 1.5 meters per second
    c. 1.5 meters per second squared
    d. 15 meters per second squared

28. Which of the following depicts a form of potential energy?
    a. The light given off by a lamp
    b. The gravitational pull of a black hole
    c. The heat from a microwaved burrito
    d. The motion of a pendulum

198

29. Which is correct for the flow of water as it passes from a pipe with a 5-inch diameter to a pipe with a 3-inch diameter?
    a. The water pressure increases.
    b. The pipe becomes clogged.
    c. The water speeds up.
    d. The same amount of water flows through both sections of pipe.

30. What property of metals lends them to be conductive materials?
    a. The protons in the outer shells are free to drift between atoms.
    b. The electrons in the outer shells are free to drift between atoms.
    c. The electrons in the outer shell are pulled in tightly by the nucleus so they do not drift away to surrounding atoms.
    d. The neutrons in the outer shell are pulled in tightly by the nucleus so they do not drift away to surrounding atoms.

Aviation and Nautical Information

1. If the cyclic pitch control is pushed to the left, which way will the rotor disk tip and which way will the helicopter move?
    a. Right; right
    b. Right; left
    c. Left; right
    d. Left; left

2. Which direction(s) are the anti-torque pedals designed to move the nose?
    a. Up and down
    b. Left and right
    c. Forward and backwards
    d. The anti-torque pedals move the nose in all of the above directions.

3. Which of the following is NOT included in a helicopter's base empty weight?
    a. The pilot
    b. The engine
    c. Optional equipment
    d. Transmission oil

4. Which of the following are dangers of overloading a helicopter?

    I. Decreased performance

    II. Structural damage

    III. Shifted center of gravity

    a. II only
    b. I, II, and III
    c. I and II
    d. I and III

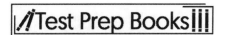

5. If the helicopter is nose down while attempting to hover, and there are no winds, then it most likely has which of the following?
    a. Front-loaded center of gravity
    b. Aft-loaded center of gravity
    c. Balanced center of gravity
    d. A changing center of gravity

6. When performing a vertical takeoff to a hover, what should be done if the heading begins to change?
    a. Quickly adjust the cyclic pitch control
    b. Slowly adjust the cyclic pitch control
    c. Slowly adjust the anti-torque pedals
    d. Quickly adjust the anti-torque pedals

7. Which of the following would make a good reference point when attempting to hover?
    a. The tail rotor
    b. Another helicopter
    c. A building
    d. A moving car

8. Which of the following should NOT need to be maintained while performing a hovering turn?
    a. Altitude
    b. RPM
    c. Heading
    d. Position

9. Which of the following is a complication unique to sideward hovering flight, as opposed to forward and rearward flight?
    a. Increased clearance needed due to dipping of the tail during the maneuver
    b. Additional pressure needed on the anti-torque pedals to deal with the weathervane
    c. Drastically-reduced visibility
    d. Decreased RPM due to the increased pitch of the rotor blades

10. When performing an air taxi, which of the following should be avoided?

    I. Flying in the shaded area of the height-velocity diagram

    II. Flying over other aircraft, vehicles, and personnel

    III. Flying in crosswind conditions

    a. I only
    b. I and II
    c. I and III
    d. I, II and III

11. Which of the following does not need to be checked *before* beginning a normal takeoff from hover?
    a. Power
    b. Balance
    c. RPM
    d. Flight controls

12. In straight-and-level flight, which control is primarily used to increase airspeed?
    a. The collective pitch control
    b. The cyclic pitch control
    c. Anti-torque pedals
    d. The throttle

13. A helicopter pilot is attempting to take off when she notices that the helicopter's nose tilts down after leaving the ground. What is most likely the problem?
    a. Too much main rotor torque
    b. Imbalanced center of gravity
    c. Insufficient power
    d. Changing winds

14. A helicopter begins a descent at 300 feet above the ground, with the intent to lower to 200 feet above the ground. The pilot begins the descent at a steady rate of 400 FPM. At what altitude should he begin leveling out the helicopter?
    a. 200 feet
    b. 220 feet
    c. 240 feet
    d. 260 feet

15. Which of the following would NOT be included in the maximum internal weight?
    a. The pilot
    b. Cargo stored in the aft of the helicopter
    c. Useable fuel
    d. An object supported by a winch

16. A pilot wishes to reposition the helicopter while hovering to get to a designated runway for a surface takeoff. After performing a hovering turn to set her bearing properly, the pilot needs to move the helicopter forward. To do this, she should do which of the following?
    a. Increase the collective
    b. Briefly apply pressure to the cyclic, then release the cyclic
    c. Apply gentle and constant pressure to the cyclic
    d. Progressively increase the throttle

17. While performing a banking left turn, the pilot notices that the helicopter has begun to skid. What can he do to get out of this?
    a. Decrease pressure on the left anti-torque pedal or increase pressure on the right anti-torque pedal
    b. Decrease pressure on the right anti-torque pedal or increase pressure on the left anti-torque pedal
    c. Apply additional leftwards cyclic pressure
    d. Apply additional rightwards cyclic pressure

18. A pilot has successfully identified that the helicopter has an aft-loaded center of balance. Which of the following methods would correct this?
    a. Removing cargo from the back of the helicopter
    b. Applying additional forward cyclic
    c. Increasing the throttle
    d. Adding additional fuel

19. A helicopter performing a takeoff from hover has just entered effective translational lift and has begun to increase the collective. Which step of the takeoff is the helicopter currently in?
    a. Step one
    b. Step two
    c. Step three
    d. Step four

20. A pilot is performing a straight and level flight when he realizes that the helicopter has drifted to the left of the intended path. What should he do?
    a. Apply pressure to the right anti-torque pedal
    b. Apply rightward pressure to the cyclic
    c. Remove cargo from the back of the helicopter
    d. Speed up the helicopter to reach the destination before the helicopter drifts further

26. Which of the following would increase the torque on the helicopter?

    I. Applying pressure on the cyclic

    II. Decreasing the collective

    III. Increasing the throttle

    a. I
    b. II
    c. III
    d. II and III

27. Which of the following is true about induced drag?
    a. It is strongest when the helicopter is moving at higher speeds.
    b. It is created by the airfoil striking the air.
    c. It always pushes in a direction perpendicular to vertical lift.
    d. All of the above are true.

28. If sufficient takeoff power is in doubt, what should the pilot do?

   I. Delay the takeoff until the aircraft is lighter

   II. Attempt the takeoff anyway to check power

   III. Wait until the density altitude has decreased

   a. I only
   b. II and III
   c. I and II
   d. I and III

29. Which of the following is not one of the four fundamental maneuvers?
   a. Turning
   b. Straight and level flight
   c. Climbing
   d. Takeoff

30. A pilot notices that as the helicopter flies, the nose slowly drops. The cyclic is in its neutral position. What is most likely the cause of this?
   a. The fuel in the rear of the helicopter is being used up, slowly shifting the center of balance forward.
   b. The cyclic is improperly calibrated and tipping the helicopter even into the neutral position.
   c. The helicopter is entering a higher density air front, pushing the nose down.
   d. The helicopter's tail rotor is creating too much torque, pushing the tail up and the nose down.

Answer Explanations

Math Skills

1. D: The total amount the company pays, y, equals the cost of the building ($50,000) plus the cost of the saws. Since the saws cost $40 each, the overall cost of the saws is $40 times x, where x is the number of saws. Putting all this together, we have $y = 50,000 + 40x$, which is equivalent to Choice D.

2. A: The function can be factored to identify the zeros. First, the term $3x$ is factored out to the front because each term contains $3x$. Then, the quadratic is factored into $(x + 3)(x - 2)$.

3. D: Denote the width as w and the length as l. Then, $l = 3w + 5$. The perimeter is $2w + 2l = 90$. Substituting the first expression for l into the second equation yields:

$$2(3w + 5) + 2w = 90$$

$$6w + 10 + 2w = 90$$

$$8w = 80$$

$$w = 10$$

Putting this into the first equation, it yields:

$$l = 3(10) + 5 = 35$$

4. B: Audit Services makes up 40% of total income, and Taxation Services makes up 30%, so together they make up $40\% + 30\% = 70\%$ of total income. To find 70% of $500,000, change the percentage to a decimal and multiply: $0.7 \times \$500,000 = \$350,000$.

5. C: When performing calculations consisting of more than one operation, the order of operations should be followed: parentheses, exponents, multiplication & division, addition & subtraction.

Parentheses:

$$7^2 - 3 \times (4 + 2) + 15 \div 5$$

$$7^2 - 3 \times (6) + 15 \div 5$$

Exponents:

$$49 - 3 \times 6 + 15 \div 5$$

Multiplication & division (from left to right):

$$49 - 18 + 3$$

Addition & subtraction (from left to right):

$$49 - 18 + 3 = 34$$

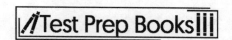

6. D: A proportion can be set up to solve for the missing value. Let d be the distance between the two cities in real life. Also, expressing the mixed number as an improper fraction is helpful: $4\frac{1}{2} = \frac{9}{2}$. Therefore, $\frac{\frac{1}{8}}{75} = \frac{\frac{9}{2}}{x}$. Cross multiply to obtain $\frac{x}{8} = \frac{675}{2}$. Cross multiply again to obtain $2x = 5,400$. Dividing by 2 results in $x = 2,700$. Therefore, the two cities are 2,700 miles apart.

7. D: Position is an antiderivative of velocity, so it must have the form:

$$h(t) = -16t^2 - 8t + C$$

At the starting time of $t = 0$, this should equal 500, so setting:

$$500 = -16 \cdot 0^2 - 8 \cdot 0 + C$$

gives $C = 500$, or:

$$h(t) = -16t^2 - 8t + 500$$

8. D: A yard is 3 feet. The equation to calculate the minimum number of yards is:

$$79 \div 3 = 26\frac{1}{3}$$

If the material is sold only by whole yards, then Mo would need to round up to the next whole yard in order to cover the extra $\frac{1}{3}$ yard. Therefore, the answer is 27 yards. None of the other choices meets the minimum whole yard requirement.

9. D: The probability of picking the winner of the race is $\frac{1}{4}$, or $\left(\frac{number\ of\ favorable\ outcomes}{number\ of\ total\ outcomes}\right)$. Assuming the winner was picked on the first selection, three horses remain from which to choose the runner-up (these are dependent events). Therefore, the probability of picking the runner-up is $\frac{1}{3}$. To determine the probability that multiple events all happen, multiply the probabilities of the events:

$$\frac{1}{4} \times \frac{1}{3} = \frac{1}{12}$$

10. A: The tip is not taxed, so he pays 5% tax only on the $10. To find 5% of $10, calculate $0.05 \times \$10 = \$0.50$. Add up $10 + $0.50 + $2 to get $12.50.

11. A: The total number of treats distributed will be the number of treats per bag $(4x + 1)$ times the number of bags given out, which can be represented by the variable n. This expression is $n(4x + 1)$. Since this is the amount of treats distributed, set it equal to $60x + 15$.

$$n(4x + 1) = 60x + 15$$

In order to figure out what n is, determine what number times 4 results in 60 (4n=60) and what number times 1 results in 15 (1n = 15). In both cases, $n = 15$. Therefore, 15 bags are given out.

12. A: The definition of an even function is that $f(-x) = f(x)$. We can plug in $-x$ to our function to see what we get:

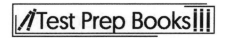

$$f(-2) = \frac{1}{2}(-x)^4 + 2(-x)^2 - 6$$

Since $(-x)^4 = x^4$ *and* $(-x)^2 = x^2$, we see that $f(-x)$ is equal to the original function, so our function is even.

The definition of an odd function is that $f(-x) = -f(x)$. We can calculate $-f(x)$:

$$-fx = -1\left(\frac{1}{2}\right)x^4 + 2x^2 - 6 = \left(-\frac{1}{2}\right)x^4 - 2x^2 + 6$$

This does not equal $f(-x)$ (which, remember, is the same as our original function), so our function is not odd.

13. C: The volume of a pyramid is $(length \times width \times height)$ divided by 3, and $(6 \times 6 \times 9)$ divided by 3 is 108 in³. Choice *A* is incorrect because 324 in³ is $(length \times width \times height)$ without dividing by 3. Choice *B* is incorrect because 6 is used for height instead of 9 ($(6 \times 6 \times 6)$ divided by 3) to get 72 in³. Choice *D* is incorrect because 18 in³ is (6×9) divided by 3 and leaving out a 6.

14. C: The average is calculated by adding all six numbers, then dividing by 6. The first five numbers have a sum of 25. This means $\frac{25+n}{6} = 6$, where n is the unknown number. Multiplying both sides by 6, we get $25 + n = 36$, which means $n = 11$.

15. B: Scientific notation takes the form $a \times 10^n$, where a is any decimal number between 1 and 10 and n is the number of decimal places it takes to reach the first digit. In this case, take the first digit 7, add a decimal point, and then include each non-zero digit after that to determine the value of a as 7.35. Next, count the place values from the position of the decimal point in standard form to the position in scientific notation in order to determine the value of n, which would be 9. Therefore, this number expressed in scientific notation would be 7.35×10^9.

16. B: The first pair of parentheses is unnecessary, and we can delete the second pair after distributing the -1 in front of them:

$$(5x^2 - 3x + 4) - 1(2x^2 - 7) = 5x^2 - 3x + 4 - 2x^2 + 7$$

Next, like terms (same variables with same exponents) are combined by adding the coefficients and keeping the variables and their powers the same:

$$5x^2 - 3x + 4 - 2x^2 + 7 = 3x^2 - 3x + 11$$

17. B: The independent variable's coordinate at the vertex of a parabola (which is the highest point when the coefficient of the squared independent variable is negative) is given by:

$$x = -\frac{b}{2a}$$

Substitute and solve for x to get:

$$x = -\frac{4}{2(-16)} = \frac{1}{8}$$

Using this value of x, the maximum height of the ball (y), can be calculated. Substituting $\frac{1}{8}$ into the equation for x yields:

$$h(t) = -16\left(\frac{1}{8}\right)^2 + 4\frac{1}{8} + 6 = 6.25$$

18. C: Because the triangles are similar, the lengths of the corresponding sides are proportional. Therefore:

$$\frac{30 + x}{30} = \frac{22}{14} = \frac{y + 15}{y}$$

Using cross multiplication on the first two terms results in the equation:

$$14(30 + x) = 22 \times 30$$

When solved, this gives:

$$x \approx 17.1$$

Using cross multiplication on the last two terms results in the equation:

$$14(y + 15) = 22y$$

When solved, this gives:

$$y \approx 26.3$$

19. C: The sample space is made up of $8 + 7 + 6 + 5 = 26$ balls. The probability of pulling each individual ball is $\frac{1}{26}$. Since there are 7 yellow balls, the probability of pulling a yellow ball is $\frac{7}{26}$.

20. B: The power of 10 by which a digit is multiplied corresponds with the number of zeros following the digit when expressing its value in standard form. Therefore:

$$(1 \times 10^4) + (3 \times 10^3) + (7 \times 10^1) + (8 \times 10^0)$$

$$10,000 + 3,000 + 70 + 8 = 13,078$$

21. D: The slope is given by the change in y divided by the change in x. The change in y is $2 - 0 = 2$, and the change in x is:

$$0 - (-4) = 4$$

The slope is $\frac{2}{4} = \frac{1}{2}$.

22. A: This vector indicates a positive relationship. A negative relationship would show points traveling from the top-left of the graph to the bottom-right. Exponential and logarithmic functions aren't linear (don't create a straight line), so these options can be immediately eliminated.

23. B: 8 squared is 64, and 6 squared is 36. These should be added together to get $64 + 36 = 100$. Then, the last step is to find the square root of 100, which is 10.

24 B: Because the 68-degree angle and angle b sum to 180 degrees, the measurement of angle b is 112 degrees. Because of corresponding angles, angle b is equal to angle f. Therefore, angle f measures 112 degrees.

25. A: To calculate the range in a set of data, subtract the lowest value from the highest value. In this graph, the range of Mr. Lennon's students is 5, which can be seen physically in the graph as having the smallest difference between the highest value and the lowest value compared with the other teachers.

26. C: Kimberley worked 4.5 hours at the rate of $10 / h$ and 1 hour at the rate of $12 / h$. The problem states that her time is rounded to the nearest hour, so the 4.5 hours would round up to 5 hours at the rate of $10/h$.

$$(5 \text{ h}) \times \left(\frac{\$10}{\text{h}}\right) + (1 \text{ h}) \times \left(\frac{\$12}{\text{h}}\right) = \$50 + \$12 = \$62$$

27. D:

$9x + x - 7 = 16 + 2x$	Combine $9x$ and x.
$10x - 7 = 16 + 2x$	
$10x - 7 + 7 = 16 + 2x + 7$	Add 7 to both sides to remove -7.
$10x = 23 + 2x$	
$10x - 2x = 23 + 2x - 2x$	Subtract $2x$ from both sides to move it to the other side of the equation.
$8x = 23$	
$\dfrac{8x}{8} = \dfrac{23}{8}$	Divide by 8 to get x by itself.
$x = \dfrac{23}{8}$	

28. B: The y-intercept of an equation is found where the x-value is zero. Plugging in zero for x in the equation, we get $0^2 + 3(0) - 4 = -4$.

29. B: An equilateral triangle has three sides of equal length, so if the total perimeter is 18 feet, each side must be 6 feet long. A square with sides of 6 feet will have an area of $6^2 = 36$ square feet.

30. A: Let the unknown score be x. The average will be:

$$\frac{5 \times 50 + 4 \times 70 + x}{10} = \frac{530 + x}{10} = 55$$

Multiply both sides by 10 to get $530 + x = 550$, or $x = 20$.

Reading Comprehension

1. B: According to the passage, Sir Isaac Newton's first law of motion is the basis for theories related to balancing drag and thrust, and this balance is one of the two objectives provided for aircraft propulsion.

Therefore, Sir Isaac Newton must be relevant for aircraft propulsion. The passage doesn't mention or reference any of Newton's other theories, so they cannot be inferred, making Choice *A* incorrect. Thrust and drag are important forces, but the passage discusses the balance of all external forces, implying that there are more than two. Even if this was untrue, the passage itself doesn't infer that thrust and drag are the only relevant forces, so Choice *C* is incorrect. The differences between acceleration and cruising aren't discussed or closely related to the passage, so Choice *D* is incorrect.

2. B: The point of this passage is to show what drowning looks like. Choice *A* is incorrect because while drowning is a danger of swimming, the passage doesn't include any other dangers. The passage is not intended for lifeguards specifically, but for a general audience, so Choice *C* is incorrect. There are a few signs of drowning, but the passage does not compare them; thus, Choice *D* is incorrect.

3. D: Abiotic components impact environment but are not living. Of the list, wind is the only one that does not include a living organism. Choice *A* and Choice *B* are incorrect because both grasses and insects are living organisms. Choice *C* is incorrect because soil, in part, includes living microorganisms.

4. C: A'a flows are laden with rock and debris, which can compound the damage caused by the heat and power of a lava flow itself. Choice *A* is incorrect because there are details in the passage to help determine this information. Choice *B* and C are incorrect. The fact that pahoehoe lava flows are fast running and the words *in contrast* were used to compare these lava flows with a'a flows, we can determine that the dangers of a'a lava flows are not speed or distance traveled.

5. C: The passage advises pilots to circumnavigate a thunderstorm rather than fly through the storm, so it can be inferred that circumnavigating is safe, at least in comparison to a direct path through. The passage advises pilots to know their personal skills and limitations, but it doesn't imply that they don't commonly know this information, so Choice *A* is incorrect. Choice *B* is incorrect because the passage doesn't directly or indirectly compare dangerous weather conditions of any kind. Choice *D* is incorrect because cloud holes are characterized as hazardous, not impenetrable.

6. B: It is stated that new word combinations such as "eye hats" are interesting. They suggest an understanding of language or vocabulary. Choice *A* and Choice *C* are incorrect. Both Koko's understood vocabulary and signed vocabulary are of interest, but the fact that she could put the two together to create language was more fascinating. Choice *D* is incorrect. Acquiring vocabulary requires repetition and mimicry, much like how a parrot can acquire vocabulary. As noted above, the ability to create new words based on an understanding of other words proves more interesting.

7. C: The passages states that he has looked forward to this vacation all year, so Choice *C* is correct. Raul has been fascinated with pyramids since childhood, not looking forward to the vacation since childhood, so Choice *A* is incorrect. The word *month* is in the passage, but the context is that Raul's vacation is next month, not that he's been excited about it for a month. Therefore, Choice *B* is incorrect. *Many years* can be found in the passage, but this in reference to how long it has been since Raul has read about the history of the pyramids, so Choice *D* is incorrect.

8. C: The passage characterizes flying as an unattainable skill and mentions that physical and mental demands can be prohibitive for potential students, so it can be inferred that some students don't become pilots. Although the passage emphasizes perseverance, it doesn't reference other attributes or make a comparison, so Choice *A* is incorrect. The passage mentions that students face physical and mental demands, but it doesn't discuss how pilots fare during their career. So, Choice *B* is incorrect. All consummate skills probably do require significant work; however, the passage doesn't reference any consummate skills other than piloting. Therefore, Choice *D* is incorrect.

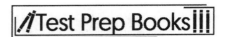

9. D: Choice D is correct. Julio broke his promise to his mother that he would clean his room. All of the other answer choices are incorrect.

10. B: The passage states that chains of separate events, not single events, cause accidents, and chains of events are referred to as *error chains*. Problems with multiple root causes are likely difficult to remedy, but the passage doesn't compare or evaluate the difficulty of problems. Additionally, "most difficult" is too strong, so Choice A is incorrect. Choice C is incorrect because the passage doesn't compare pilot errors and mechanical problems in terms of difficulty to solve. The passage doesn't discuss isolated problems with single root causes, and it doesn't imply such problems couldn't cause air disasters, although the author of the passage would probably seek to look at the broader context of the isolated problem. As such, Choice D is incorrect.

11. A: Tropical zones are dubbed tropical because of their climate. It is the wet and warm weather that creates the climate. Choice B is incorrect because the climate is largely responsible for the biodiversity rather than the biodiversity defining the zone itself. Choice C is incorrect because tropical zones occur in multiple regions, so geography is not the feature for which they are best known. Choice D is incorrect because, much like regions, tropical zones feature varying elevations and occur in lowlands as well. As the passage suggests, tropical zones are noted for their climate.

12. A: The passage states that flying at higher altitudes can be smoother and subject to less turbulence. Because turbulence is a disruption in airflow, it can be inferred that flying at higher altitudes involves fewer disruptions in airflow. The passage states that turbulence can be manageable and doesn't allude to any exceptions, so Choice B is incorrect. Choice C is incorrect because the passage doesn't discuss whether severe turbulence is common, although it does infer that it's manageable. Aircraft definitely do experience less turbulence while taxiing, but the passage doesn't mention taxiing or turbulence on the ground. As such, Choice D is incorrect.

13. A: The Fifteenth Amendment expanded democracy by prohibiting the denial of voting rights based on "race, color, or previous condition of servitude," which increased the number of eligible voters. The Seventeenth Amendment expanded democracy by establishing the popular election of U.S. Senators, which gave the public more input. Thus, Choice A is correct. Choice B is incorrect because the right to vote for people regardless of sex is not mentioned in the passage. Choice C is incorrect because the Fourteenth Amendment prohibited discrimination based on race, and the Eighteenth Amendment prohibited the sale of alcohol, and neither of these are mentioned in the passage. Choice D is incorrect because the Twenty-Sixth Amendment lowered the eligible voting age, and the Twelfth Amendment reformed the Electoral College, and neither of these are mentioned in the passage.

14. D: The passage ends by stating that production did not decline until the 1970s, so Choice D is correct. If production did not decline until the 1970s, then it could not have declined one hundred years ago. Therefore, Choice A in incorrect. Evidence was presented that asbestos was dangerous early on, and asbestos was produced for over one hundred years, so it can be reasoned that the evidence was around long before the decline in production during the 1970s. This means that Choice B is incorrect. The passage does not state that the durability of asbestos ever declined, so Choice C is incorrect.

15. B: The cyclic control and collective lever control both affect the pitch angle, and both are related to maintaining equilibrium. So, it can be inferred that a helicopter's pitch angle affects the equilibrium. The nose of the helicopter affects an aircraft's equilibrium, and the passage doesn't imply that this also works in the reverse. So, Choice A is incorrect. Choice C is incorrect because the anti-torque pedals

210

affect the nose of the helicopter. The passage lists three factors that impact equilibrium in flight and doesn't reference any additional factors. As such, Choice *D* is incorrect.

16. C: Choice *C* is correct. The documents can be used to conduct background checks. Choice *A* is incorrect since only the majority, not all, of records are part of the public domain. Choice *B* is incorrect because records that are part of the public domain can be viewed by anyone who asks for access. It is not stated in the passage that they can only be accessed to conduct background checks. Choice *D* is incorrect. Some can be found by searching state and county databases, and others can be accessed through the appropriate department.

17. C: The passage states that the main asteroids that lie in a tight belt between Mars and Jupiter are theorized to be fragments of a planet that was forming but broke into pieces due to a collision. Choice *A* is incorrect. These are thought to have been created from a giant cloud of gas and dust. Choice *B* is incorrect. Mars and Jupiter are the planets that have a tight belt of asteroids between them. Choice *D* is incorrect. Comets are thought to be remnants from that giant cloud of gas and dust that created the Sun, planets, and moons.

18. D: The main point of this passage is to define osteoporosis. Choice *A* is incorrect because the passage does not list ways that people contract osteoporosis. Choice *B* is incorrect because the passage does not mention any treatment options. While the passage does briefly mention prevention, it does not explain how, so Choice *C* is incorrect.

19. D: The synchropter arrangement uses an intermeshing rotor configuration, which allows the helicopter to save power. Choice *A* is incorrect because helicopters require less power when using an intermeshing rotor configuration. Helicopters don't rely on a tail rotor for power because the intermeshing rotor configuration allows a helicopter to operate without a tail rotor. As such, Choice *B* is incorrect. The synchropter arrangement involves two oppositional rotors; therefore, Choice *C* is incorrect.

20. C: Choice *C* is correct because there are not enough details in the passage to determine the answer to this question. There is no mention of his performance after half of his tutoring sessions or after his last session, so Choices *A* and *B* are incorrect. It might be tempting to guess that he showed improvement after the last session since his ability to pass was unclear after several sessions but he was able to pass during the last week of class. However, the question asks us to determine when he began to show improvement. There is no indication that his last tutoring session had already occurred. Choice *D* is incorrect. Jason did buckle down during the last week of class and ended up passing, but we do not know if he had already shown some improvement before the last week of class.

Mechanical Comprehension

1. C:

$$(Desired\ Distance\ in\ km\ \times\ conversion\ factor\ (m\ to\ km))/current\ velocity\ in\ \frac{m}{s}$$

$$\left(45\ km\times\frac{1000\ m}{km}\right)\bigg/25\frac{m}{s}=1800\ seconds$$

2. C: The equation $F = ma$ should be memorized. All of the values are given in the correct units (kilogram-meter-second) so plug them in to the equation:

$$F = 100,000 \text{ kg} \times 0.5\frac{\text{m}}{\text{s}^2} = 50,000 \text{ N}$$

3. A: The acceleration due to gravity reduces the upward velocity every moment thereafter. The speed is the same at points A and E, but the velocity is different. At point E, the velocity has a maximum negative value.

4. C: Choice *A* is incorrect. Even though the total energy is at a maximum at Points A and E, it isn't equal at only those points. The total energy is the same at *all* points. Choice *B* is incorrect. The kinetic energy is at a maximum at C, but not the *total* energy. The correct answer is Choice *C*. The total energy is conserved, so it's the same at *all* points on the arc.

5. C: The answer is 10kg x 2m x 9.81m/s².

6. C: The pressure created by the load is:

$$\frac{50 \text{ N}}{0.1 \text{ m}^2} = 500\frac{\text{N}}{\text{m}^2}$$

This pressure acts throughout the jack, including the large cylinder. Force is pressure times area, so the area equals pressure divided by force:

$$\frac{800 \text{ N}}{500\frac{\text{N}}{\text{m}^2}} = 1.6 \text{ m}^2$$

7. C: The driver gear is turning clockwise, and the gear meshed with it turns counter to it. Because of the 2:1 gear ratio, every revolution of the driver gear causes half a revolution of the follower.

8. C: According to the *ideal gas law* ($PV = nRT$), if volume is constant, the temperature is directly related to the pressure in a system. Therefore, if the pressure increases, the temperature will increase in direct proportion. Choice *A* would not be possible, since the system is closed and a change is occurring, so the temperature will change. Choice *B* incorrectly exhibits an inverse relationship between pressure and temperature, or $P = 1/T$.

9. C: As long as there is a closed path for electrons and a voltage, current will flow. Voltage, which is essentially the electromotive potential, causes current. However, if there is a suitable path for electrons but no voltage, or voltage in the absence of a viable path, current will cease.

10. D: Circular motion occurs around an invisible line around which an object can rotate; this invisible line is called an axis. Choice *A*, center of mass, is the average placement of an object's mass. Choice *B* is not a real term. Choice *C*, elliptical, describes an elongated circle and is not a viable selection.

11. C: This question tests knowledge of Boyle's law, which states that for a fixed amount of an ideal gas kept at a fixed temperature, pressure and volume are inversely proportional. With the amount of air and temperature constant as the plunger is pulled back, the volume inside of the syringe increases. The inverse relationship between pressure and volume means that as one increases, the other decreases. This means that pressure of the air decreases as the plunger is pulled back, making Choice *C* the correct answer. Choices *A*, *B*, and *D* are incorrect because they do not reflect Boyle's law surrounding an ideal gas. Temperature and density would be unchanged in this scenario, and pressure must decrease if the volume of a container of gas increases.

12. A: This question focuses on the principles of potential and kinetic energy. The potential energy of the snowboarder is equal to the work that's required to lift them from the base of the mountain to their current position, while their kinetic energy is related to their mass and velocity. Standing still on top of the mountain, the snowboarder has no kinetic energy and the greatest amount of potential energy, making Choice A the correct answer. Choices B, C, and D are incorrect because the snowboarder at these points has less potential energy than in Choice A.

13. A: The answer is 30 $\frac{m^3}{s}$. One of the few equations that must be memorized is the flow rate formula, $Q = v \times A$, to find volumetric flow rates. This represents the volume of fluid passing through a channel in a given timeframe, which is equivalent to the velocity of a fluid passing through a fixed area, as shown below:

$$Q = v \times A$$

$$Q = \frac{s}{t} \times s^2$$

$$Q = \frac{s^3}{t}$$

$$Q = V/t$$

The length of the canal is unnecessary because the flow rate can be found from the velocity at a two-dimensional slice of the canal. The area of flow is $1\ m \times 10\ m$ because only half the depth of the channel is full of water, therefore: $Q = 3\ \frac{m}{s} \times 10\ m^2 = 30\ \frac{m^3}{s}$.

14. C: In any system, the total mechanical energy is the sum of the potential energy and the kinetic energy. Either value could be zero, but it still must be included in the total. Choices A and B only give the total potential or kinetic energy, respectively.

15. C: Motion with one dimension or measurement is known as a *scalar quantity*, and includes things such as length, speed, or time. Motion with two dimensions is known as a *vector quantity*. This would be speed with a direction, or velocity. Choices A, B, D, and E (mass, length, speed, and frequency) are all measurements of magnitudes—one-dimensional scalar quantities.

16. B: The mechanical advantage of the multiple-sheave block and tackle is approximated by counting the number of ropes going to and from the moving block. Because there are two ropes connecting the moving block to the fixed block in warehouse's pulley system, the mechanical advantage is 2:1. This means that the force needed to lift the item is one-half the weight of the item. Thus, 10 kg of force is needed to lift a 20-kg bag of garden mulch.

17. C: The mechanical advantage of a system or machine can be calculated by comparing the force input by the user to the machine with the force output from the use of the machine such that:

$$Mechanical\ Advantage = \frac{output\ force}{input\ force}$$

or

$$MA = \frac{F_{out}}{F_{in}}$$

Therefore, Choice *C* is correct.

18. C: Total resistance in a circuit that has both series and parallel elements is calculated by calculating the equivalent resistance of the parallel portion, then finding total resistance in series. First, the simplify the parallel section:

$$\frac{1}{R_{equivalent}} = \frac{1}{150\ \Omega} + \frac{1}{100\ \Omega}$$

$$R_{equivalent} = \frac{1}{\frac{1}{150\ \Omega} + \frac{1}{100\ \Omega}} = \frac{1}{\frac{2}{300\ \Omega} + \frac{3}{300\ \Omega}} = \frac{1}{\frac{5}{300\ \Omega}} = \frac{1}{\frac{1}{60\ \Omega}} = 60\ \Omega$$

Now that the parallel portion has been simplified, the total resistance can be calculated:

$$R_{total} = 85\ \Omega + 175\ \Omega + 60\ \Omega = 320\ \Omega$$

The total resistance of the circuit is 320 ohms.

19. B: The total resistance for the circuit was found in the previous problem (320 ohms), so this value is plugged into the equation as well as the voltage from the battery source (80 volts).

$$I = \frac{V}{R} = \frac{80\ V}{320\ \Omega} = 0.25\ A$$

Choices *A*, *C*, and *D* do not manipulate the equation appropriately, leaving Choice *B* as the correct answer.

20. C: The voltage drop, or decrease, across a resistor is equal to the current passing that resistor, times its resistance. However, with resistors in parallel, the voltage drop across each resistor is the same, regardless of which resistor is examined; the voltage before and after the 100-ohm resistor is the same as across the 150-ohm resistor. Calculating the voltage drop across parallel resistors takes the *equivalent* resistance (60 ohms) of the parallel resistors and multiplies it by the current:

$$V = I \times R = 0.25\ A \times 60\ \Omega = 15\ V$$

Therefore, the voltage drop across the 100-ohm resistor is 15 volts. This can be checked by calculating the voltage drops of the 85-ohm and 175-ohm resistors and subtracting them from the total voltage (80 volts):

$$V_{85\Omega} = 0.25\ A \times 85\ \Omega = 21.25\ V$$

$$V_{175\Omega} = 0.25\ A \times 175\ \Omega = 43.75\ V$$

$$V = 80\ V - (21.25\ V + 43.75\ V) = 80\ V - 65\ V = 15\ V$$

21. D: The higher the frequency of a wave, the higher its energy. Gamma waves radiate at a higher frequency than the other forms of electromagnetic radiation, while radio waves are the lowest energy, and thus lowest frequency, waves listed.

22. B: For charges, like charges repel each other and opposite charges attract each other. Negatives and positives will attract, while two positive charges or two negative charges will repel each other. Charges have an effect on each other, so Choices *C* and *D* are incorrect.

23. B: This question looks for understanding of pressure in a system, expressed as Pressure equals Force divided by Area, or $P = \frac{F}{A}$. The force of the water is equal to its weight, which is

$10 \times 8 = 80$ pounds. The area of the fish tank is $1 \times 4 = 4$ square feet. Plugging these values into the equation yields $P = \frac{80}{4} = 20$ pounds per square foot, making Choice *B* the correct answer. Choices *A*, *C*, and *D* are incorrect because they describe either insufficient or excessive pressure for the values given in the problem.

24. C: Mass refers to the amount or quantity there is of an object. Light, sound, heat, and microwaves are all forms of energy that can travel in waves.

25. D: Ohm's Law describes the relation between voltage and amperage, where voltage is a measure of electromotive potential much like potential energy of motion in kinetics. Amperage measures the electric current or the flow rate of 1 coulomb of electrons in a second. The basic law is $V = I \times R$, but this can be manipulated in the following ways:

$$I = \frac{V}{R} \quad \text{or} \quad V = I \times R \quad \text{or} \quad R = \frac{V}{I}$$

26. B: This question calls upon the basics of lever systems. Since a wheelbarrow places the load between the fulcrum and effort, it is a Class II lever, making Choice *B* the correct answer. Choices *A* and *C* are incorrect because they describe other types of levers. Choice *D* is incorrect because there is no such thing as a Class IV lever.

27. C: This question relies on Newton's second law of motion, typically expressed as $Force = Mass \times Acceleration$. However, in this problem, we are given the force and the mass and are tasked with finding the acceleration. This requires shifting the equation to $Acceleration = \frac{Force}{Mass}$. Plugging in the car's mass and Jerome's force gives us $\frac{1,500}{1,000} = 1.5$. With both speed and direction, acceleration is a vector quantity, so the answer will be expressed in meters per second squared, making Choice *C* the correct answer. Choices *A*, *B*, and *D* are incorrect because the values and/or units do not match the result of the force calculation.

28. B: In broad terms, energy is divided into kinetic and potential energy. Kinetic energy refers to an object in motion. It is the product of mass and velocity:

$$KE = \frac{1}{2}mv^2$$

Potential energy refers to the capacity for doing work. Its gravitational configuration is the product of mass, acceleration due to gravity, and height ($PE = mgh$). Examples of kinetic energy include heat (which is the thermal energy from atoms and molecules moving around), waves like light, and physical motion. Potential energy examples include gravitational energy and chemical energy stored in bonds.

29. D: This question relies on the fundamentals of fluid dynamics. Water is an incompressible liquid, meaning that there cannot be areas of differing pressure throughout a hydraulic system. This also

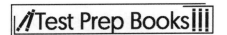
means that water cannot be traveling at different speeds throughout a closed system. Since the water cannot be compressed and travels at the same speed throughout the system, the same amount of water will pass through both sections of pipe, making Choice *D* the correct answer. Choices *A*, *B*, and *C* are incorrect because they do not reflect the flow qualities of an incompressible fluid.

30. B: Physical properties of atoms are influenced to some degree by the number and arrangement of electrons in the shells around the nucleus. The electrons in the outer shells in metals are free to drift between atoms. This movement potential allows them to jump between atoms, creating an electric current or flow, when subjected to an external force such as a magnetic field.

Aviation and Nautical Information

1. D: The tilt of the disk and the direction of horizontal movement are both directional with the cyclic pitch control. Therefore, both will go in the same direction that the cyclic pitch control is pushed, which, in this case, is left.

2. B: The anti-torque pedals allow the helicopter to alter its heading left and right. The pedals cannot move the nose up and down, nor can they create forward or backwards thrust. The cyclic is the instrument that controls the helicopter's attitude and is responsible for creating the thrust that moves the helicopter forwards and backwards.

3. A: All of the listed items are included in a basic empty weight except for the pilot. Had the question asked about the licensed empty weight, both *A* and *D* would have been correct, as the transmission oil is not included in that case.

4. C: While overloading a helicopter can cause a shifted center of gravity (if the helicopter is not properly managed), that is not a direct effect of overloading a helicopter. Structural damage and decreased performance, however, are both potential effects of overloading, regardless of how the weight is distributed.

5. A: A nose-down position means that there is more weight located near the front of the helicopter; thus, the helicopter is front-loaded. Had the helicopter been aft-loaded, the nose would have pointed up, and a centrally-balanced helicopter would be parallel with the ground.

6. C: If the heading is moving, the anti-torque pedals are used to compensate. The cyclic pitch control would be used to counteract a horizontal shift in position, rather than heading. Additionally, like all controls, the anti-torque pedals should be adjusted slowly to avoid over-controlling.

7. C: A moving object like a car would make a poor point of reference as it would be difficult—if not impossible—to figure out whether its shift relative to the current position is a result of its movement on the ground or the movement in the air. Likewise, using another helicopter as reference, even if that helicopter is also in hover, is ill-advised, as there is no guarantee its position is stable. Using one's own tail rotor is incorrect, given that this piece is attached solidly to the helicopter and will always appear stationary relative to the rest of the helicopter. A building, however, is fixed to the ground, which makes it an excellent point of reference.

8. C: Altitude, RPM, and position should ideally remain constant while performing a turn. Changing the heading, however, is the purpose of the maneuver.

9. B: Increased clearance is only necessary for rearward flight, and though there is some loss of visibility in making sideward motion versus forward motion, this is a more significant issue in rearward hovering flight. While RPM does decrease when adjusting the pitch of the blades, this is true of all maneuvers. Only the weathervane effect of the tail is truly unique to sideward hovering flight.

10. D: The first two items should be avoided whenever possible as they can increase the risk of damage, either to the helicopter itself or to objects around it. While additional precautions must be taken due to reduced effectiveness of the tail rotor in a crosswind, crosswinds do not need to be avoided to air taxi.

11. C: The power, balance, and flight controls must be checked before takeoff to ensure the helicopter can safely perform the maneuver. Fuel levels should also be sufficient for the planned mission. In contrast, the RPM should not be significantly changing during a hover, although it will need to be checked while performing the maneuver.

12. B: The cyclic pitch control is used to control airspeed. The anti-torque pedals are used to control heading, the throttle controls RPM, and the collective pitch controls altitude.

13. B: A nose-down helicopter is most often the result of a front-loaded center of gravity. Excessive torque results in the helicopter spinning, while insufficient power prevents the helicopter from successfully taking off.

14. C: By using the 10% rule, it is clear that leveling out at 240 feet is ideal. If the helicopter does not begin leveling out until 220 or 200 feet, the helicopter will almost certainly overshoot the target, while stopping too early may result in ending short of the desired destination.

15. D: The pilot, cargo, and the fuel are all inside the helicopter and are counted towards the maximum internal weight. An object supported by a winch, however, is outside the helicopter and is instead applied to the maximum external weight.

16. B: The cyclic is an acceleration control and holding the cyclic down will cause the helicopter to continuously accelerate. Since the helicopter is in a hover, and high speeds should be avoided while performing forward flight, the correct method is to apply brief pressure, allowing the helicopter to accelerate to some speed and then release the cyclic to maintain that speed. Increasing the collective would only work to increase speed if the helicopter already had a forward attitude.

17. A: Skidding is caused when the rate of turn is too great for the angle of bank. Therefore, the solution to skidding is to decrease the rate of turn, which requires either less pressure on the pedal in the direction of the turn (in this case, left) or more pressure on the pedal in the opposite direction. While increasing the banking angle (by applying additional left pressure on the cyclic) would also stop the skidding, it would also make the banking angle greater, which would have numerous other effects. For this reason, correcting the anti-torque pedals is the preferred method.

18. A: Removing the offending weight is the simplest way to correct a bad center of balance. While applying forward cyclic would treat the symptoms of the problem, doing so would not do anything to resolve the root of the issue and would still result in reduced performance. The throttle has nothing to do with the center of balance and given that most fuel reserves are in the rear of the helicopter, adding fuel would likely exacerbate the problem.

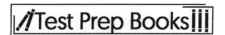

19. C: Once effective translational lift has been reached, step two has officially ended, but since the pilot has only just entered ETL and applied the cyclic, the helicopter has not yet reached step four. Therefore, the helicopter is currently at step three.

20. B: Using the anti-torque pedals would help if the nose was drifting to the side, but if the helicopter itself is displaced from the flight path, the anti-torque pedals wouldn't help. Likewise, ignoring the problem or trying to hurry past the problem won't solve anything. Removing cargo will also not help in this situation. Using the cyclic to nudge the helicopter back solves the problem without creating any new ones and is the ideal answer.

26. C: Increasing the throttle will increase the power, which creates more torque. Decreasing the collective would actually decrease the torque, assuming that the throttle was appropriately controlled to keep RPM constant. The cyclic primarily rotates the rotor disk to convert lift to thrust and does not directly increase the torque of the helicopter.

27. C: Parasitic drag, not induced drag, is strongest at higher speeds, and profile drag is created by the airfoil striking the air. Induced drag actually generally gets less potent as airspeed increases. This is created by the vacuum left behind by the airfoils and the air rushing to fill that hole. Induced drag does, however, create the drag horizontally in the direction of lift and perpendicular to the vertical lift, which is why induced drag's significance depends on the attitude of the helicopter.

28. D: If takeoff power is in question, the pilot should wait until the temperature cools off, and the density altitude will decrease. Also, departures should be planned either in the morning or later in the day. If possible, the load on the aircraft should be reduced or fuel burned off to reduce weight. If the takeoff is attempted and the aircraft does not have sufficient power, it could put the aircraft in an unsafe flight profile.

29. D: Takeoff, while a common maneuver, is not considered a fundamental maneuver, primarily because takeoff is at most performed once per flight, while turning, climbing, descending, and flying straight will be performed constantly.

30. A: While an improperly-calibrated cyclic is possible, something like that would most likely be noticed immediately, and the cyclic somehow getting more uncalibrated during flight would not explain why the pilot saw the helicopter slowly dropping. A higher air density would indeed have an impact on a helicopter's flight, but air density would change at such a slow gradient that the change would be imperceptible to the human eye. If the tail was producing too much torque, the tail would move horizontally, not vertically. Fuel, however, does have weight, and as the fuel is consumed, the weight of the remaining fuel would decrease.

Practice Test #2

Math Skills

1. At the beginning of the day, Xavier has 20 apples. At lunch, he meets his sister Emma and gives her half of his apples. After lunch, he stops by his neighbor Jim's house and gives him 6 of his apples. He then uses $\frac{3}{4}$ of his remaining apples to make an apple pie for dessert at dinner. At the end of the day, how many apples does Xavier have left?
   a. 4
   b. 6
   c. 2
   d. 1

2. What is the product of two irrational numbers?
   a. Irrational
   b. Rational
   c. Irrational or rational
   d. Complex and imaginary

3. The graph shows the position of a car over a 10-second time interval. Which of the following is the correct interpretation of the graph for the interval 1 to 3 seconds?

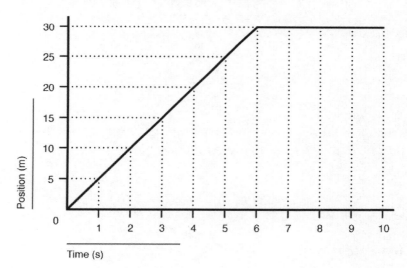

   a. The car remains in the same position.
   b. The car is traveling at a speed of 5 m/s.
   c. The car is traveling up a hill.
   d. The car is traveling at 5 mph.

219

Practice Test #2

4. Being as specific as possible, how is the number −4 classified?
    a. Real, rational, integer, whole, natural
    b. Real, rational, integer, natural
    c. Real, rational, integer
    d. Real, irrational, complex

5. After a 20% discount, Frank purchased a new refrigerator for $850. How much did he save compared to the original price?
    a. $170
    b. $212.50
    c. $105.75
    d. $200

6. Store-brand coffee beans cost $1.23 per pound. A local coffee bean roaster charges $1.98 per $1\frac{1}{2}$ pounds. How much more would 5 pounds from the local roaster cost than 5 pounds of the store brand?
    a. $0.55
    b. $1.55
    c. $1.45
    d. $0.45

7. What is the solution to the following problem in decimal form?

$$\frac{3}{5} \times \frac{7}{10} \div \frac{1}{2}$$

    a. 0.042
    b. 84%
    c. 0.84
    d. 0.42

8. Dwayne has received the following scores on his math tests: 78, 92, 83, and 97. What score must Dwayne get on his next math test to have an overall average of 90?
    a. 89
    b. 98
    c. 95
    d. 100

9. What are all the factors of 12?
    a. 12, 24, 36
    b. 1, 2, 4, 6, 12
    c. 12, 24, 36, 48
    d. 1, 2, 3, 4, 6, 12

220

10. Which of the following augmented matrices represents the system of equations below?

$$2x - 3y + z = -5$$

$$4x - y - 2z = -7$$

$$-x + 2z = -1$$

a. $\begin{bmatrix} 2 & -3 & 1 & 5 \\ 4 & -1 & 0 & -7 \\ -1 & 0 & 2 & 1 \end{bmatrix}$

b. $\begin{bmatrix} 2 & 4 & -1 \\ -3 & -1 & 0 \\ 1 & -2 & 2 \\ -5 & -7 & -1 \end{bmatrix}$

c. $\begin{bmatrix} 2 & 4 & -1 & -5 \\ -3 & -1 & 0 & -7 \\ 2 & -2 & 2 & -1 \end{bmatrix}$

d. $\begin{bmatrix} 2 & -3 & 1 & -5 \\ 4 & -1 & -2 & -7 \\ -1 & 0 & 2 & -1 \end{bmatrix}$

11. What are the zeros of the function: $f(x) = x^3 + 4x^2 + 4x$?
   a. -2
   b. $0, -2$
   c. 2
   d. $0, 2$

12. If $g(x) = x^3 - 3x^2 - 2x + 6$ and $f(x) = 2$, then what is $g(f(x))$?
   a. -26
   b. 6
   c. $2x^3 - 6x^2 - 4x + 12$
   d. -2

13. What is the solution to the following system of equations?

$$x^2 - 2x + y = 8$$

$$x - y = -2$$

   a. $(-2, 3)$
   b. There is no solution.
   c. $(-2, 0) \ (1, 3)$
   d. $(-2, 0) \ (3, 5)$

14. Which of the following is the result after simplifying the expression: $(7n + 3n^3 + 3) + (8n + 5n^3 + 2n^4)$?
   a. $9n^4 + 15n - 2$
   b. $2n^4 + 5n^3 + 15n - 2$
   c. $9n^4 + 8n^3 + 15n$
   d. $2n^4 + 8n^3 + 15n + 3$

15. What is the product of the following expression?

$$(4x - 8)(5x^2 + x + 6)$$

a. $20x^3 - 36x^2 + 16x - 48$
b. $6x^3 - 41x^2 + 12x + 15$
c. $20x^4 + 11x^2 - 37x - 12$
d. $2x^3 - 11x^2 - 32x + 20$

16. How could the following equation be factored to find the zeros?

$$y = x^3 - 3x^2 - 4x$$

a. $0 = x^2(x - 4), x = 0, 4$
b. $0 = 3x(x + 1)(x + 4), x = 0, -1, -4$
c. $0 = x(x + 1)(x + 6), x = 0, -1, -6$
d. $0 = x(x + 1)(x - 4), x = 0, -1, 4$

17. The hospital has a nurse-to-patient ratio of $1 : 25$. If there are a maximum of 325 patients admitted at a time, how many nurses are there?
a. 13 nurses
b. 25 nurses
c. 325 nurses
d. 12 nurses

18. Which of the following is the solution for the given equation?

$$\frac{x^2 + x - 30}{x - 5} = 11$$

a. $x = -6$
b. All real numbers.
c. $x = 16$
d. There is no solution.

19. Mom's car drove 72 miles in 90 minutes. How fast did she drive in feet per second?
a. 0.8 feet per second
b. 48.9 feet per second
c. 0.009 feet per second
d. 70.4 feet per second

20. Solve $V = lwh$ for h.
a. $lwV = h$

b. $h = \dfrac{V}{lw}$

c. $h = \dfrac{Vl}{w}$

d. $h = \dfrac{Vw}{l}$

21. What is the domain for the function $y = \sqrt{x}$?
    a. All real numbers
    b. $x \geq 0$
    c. $x > 0$
    d. $y \geq 0$

22. If Sarah reads at an average rate of 21 pages in four nights, how long will it take her to read 140 pages?
    a. 6 nights
    b. 26 nights
    c. 8 nights
    d. 27 nights

23. The phone bill is calculated each month using the equation $c = 50g + 75$. The cost of the phone bill per month is represented by c, and g represents the gigabytes of data used that month. Identify and interpret the slope of this equation.
    a. 75 dollars per day
    b. 75 gigabytes per day
    c. 50 dollars per day
    d. 50 dollars per gigabyte

24. What is the function that forms an equivalent graph to $y = \cos(x)$?
    a. $y = \tan(x)$
    b. $y = \csc(x)$
    c. $y = \sin\left(x + \frac{\pi}{2}\right)$
    d. $y = \sin\left(x - \frac{\pi}{2}\right)$

25. If $\sqrt{1 + x} = 4$, what is x?
    a. 10
    b. 15
    c. 20
    d. 25

26. What is the inverse of the function $f(x) = 3x - 5$?
    a. $f^{-1}(x) = \frac{x}{3} + 5$
    b. $f^{-1}(x) = \frac{5x}{3}$
    c. $f^{-1}(x) = 3x + 5$
    d. $f^{-1}(x) = \frac{x+5}{3}$

27. What are the zeros of $f(x) = x^2 + 4$?
    a. $x = -4$
    b. $x = \pm 2i$
    c. $x = \pm 2$
    d. $x = \pm 4i$

28. 20 is 40% of what number?
    a. 60
    b. 8
    c. 200
    d. 50

29. Simplify $1.2 \times 10^{12} \div 3.0 \times 10^8$?
    a. 0.4×10^4
    b. 4.0×10^4
    c. 4.0×10^3
    d. 3.6×10^{20}

30. You measure the width of your door to be 36 inches. The true width of the door is 35.75 inches. What is the relative error in your measurement?
    a. 0.7%
    b. 0.007%
    c. 0.99%
    d. 0.1%

Reading Comprehension

Directions: Assume each passage below to be true. Then, pick the answer choice that best answers the question.

1. One of the four forces that affects aerodynamics is weight. The total weight of an aircraft must be factored into the mechanics of flight. Weight must include the craft itself, accompanying gear, the fuel load, and any personnel. Carefully assessing weight will help a pilot calculate how to oppose the downward force of weight during flight.

According to the passage, which of the following answer choices is true?
    a. Opposing the downward force of weight is necessary to fly.
    b. Drag and thrust have a profound effect on aerodynamics.
    c. Personnel are included in the total weight of an aircraft.
    d. The mechanics of flight are most impacted by aircraft weight.

2. Technology has been invading cars for the last several years, but there are some new high-tech trends that are pretty amazing. It is now standard in many car models to have a rear-view camera, hands-free phone and text, and a touch screen digital display. Music can be streamed from a paired cell phone, and some displays can even be programmed with a personal photo. Sensors beep to indicate there is something in the driver's path when reversing and changing lanes. Rain-sensing windshield wipers and lights are automatic, leaving the driver with little to do but watch the road and enjoy the ride. The next wave of technology will include cars that automatically parallel park, and self-driving cars are on the horizon. These technological advances make it a good time to be a driver.

Based on the passage, which of the following can be concluded?
    a. Technology will continue to influence how cars are made.
    b. Windshield wipers and lights are always automatic.
    c. It is standard to have a rear-view camera in all cars.
    d. Technology has reached its peak in cars.

3. Proponents of humanities education are starting to push back in the face of both budget and faculty cuts. With STEM subjects and professors bringing in more grant money to research universities, it's easy to see why many of them feel as if they're fighting an uphill battle.

What is implied in this passage?
   a. More students take STEM classes than humanities courses.
   b. Research universities invest in fields that bring in grants.
   c. Humanities professors need to bring in more grant money.
   d. STEM is more valuable than humanities.

4. Everyone had said his piloting acumen was not to be questioned. He had a knack for feeling the aircraft, as if it was an instinctual part of himself. He had a knowledge base he'd built up over years of study and thousands of flying hours, but moreover, he had the ability to think and act quickly in the most unexpected circumstances.

According to the passage, which of the following answer choices is true?
   a. Anybody who questions a pilot's acumen is ignorant.
   b. Instincts are more indicative of a pilot's acumen than practical knowledge.
   c. Pilot acumen can be improved over time through study and practice.
   d. A pilot must fly for 2000 miles before being considered an expert.

5. On his initial journey, de León set anchors first on the east coast of Florida but moved on to the Keys and ultimately the Gulf of Mexico, discovering the Gulf Stream, which fed his sails, speeding up his return trip.

What is the Gulf Stream?
   a. A tidal current that passes from the Gulf to the Atlantic
   b. The name of de León's ship
   c. A wind pattern, strong enough to fill de León's sails
   d. A water passage out of Tampa Bay

6. Golden Rice is modified to include more beta carotene, which the body can convert to vitamin A. Vitamin A deficiency, which can cause malnourishment, is a significant problem across the globe, with nearly 200 million children and 20 million pregnant or lactating women lacking this essential vitamin. Golden Rice also hopes to address iron and zinc deficiencies, which can stunt a child's growth.

What is the risk of a vitamin A deficiency?
   a. Poor iron absorption
   b. Trouble for lactating mothers
   c. Stunted growth in children
   d. Malnourishment

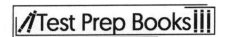

7. Worldwide, fungal infections of the lung account for significant mortality in individuals with compromised immune function. Three of the most common infecting agents are *Aspergillus, Histoplasma*, and *Candida*. Successful treatment of infections caused by these agents depends on an early and accurate diagnosis.

Which statement is true?
   a. Aspergillus, Histoplasma, and Candida are known to compromise the immune system when they infect the lungs.
   b. Fungal infections of the lung are always fatal.
   c. *Candida* is the only treatment available for infections of the lung.
   d. Infections from *Aspergillus, Histoplasma*, and *Candida* can be treated if an accurate diagnosis is made early.

8. Predators are animals that eat other animals. Prey are animals that are eaten by a predator. Predators and prey have a distinct relationship. Predators rely on the prey population for food and nutrition. The prey population may develop features that allow them to escape and hide from their predators.

If a cat is a predator and a mouse is its prey, which of the following are true?
   a. Cats are eaten by mice.
   b. Cats have developed features that allow them to escape from mice.
   c. Cats rely on mice for food and nutrition.
   d. Cats and mice have an extinct relationship.

9. Aviation's history expands more than 2000 years. (A) Eventually, Leonardo da Vinci studied the flight of birds and began noting some basic principles of aerodynamics. (B) It is said that kites were the first airborne, man-made "vehicles." They existed in China around the fifth century BCE and were capable of carrying a person into the air. (C) The first recorded attempt at flight was made by a Spanish citizen who covered his arms in feathers and jumped. (D) The late eighteenth century saw a major development in ballooning, and the steerable airship, or dirigible, was developed. (E) Sir George Cayley significantly impacted aerodynamics in the early nineteenth century by contributing key ideas to flight physics. (F) In 1903, Orville Wright flew 130 feet in twelve seconds.

According to the passage, which of the following answer choices is true?
   a. Orville Wright was the first man to fly a motor-powered airplane.
   b. Historical events can take several centuries to develop.
   c. Aviation's history officially began in the twentieth century.
   d. Kites were the first man-made aircraft.

10. Invasive species, both plants and animals, tend to crowd out native species, utilizing or depleting the resources they need to survive. In some cases, such as Burmese pythons in the Everglades, they become the apex predator, leading to a significant decline in several native animal species.

What do invasive species do?
   a. Exist alongside native species
   b. Form symbiotic relationships
   c. Crowd out native species
   d. Starve due to non-native conditions

226

11. Matter generally exists in three states: gas, solid, and liquid. Solids contain atoms that are packed into a fixed crystalline state. Liquids contain atoms or molecules that move past one another and are less dense than solids. However, the exception is water, where the solid phase is less dense compared to the liquid phase. Gases contain atoms or molecules with the most kinetic energy; the atoms are much further apart and are less dense with respect to solids and liquids.

Which of the following is true?
   a. Atoms or molecules with the most kinetic energy are in liquids.
   b. Atoms and molecules in liquids are able to move past one another.
   c. All liquids are less dense than solids.
   d. Gases have the most tightly packed atoms.

12. The body needs fuel and some time in the gym to power through a busy day, so restricting calories and macronutrients—the primary building blocks of your diet, which includes carbohydrates—can actually backfire on weight loss efforts.

Based on the sentence, which of the following best describes macronutrients?
   a. Carbohydrates, such as grains and breads
   b. The primary and major nutrients in your diet
   c. Vitamins and minerals found in whole foods
   d. Foods found at the top of the food pyramid

13. Although turbulence can be dangerous, it is common and manageable during flight. Turbulence is a disruption in airflow. Think of it as a bump on the road while driving to work. It happens all the time, and, when managed effectively, it's fairly benign. One type of turbulence is CAT. It cannot be seen, and one way to avoid it is to fly at a higher, and likely smoother, altitude. Severe turbulence, a disturbance that results in an altitude deviation of 100 feet, is uncomfortable but not dangerous. A disruptive airflow that causes turbulence doesn't have to result in difficulty for the pilot. A well-trained pilot and crew can manage turbulence so that it isn't disruptive to passengers in flight.

According to the passage, which of the following answer choices is true?
   a. Pilots can train for turbulence by driving on a bumpy road.
   b. Flying at higher altitudes is often more comfortable for passengers.
   c. CAT occurs more frequently at higher altitudes.
   d. CAT is the most dangerous type of turbulence.

14. Home improvement projects can be pricey, but there are ways to keep costs down such as "Do It Yourself," or DIY; comparing prices of the materials and workers that will be used; and keeping the original layout for plumbing and electrical.

What is the subject of this sentence?
   a. DIY home improvement
   b. Keeping costs of home improvement down
   c. Comparing the cost of workers and materials
   d. Plumbing and electrical layout

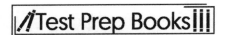

15. Conducting a traffic stop can be one of the most dangerous parts of being a police officer. In light of the many traffic stop incidents that have occurred all over the country, many states are looking at how to address the problem. Recently, the state of Illinois passed a new law that adds traffic stop training to their driver's education courses. As this new driver's education component gains popularity, it could be seen in more states across the US, and hopefully reduce the amount of traffic stop incidents.

According to the passage, where is traffic stop training required by law?
   a.   In driver's education classes in Illinois
   b   During police officer training in Illinois
   c.   While conducting a traffic stop
   d.   In driver's education classes in every state

16. The pilot looked to the left, and there it was: a tiny glimmer of white on the left wing. He was on the leading edge of it. He knew the temperature had dropped. He'd checked it repeatedly. He had been cleared at 9000 feet but needed to go down. He needed to get to warmer air and get there quickly. He checked the terrain clearance and decided it was now or never. He popped out of the clouds and began his descent, chunks of ice flying off the fuselage.

According to the passage, which of the following answer choices is true?
   a.   The air is warmer at lower altitudes.
   b.   Terrain clearance cannot prevent a descent.
   c.   Temperatures sometimes drop randomly.
   d.   Fuselage is located on the left wing.

17. The mimic octopus is an impressive example of biological mimicry. It can mimic three different dangerous animals in the ocean. It changes its colors and poses on demand. It can resemble a lionfish, sea snake, or banded sole. All of these mimicked sea creatures are either venomous or poisonous. Predators now avoid the harmless mimic octopus due to this deception.

Based on the information in the passage, which of the following answer choices is true?
   a.   Sea snakes are harmless creatures found in the ocean.
   b.   The mimic octopus avoids predators by resembling venomous as well as nonpoisonous sea creatures.
   c.   The mimic octopus deceives its predators by mimicking other sea creatures that are venomous.
   d.   Biological mimicry allows nonpoisonous creatures to evolve into poisonous creatures.

18. Coaches of kids' sports teams are increasingly concerned about the behavior of parents at games. Parents are screaming and cursing at coaches, officials, players, and other parents. Physical fights have even broken out at games. Parents need to be reminded that coaches are volunteers, giving up their time and energy to help kids develop in their chosen sport. The goal of kids' sports teams is to learn and develop skills, but it's also to have fun. When parents are out of control at games and practices, it takes the fun out of the sport.

What can be concluded from this passage?
   a.   Coaches are modeling good behavior for kids.
   b.   Organized sports are not good for kids.
   c.   Parents' behavior at their kids' games needs to change.
   d.   Parents and coaches need to work together.

19. Proper risk assessment for flight is critical for avoiding air disasters. Because most events in the error chain can be addressed and controlled by the pilot, it's essential for the pilot to consider all risks before and during flight. A pilot must perform all necessary informational checks prior to a scheduled flight. The flight path itself must be registered and approved. During the flight, a pilot must communicate regularly with others in the air and on the ground. Making sudden, unapproved changes during flight can lead to a negative chain of events. Being unprepared, uncommunicative, and unaware are all mistakes a pilot can make while on the job. Constant risk assessment is necessary to a successful and happily uneventful flight.

According to the passage, which of the following answer choices is true?
   a.   The FAA reviews, registers, and approves flight paths to ensure the safety of all aircraft.
   b.   A lack of preparation is more deleterious to safety than a lack of communication.
   c.   Pilots need to adapt to changing circumstances while flying.
   d.   Informational checks and regular communication make up the entirety of a proper risk assessment.

20. Tornadoes are dangerous funnel clouds that occur during large thunderstorms. When warm, humid air near the ground meets cold, dry air from above, a column of the warm air can be drawn up into the clouds. Winds at different altitudes blowing at different speeds make the column of air rotate. As the spinning column of air picks up speed, a funnel cloud is formed. This funnel cloud moves rapidly and haphazardly. Rain and hail inside the cloud cause it to touch down, creating a tornado. Tornadoes move in a rapid and unpredictable pattern, making them extremely destructive and dangerous.

What causes the rotation of the column of warm air?
   a.   Various speeds of wind blowing at different altitudes
   b.   Warm and humid air near the ground meeting dry air from above
   c.   Rain and hail inside the funnel cloud
   d.   Rapid and unpredictable movement

Mechanical Comprehension

1. A ship is traveling due east at a speed of 1 m/s against a current flowing due west at a speed of 0.5 m/s. How far has the ship travelled from its point of departure after two hours?
   a.   1.8 kilometers west of its point of departure
   b.   3.6 kilometers west of its point of departure
   c.   3.6 kilometers east of its point of departure
   d.   1.8 kilometers east of its point of departure

2. The gravitational acceleration on Earth averages 9.81 m/s^2. An astronaut weighs 1,962 N on Earth. The diameter of Earth is six times the diameter of its moon. What's the mass of the astronaut on Earth's moon?
   a.   100 kilograms
   b.   200 kilograms
   c.   300 kilograms
   d.   400 kilograms

3. The skater is shown spinning in Figure (a), then bringing in her arms in Figure (b). Which sequence accurately describes what happens to her angular velocity?

(a)   (b)

   a. Her angular velocity decreases from (a) to (b).
   b. Her angular velocity doesn't change from (a) to (b).
   c. Her angular velocity increases from (a) to (b).
   d. It's not possible to determine what happens to her angular velocity if her weight is unknown.

4. At what point is the potential energy of the pendulum equal to its kinetic energy, where the height of the pendulum at point B is half that of point A?

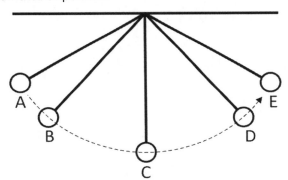

   a. Point A
   b. Point C
   c. Point D
   d. Point E

230

5. A steel spring is loaded with a 10-newton weight and is stretched by 0.5 centimeters. What is the deflection if it's loaded with two 10-newton weights?

0.5 cm

?

10 N

10 N

10 N

a. 0.5 centimeter
b. 1 centimeter
c. 2 centimeters
d. 3 centimeters

6. Pascal's law states that a change in pressure, applied to an enclosed fluid, is transmitted undiminished to every portion of the fluid and to the walls of its containing vessel. This principle is used in the design of hydraulic jacks.

The figure above shows two pistons connected by a sealed hydraulic system. If 100 psi of downward pressure is exerted on piston A, how much pressure is used to lift piston B?
   a.   50 psi
   b.   10 psi
   c.   100 psi
   d.   None, piston B experiences no pressure.

7. How much energy is needed to run a 6000-watt air conditioner for 3 hours?
   a.   18 kilowatts
   b.   18 kilowatt-hours
   c.   18,000 kilowatt-hours
   d.   18,000 kilowatts

8. A 150-kilogram mass is placed on the left side of the lever as shown. What force must be exerted on the right side (in the location shown by the arrow) to balance the weight of this mass?

   a.   675 kg·m
   b.   735.75 N
   c.   1471.5 N

Practice Test #2 ///Test Prep Books!!!

d. 2207.25 N·m

9. The three steel wheels shown are connected by rubber belts. The two wheels at the top have the same diameter, while the wheel below is twice their diameter. If the driver wheel at the upper left is turning clockwise at 60 RPM, at what speed and in which direction is the large bottom wheel turning?

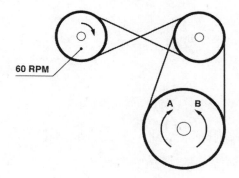

a. 30 RPM, clockwise (A)
b. 30 RPM, counterclockwise (B)
c. 120 RPM, clockwise (A)
d. 120 RPM, counterclockwise (B)

10. What is the current when a 3.0 V battery is wired across a lightbulb that has a resistance of 6.0 ohms?
a. 0.5 A
b. 18.0 A
c. 0.5 J
d. 18.0 J

11. Which of the following statements about parallel circuits is FALSE?
a. If the resistance is different in each load, more current passes through the load with the lower resistance.
b. If the resistance is different in each load, more current passes through the one with higher resistance.
c. If the resistance is the same in both loads, then the same amount of current passes through each one.
d. The voltage is the same across each resistor.

12. Current is typically measured in which of the following units?
a. Volts
b. Amperes
c. Ohms
d. Watts

13. A small gear has 12 teeth and a large one has 24 teeth. They are connected. If the large gear makes 8 rotations, how many does the small gear make?
    a. 4
    b. 8
    c. 12
    d. 16

14. Lifting a box using a pulley increases its _____
    a. Weight
    b. Potential energy
    c. Gravitational pull
    d. Torque

15. The energy from electricity results from which of the following?
    a. The atomic structure of matter
    b. The ability to do work
    c. The neutrons in an atom
    d. Conductive materials like metals

16. For circular motion, what is the name of the actual force pulling toward the axis of rotation?
    a. Centrifugal force
    b. Gravity
    c. Centripetal force
    d. Friction

17. Which of the following describes the doppler effect?
    a. The absorption of energy from a wave as it collides with another medium
    b. The observed frequency of waves changes based on velocities of the source and observer
    c. The bending of radiant waves as they pass through a different medium than their source
    d. The deformation of crystalline solids in the presence of an electric potential

18. Which of the following best describes the function of and symbol for a diode?

    a. It is a type of variable resistor that controls voltage, and it is represented as: ─▷┼

    b. It is a type of variable resistor that controls voltage, and it is represented as: ▯◀

    c. It ensures that current flows one way only, and it is represented as: ─▷┼

    d. It ensures that current flows one way only, and it is represented as: ▯◀

234

19. The energy of motion is also referred to as what?
    a. Potential energy
    b. Kinetic energy
    c. Solar energy
    d. Heat energy

20. Mark needs to load a 500 N box into a truck using a ramp. If the truck bed is 1 meter high and the ramp is 5 meters long, how much force (ignoring friction) is needed to load the box?
    a. 100 N
    b. 200 N
    c. 1,000 N
    d. 2500 N

21. Circuits in which the current flows in one direction with a constant voltage source are called
    a. directional circuits.
    b. AC/DC circuits.
    c. alternating currents.
    d. direct current circuits.

22. A ramp leading up to a loading dock would be considered which type of simple machine?
    a. Screw
    b. Lever
    c. Inclined plane
    d. Pulley

23. A tank starts out with 100 gallons of water. The lower valve is opened, pouring out water at a rate of 50 gallons an hour. At the same time, water is poured into the tank at a rate of 4 gallons a minute. How much water is in the tank after 3 hours?
    a. 670 gallons
    b. 190 gallons
    c. 100 gallons
    d. None, the tank is empty.

24. Electric power can be measured in which of the following units?
    a. Volts
    b. Amperes
    c. Ohms
    d. Watts

25. Which of the following statements is true?
    a. Conductors have high resistance because the electrons are easily detached from the atoms.
    b. Conductors have high resistance because the electrons are not easily detached from the atoms.
    c. Conductors have low resistance because the electrons are easily detached from the atoms.
    d. Conductors have low resistance because the electrons are not easily detached from the atoms.

26. What is the formula used in an Ohm's Law calculation?
    a. Current (I) = voltage (V) ⊠ resistance (R)
    b. Voltage (V) = current (I) ⊠ resistance (R)
    c. Voltage (V) = current (I) ⊠ resistance (R)
    d. Current (I) = voltage (V) + resistance (R)

27. Relatively how much force is needed to raise a 10 Newton box straight up into trailer A compared to using a ramp as on trailer B?

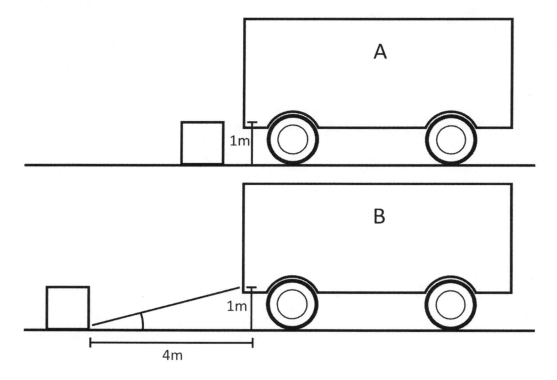

a. The same force is required.
b. Twice as much force is required.
c. Half as much force is required.
d. Four times as much force is required.

28. Closed Basins A and B each contain a 10,000-ton block of ice. The ice block in Basin A is floating in sea water. The ice block in Basin B is aground on a rock ledge (as shown). When all the ice melts, what happens to the water level in Basin A and Basin B?

a. Water level rises in A but not in B
b. Water level rises in B but not in A
c. Water level rises in neither A nor B
d. Water level rises in both A and B

29. A 1,000-kilogram weight is raised 30 meters in 10 minutes. What is the approximate power expended in the period?
a. $1,000 \text{ Kg} \times \text{m/s}^2$
b. $500 \text{ N} \cdot \text{m}$
c. 500 J/s
d. 100 watts

30. The following diagram illustrated a slope and a block of mass m at rest. Which equation represents the force of friction, F_f, holding the block in place?

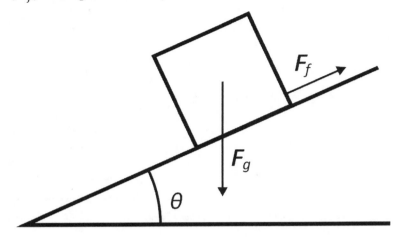

a. $F_2 = 9.81 \frac{m}{s^2} \times m \times \sin \theta$

b. $F_2 = \dfrac{9.81 \frac{m}{s^2} \times m}{\sin \theta}$

c. $F_2 = 9.81 \frac{m}{s^2} \times m \times \cos \theta$

d. $F_2 = \dfrac{9.81 \frac{m}{s^2} \times m}{\cos \theta}$

Aviation and Nautical Information

1. Lowering the collective while the helicopter is flying straight and level will have what effect, assuming everything else remains constant?
    a. It will cause the nose to pitch down, the helicopter's airspeed to increase, and it will produce left yaw.
    b. It will cause the nose to pitch up, the helicopter's airspeed to decrease, and it will produce right yaw.
    c. It will cause the nose to pitch down and the helicopter's airspeed will decrease.
    d. It will have no appreciable effect on the airspeed of the helicopter.

2. While hovering, a pilot wishes to increase her altitude, so she uses the collective. Which control will the pilot NOT need to use while doing so, assuming ideal conditions?
    a. The cyclic
    b. The anti-torque pedals
    c. The throttle
    d. All the above are needed while raising the collective

3. After achieving the desired altitude, the pilot decides to perform a takeoff from a hover and applies forward pressure on the cyclic to begin forward movement. Which control/s will he need to use while doing so, assuming ideal conditions?

      I. The collective

      II. The anti-torque pedals

      III. The throttle

   a. II only
   b. I and II
   c. I and III
   d. I, II and III

4. Although both parasitic drag and profile drag increase as speed increases, which of the following correctly identifies the difference between the two?
   a. Profile drag starts out as more significant than parasitic drag and remains more significant at all speeds.
   b. Parasitic drag starts out as more significant than profile drag and remains more significant at all speeds.
   c. Profile drag starts out as more significant, but parasitic drag becomes more significant at higher speeds.
   d. Parasitic drag starts out as more significant, but profile drag becomes more significant at higher speeds.

5. When performing a hovering turn on a windy day, at what point is weathervane most likely to cause problems?
   a. When the helicopter's heading is into the wind
   b. When the helicopter's heading is with the wind
   c. At the end of the turn
   d. At the beginning of the turn

6. When climbing at cruising speed, in addition to raising the collective, the rate of climb can be increased by which of the following actions?

      I. Applying rearward cyclic pressure to reduce airspeed

      II. Increasing the throttle to increase power

      III. Applying forward cyclic pressure to increase airspeed

   a. I only
   b. II only
   c. III only
   d. I and II

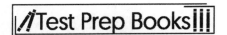

7. Which of the following maneuvers should be avoided when flying with a heavy load?

      I. Large angle banking turns

      II. High speed straight and level flight

      III. Takeoff from hover

   a. I
   b. II only
   c. III only
   d. I, II and III

8. Which of the following influences the G load?

      I. The weight of the helicopter

      II. The weather

      III. Air density

   a. I only
   b. I and II
   c. I and III
   d. II and III

9. At what pace should a helicopter in forward flight move?
   a. About as fast as a brisk walk
   b. No faster than jogging speed
   c. As fast as desired as long as control can be maintained
   d. Not faster than a run, and even slower if the area is uneven

10. Which control is a rate-controlled instrument?
   a. The collective
   b. The throttle
   c. The cyclic
   d. The anti-torque pedals

11. Which of the following will create lift?
   a. Airflow against the tail section of the aircraft
   b. Faster flow of air over the wing than beneath it
   c. Raised ailerons
   d. Helium in the wings

12. Which of the following axes is controlled by ailerons?
   a. Lateral
   b. Longitudinal
   c. Vertical
   d. Equatorial

13. Which of the following axes is controlled by elevators?
    a. Lateral
    b. Longitudinal
    c. Vertical
    d. Equatorial

14. Which of the following axes is controlled by a rudder?
    a. Lateral
    b. Longitudinal
    c. Vertical
    d. Equatorial

15. Which of the following is not a secondary or auxiliary flight control?
    a. Flap
    b. Spoiler
    c. Aileron
    d. Slat

16. What component is not part of an empennage?
    a. Stabilizer
    b. Rudder
    c. Elevator
    d. Slats

17. Which of the following is not a type of landing gear?
    a. Ski
    b. Skate
    c. Skid
    d. Float

18. Which is not a type of fuselage?
    a. Monocoque
    b. Semicoque
    c. Semi-Monocoque
    d. Truss

19. Who should be the most concerned about an aircraft's flight envelope?
    a. The pilot
    b. Air traffic controller
    c. Passengers
    d. Aircraft mechanic

20. What is the minimum speed at which an aircraft can maintain level flight?
    a. Ceiling speed
    b. Cruising speed
    c. Stalling speed
    d. Mach 1

21. Which of the following forces is a helicopter subjected to, but not a fixed-wing aircraft?
    a. Lift
    b. Torque
    c. Weight
    d. Drag

22. Which term describes a reduced drag coupled with an increased lift experienced by an aircraft due to extremely close proximity to land?
    a. Center of gravity
    b. Coriolis effect
    c. Effective translational lift
    d. Ground effect

23. Which of the following lights are green lights that indicate the beginning of a runway?
    a. Taxiway centerline lights
    b. Runway edge lights
    c. Approach lighting systems
    d. Threshold lights

24. Which parts of fixed-wing aircrafts are utilized to create a rolling motion?
    a. Stabilizers
    b. Ailerons
    c. Wing tips
    d. Elevators

25. Which of the following is NOT considered an airfoil?
    a. Spoiler
    b. Elevator
    c. Aileron
    d. Fuselage

26. Which statement is true when an airplane increases its lift?
    a. Atmospheric pressure decreases.
    b. Airplane temperature increases.
    c. Air pressure below the wing increases.
    d. The airplane loses altitude.

27. What turning angle is considered a medium turn?
    a. 30°
    b. 75°
    c. 15°
    d. 10°

28. A vertical stabilizer controls which of the following motions?
    a. Roll
    b. Thrust
    c. Pitch
    d. Yaw

29. What force is opposed by parasitic drag?
    a. Lift
    b. Weight
    c. Gravity
    d. Thrust

30. Which instrument functions by measuring the differential between static and ram pressure?
    a. Heading indicator
    b. Vertical speed indicator
    c. Turn coordinator
    d. Airspeed indicator

Answer Explanations

Math Skills

1. D: This problem can be solved using basic arithmetic. Xavier starts with 20 apples, then gives his sister half, so 20 is divided by 2.

$$\frac{20}{2} = 10$$

He then gives his neighbor 6, so 6 is subtracted from 10.

$$10 - 6 = 4$$

Finally, he uses $\frac{3}{4}$ of his remaining apples to make a pie. Since $\frac{3}{4}$ of 4 is 3, he uses 3 apples, so 3 is subtracted from 4. $4 - 3 = 1$.

2. C: The product of two irrational numbers can be rational or irrational. Sometimes the irrational parts of the two numbers cancel each other out, leaving a rational number. For example, $\sqrt{2} \times \sqrt{2} = 2$ because the roots cancel each other out. Technically, the product of two irrational numbers is a complex number, because real numbers are a type of complex number. However, Choice *D* is incorrect because the product of two irrational numbers is not an imaginary number.

3. B: The car is traveling at a speed of 5 meters per second. On the interval from 1 to 3 seconds, the position changes by 10 meters. This is 10 meters in 2 seconds, or 5 meters in each second.

4. C: The terms "whole numbers" and "natural numbers" include all the ordinary counting numbers (1, 2, 3, 4, 5, ...), and sometimes zero depending on the definition used, but no negative numbers. The term "integers" includes all those numbers, their negatives, and zero. So –4 is not a whole number or a natural number, but it is an integer. It is also rational because it can be written as a ratio of two integers (–4/1); all integers are rational. It is a real number because it does not have an imaginary component (symbolized by the letter i); all integers are real numbers.

5. B: Since $850 is the price after a 20% discount, $850 represents 80% of the original price. In other words, $850 = 0.8x$ (where x is the original price).

Solving this, we find:

$$x = \frac{850}{0.8} = 1{,}062.5$$

Now, to find the savings, calculate the original price minus the sale price:

$$\$1{,}062.50 - \$850 = \$212.50.$$

6. D: 5 pounds of store-brand coffee would cost $\frac{\$1.23}{1\ lbs} \times 5\ lbs = \$6.15$. For 5 pounds of local coffee, the cost would be $\frac{\$1.98}{1.5\ lbs} \times 5\ lbs = \$6.60$. Calculate the price difference: $\$6.60 - \$6.15 = \$0.45$.

244

7. C: The first step in solving this problem is expressing the result in fraction form. Multiplication and division are typically performed in order from left to right, but they can be performed in any order. For this problem, let's start with the division operation between the last two fractions. When dividing one fraction by another, invert or flip the second fraction and then multiply the numerators and denominators.

$$\frac{7}{10} \times \frac{2}{1} = \frac{14}{10}$$

Next, multiply the first fraction by this value:

$$\frac{3}{5} \times \frac{14}{10} = \frac{42}{50}$$

Decimals are expressions of 1 or 100%, so Multiply both the numerator and denominator by 2 to get the fraction into the form 100.

$$\frac{42}{50} \times \frac{2}{2} = \frac{84}{100}$$

In decimal form, this would be expressed as 0.84.

8. D: To find the average of a set of values, add the values together and then divide by the total number of values. In this case, include the unknown value, x, of what Dwayne needs to score on his next test. The average must equal 90. Set up the equation and solve:

$$\frac{78 + 92 + 83 + 97 + x}{5} = 90$$

$$\frac{350 + x}{5} = 90$$

$$350 + x = 90$$

$$x = 100$$

Dwayne would need to get a perfect score of 100 in order to get an average of at least 90.

Test this answer by substituting back into the original formula:

$$\frac{78 + 92 + 83 + 97 + 100}{5} = 90$$

9. D: A given number divides evenly by each of its factors to produce an integer (no decimals). To find the factors of 12, determine what whole numbers when multiplied equal 12. 1 × 12, 2 × 6, and 3 × 4 are all the ways to multiply to 12 using whole numbers, so the factors of 12 are: 1, 2, 3, 4, 6, 12.

10. D: The augmented matrix that represents the system of equations has dimensions 4 × 3 because there are three equations with three unknowns. The coefficients of the variables make up the first three columns, and the last column is made up of the numbers to the right of the equals sign. This system can be solved by reducing the matrix to row-echelon form, where the last column gives the solution for the unknown variables.

11. B: There are two zeros for the function: $x = 0, -2$.

The zeros can be found several ways, but this particular equation can be factored into:

$$f(x) = x(x^2 + 4x + 4) = x(x + 2)(x + 2)$$

By setting each factor equal to zero and solving for x, there are two solutions: $x = 0$ and $x = -2$. On a graph these zeros can be seen where the line crosses the x-axis.

12. D: This problem involves a composition function, where one function is plugged into the other function. In this case, the $f(x)$ function is plugged into the $g(x)$ function for each x-value. Since $f(x) = 2$, the composition equation becomes:

$$g(f(x)) = g(2) = (2)^3 - 3(2)^2 - 2(2) + 6$$

Simplifying the equation gives the answer:

$$g(f(x)) = 8 - 3(4) - 2(2) + 6$$

$$g(f(x)) = 8 - 12 - 4 + 6$$

$$g(f(x)) = -2$$

13. D: This system of equations involves one quadratic equation and one linear equation. One way to solve this is through substitution.

Solving for y in the second equation yields:

$$y = x + 2$$

Plugging this equation in for the y of the quadratic equation yields:

$$x^2 - 2x + x + 2 = 8$$

Simplify the equation:

$$x^2 - x + 2 = 8$$

Set this equal to zero and factor:

$$x^2 - x - 6 = 0 = (x - 3)(x + 2)$$

Solving these two factors for x gives the zeros:

$$x = 3, -2$$

To find the y-value for the point, plug in each number to either original equation. Solving each one for y yields the points $(3, 5)$ and $(-2, 0)$.

14. D: The expression is simplified by collecting like terms. Terms with the same variable and exponent are like terms, and their coefficients can be added.

15. A: Finding the product means distributing one polynomial onto the other. Each term in the first polynomial must be multiplied by each term in the second polynomial. Then, like terms can be collected. Multiplying the factors yields the expression:

$$20x^3 + 4x^2 + 24x - 40x^2 - 8x - 48$$

Collecting like terms means adding the x^2 terms and adding the x terms. The final answer after simplifying the expression is:

$$20x^3 - 36x^2 + 16x - 48$$

16. D: Finding the zeros for a function by factoring is done by setting the equation equal to zero, then completely factoring. Since there is a common x for each term in the provided equation, that should be factored out first to get $x(x^2 - 3x - 4)$. Then the quadratic that is left can be factored into two binomials, which are $(x + 1)(x - 4)$. This gives the factored equation $0 = x(x + 1)(x - 4)$.

17. A: Using the given information of 1 nurse to 25 patients and 325 patients, set up an equation to solve for the number of nurses (N):

$$\frac{N}{325} = \frac{1}{25}$$

Multiply both sides by 325 to get N by itself on one side.

$$\frac{N}{1} = \frac{325}{25} = 13 \; nurses$$

18. D: The equation can be solved by factoring the numerator into $(x + 6)(x - 5)$.

Since the factor $(x - 5)$ is on the top and bottom, it cancels out.

This leaves the equation $x + 6 = 11$.

Solving the equation gives the answer $x = 5$. When this value is plugged into the equation, it yields a zero in the denominator of the fraction. Since this is undefined, there is no solution.

19. D: This problem can be solved by using unit conversion. The initial units are miles per minute. The final units need to be feet per second. Converting miles to feet uses the equivalence statement 1 mi = 5,280 ft. Converting minutes to seconds uses the equivalence statement 1 min = 60 s. Setting up the ratios to convert the units is shown in the following equation:

$$\frac{72 \text{ mi}}{90 \text{ min}} \times \frac{1 \text{ min}}{60 \text{ s}} \times \frac{5{,}280 \text{ ft}}{1 \text{ mi}} = 70.4 \frac{\text{ft}}{\text{s}}$$

The initial units cancel out, and the new units are left.

20. B: The formula can be manipulated by dividing both the length, l, and the width, w, on both sides. The length and width will cancel on the right, leaving height, h, by itself.

21. B: The domain is all possible input values, or x-values. For this equation, the domain is every number greater than or equal to zero. There are no negative numbers in the domain because taking the square root of a negative number results in an imaginary number.

22. D: This problem can be solved by setting up a proportion involving the given information and the unknown value. The proportion is:

$$\frac{21 \text{ pages}}{4 \text{ nights}} = \frac{140 \text{ pages}}{x \text{ nights}}$$

We can cross-multiply to get $21x = 4 \times 140$. Solving this, we find $x \approx 26.67$. Since this is not an integer, we round up to 27 nights. 26 nights would not give Sarah enough time.

23. D: The slope from this equation is 50, and it is interpreted as the cost per gigabyte used. Since the g-value represents the number of gigabytes and the equation is set equal to the cost in dollars, the slope relates these two values. For every gigabyte used on the phone, the bill goes up 50 dollars.

24. C: Graphing the function $y = \cos(x)$ shows that the curve starts at $(0, 1)$, has an amplitude of 2, and a period of 2π. This same curve can be constructed using the sine graph, by shifting the graph to the left $\frac{\pi}{2}$ units. This equation is in the form:

$$y = \sin\left(x + \frac{\pi}{2}\right)$$

25. B: Start by squaring both sides to get $1 + x = 16$. Then subtract 1 from both sides to get $x = 15$.

26. D: This inverse of a function is found by switching the x and y in the equation and solving for y. In the given equation, solving for y is done by adding 5 to both sides, then dividing both sides by 3. This answer can be checked on the graph by verifying the lines are reflected over $y = x$.

27. B: The zeros of this function can be found by setting $f(x)$ equal to 0 and solving for x:

$$0 = x^2 + 4$$

$$-4 = x^2$$

$$\sqrt{-4} = x$$

Taking the square root of a negative number results in an imaginary number, so the solution is:

$$x = +- 2i$$

28. D: Setting up a proportion is an easy way to represent this situation. The proportion is $\frac{20}{x} = \frac{40}{100}$, and cross-multiplication can be used to solve for x. Here, $40x = 2,000$, so $x = 50$.

29. C: Division with scientific notation can be solved by grouping the first terms together and grouping the tens together. The first terms can be divided, and the tens terms can be simplified using the rules for exponents. The initial expression becomes 0.4×10^4. This is not in scientific notation because the first number is not between 1 and 10. Shifting the decimal and subtracting one from the exponent yields 4.0×10^3.

30. A: The relative error can be found by finding the absolute error and making it a percent of the true value. The absolute error is $36 - 35.75 = 0.25$. This error is then divided by 35.75—the true value—to find 0.7%.

Reading Comprehension

1. A: The last sentence references the importance of opposing downward weight during flight, so it can be inferred that this balance is a necessary part of flight. Although drag and thrust do have a profound effect on aerodynamics, this concept is not described or alluded to in the passage, so Choice *B* is incorrect. Choice *C* is incorrect because the passage directly states that personnel are included in weight calculations, so it cannot be an inference. According to the passage, aircraft weight impacts the mechanics of flight, but "most important" is too strong and unsupported based on the lack of reference to other factors. Therefore, Choice *D* is incorrect.

2. A: The passage discusses recent technological advances in cars and suggests that this trend will continue in the future with self-driving cars. Choice *B* and *C* are not true, so these are both incorrect. Choice *D* is also incorrect because the passage suggests continuing growth in technology, not a peak.

3. B: The juxtaposition of the statement regarding research money with the author's suggestion that humanities face an uphill battle suggests a correlation between the two. In other words, humanities do not bring in the kind of funding that science, technology, engineering, and mathematics (STEM) subjects and research do. As a result, universities don't fund them the same way. Choice *A* is incorrect. There is no indication that this is true. Choice *C* is incorrect. Although it might solve the problem, that solution is not the focus of this passage. Choice *D* is incorrect. Although there is an implication that STEM receives more money, money is not the only valuable aspect of education or universities.

4. C: Although the passage mentions an instinctive part of piloting acumen, it also emphasizes the importance of studying and practicing. If study and practicing is important to developing pilot acumen, it can be inferred that pilot acumen can be improved. The first sentence states that the pilot's acumen was beyond questioning, but it doesn't mention other pilots' acumen or characterize those questions as coming from a place of ignorance, so Choice *A* is incorrect. Choice *B* is incorrect because the passage doesn't compare the relative importance of instincts and practical knowledge. The passage states that pilots need thousands of flying hours to improve, but it doesn't reference expertise or the number of hours necessary to attain expertise. As such, Choice *D* is incorrect.

5. C: The passage notes that the Gulf Stream was able to fill de León's sails, indicating that it is a wind pattern. Choice *A* is incorrect. Although tides would have helped, they do not fill sails. Choice *B* is incorrect. There is no mention of the name of de León's ship. Choice *D* is incorrect. Although de León was in the Gulf, it's not clear in the passage if he is in Tampa Bay (in fact, he was south of there).

6. D: A lack of vitamin A can result in malnourishment. Choice *A* is incorrect. In the passage, a connection was not made between vitamin A deficiency and iron absorption. Iron deficiency was mentioned as another problem that Golden Rice might be able to address. Choice *B* is incorrect. Lactating mothers are one of the populations at risk for vitamin A deficiency, which may cause trouble for them, but that's not explicitly stated here. Choice *C* is incorrect. A lack of zinc and iron will result in stunted growth.

7. D: The passage states that successful treatment depends on an early and accurate diagnosis, so Choice *D* is correct. Choice *A* is incorrect because it has taken facts found in the passage and made a statement that is inaccurate. People with lung infections and who have compromised immune function are at higher risk of mortality. The agent causing the lung infection isn't necessarily the cause of the compromised immune function. Choice *B* is incorrect because early and accurate diagnosis can lead to successful treatment. Choice *C* is incorrect because *Candida* is not a treatment, it is an infecting agent.

8. C: Choice *C* is correct, if predators rely on prey for food and nutrition and if cats are predators of mice, then cats rely on mice for food and nutrition. Choice *A* is incorrect. The prey is eaten by the predator. Choice *C* is incorrect. The prey (the mice) are the ones who develop the feature that allow them to escape from the predators (the cats). Choice *D* is incorrect. *Extinct relationship* is not an actual term. The term used in the passage is *distinct relationship*.

9. B: The passage lists a number of important historical events that occurred over 2000 years, and it can be inferred that some of these events influence later developments. It's true that Orville Wright was the first man to fly a motor-powered plane, but the type of plane isn't referenced in the passage. So, Choice *A* is incorrect. Choice *C* is incorrect because it contradicts the passage, which states that aviation's history dates back 2000 years. The passage directly states that kites were likely the first man-made aircraft, so it cannot be an inference. As such, Choice *D* is incorrect.

10. C: The sentence clearly states that they tend to crowd out native species. Choice *A* is incorrect because it is the opposite of what invasive species do. Choice *B* is incorrect because symbiotic relationships require coexistence, and crowding out is not coexistence. Choice *D* is incorrect because invasive species can often find a way to thrive, as demonstrated by the example of the Everglades pythons.

11. B: Choice *B* is correct. The passage clearly states that liquids contain atoms or molecules that move past one another. Choice *A* is incorrect. Gases, not liquids, contain atoms with the most kinetic energy. Choice *C* is incorrect. Not all liquids are less dense than solids. The exception is water. Choice *D* is incorrect. The type of matter that have the most tightly packed atoms are solids, not gases.

12. B: The sentence specifically states that macronutrients are the building blocks of one's diet. Choice *A* is incorrect because carbohydrates are included as a specific example rather than a larger category. Choice *C* is incorrect because the sentence does not mention vitamins. Choice *D* is incorrect. Macronutrients form the base of the pyramid; however, the pyramid isn't noted in the passage at all.

13. B: The last sentence states that passengers are more comfortable flying with minimal turbulence, and flying at higher altitude reduces turbulence. Choice *A* is incorrect because the bumpy road is a metaphor, not a training exercise. According to the passage, CAT occurs less frequently at higher altitudes, so Choice *C* is incorrect. CAT seems dangerous based on its description, but "the most dangerous" is too strong and unsupported by the passage. Therefore, Choice *D* is incorrect.

14. B: The overall subject of the sentence is keeping the costs of home improvement down, with suggestions for doing so listed. Choices *A*, *C*, and *D* are incorrect. These are the ways to keep costs down, but independently, none of these are the subject of the sentence.

15. A: Choice *A* is correct. According to the passage, the state of Illinois passed a law that added traffic stop training to driver's education courses. Choice *B* is incorrect. Although traffic stop training is most likely required as part of police training, the question asks which choice is correct according to the passage, and the passage does not discuss police officer training. Choice *C* is incorrect. This information is found nowhere in the passage. Choice *D* is incorrect. The last sentence states that this component of driver's education could eventually be seen in more states, therefore it can be reasoned that it's not yet a law in all states.

16. A: The pilot tries to make an emergency descent because ice is forming on the aircraft, so it can be inferred that the air is warmer at the lower altitude. The pilot checks terrain clearance before his descent, so it can be inferred that clearance can prevent a descent. Therefore, Choice *B* is incorrect. Choice *C* is incorrect because the passage clearly discusses how flying at a high altitude caused the freezing issue. Fuselage is the main body of an aircraft, and, in any event, the passage doesn't indicate that it's located on the left wing. As such, Choice *D* is incorrect.

17. C: Choice *C* is correct. Biological mimicry occurs when an animal can make itself look like another animal that is poisonous in order to avoid its predators. Choice *A* is incorrect. Since sea snakes are one of the creatures that a mimic octopus will mimic, it can be concluded that this creature is venomous or poisonous rather than harmless. Choice *B* is incorrect. The passage states that the animals that are mimicked are venomous and poisonous. This answer choice says they can be either venomous or nonpoisonous, which, according to the passage, is not correct. Choice *D* is incorrect. Animals that use biological mimicry to deceive their predators are only temporarily changing their appearance to look like a poisonous creature. They are not evolving and becoming poisonous.

18. C: The main point of this paragraph is that parents need to change their poor behavior at their kids' sporting events. Choice *A* is incorrect because the coaches' behavior is not mentioned in the paragraph. Choice *B* suggests that sports are bad for kids, when the paragraph is about parents' behavior, so it is incorrect. While Choice *D* may be true, it offers a specific solution to the problem, which the paragraph does not discuss.

19. C: The passage states that pilots need to conduct constant risk assessments while flying, so it can be inferred that the pilots are using these assessments to adapt to changing circumstances. The passage doesn't state who or what registers and approves flight paths, so Choice *A* is incorrect. Choice *B* is incorrect because the passage never compares the consequences of a lack of preparation with the consequences of a lack of communication. Informational checks and regular communication are part of risk assessment procedures, but based on the passage, it cannot be inferred that they constitute the entire procedure. As such, Choice *D* is incorrect.

20. A: Choice *A* is correct. The passage states, "Winds at different altitudes blowing at different speeds make the column of air rotate." Choice *B* is incorrect. This is what causes a column of warm air to be drawn up into the clouds. Choice *C* is incorrect. This is what causes the funnel cloud to touch down. Choice *D* is incorrect. This is the movement of tornadoes that causes them to be destructive and dangerous.

Mechanical Comprehension

1. C: The ship is traveling faster than the current, so it will be east of the starting location. Its net forward velocity is 0.5 m/s which is 1.8 kilometers/hour, or 3.6 kilometers in two hours.

2. B: This is actually a trick question. The mass of the astronaut is the same everywhere (it is the weight that varies from planet to planet). The astronaut's mass in kilograms is calculated by dividing his weight on Earth by the acceleration of gravity on Earth:

$$\frac{1962 \text{ N}}{9.81 \text{ m/s}^2} = 200 \text{ kg}$$

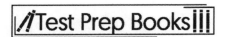

3. C: The answer is her angular velocity increases from (a) to (b) as she pulls her arms in close to her body and reduces her moment of inertia.

4. C: The potential energy of the pendulum can be graphed as a sine wave, reaching its maximum at the ends of its arc, and the minimum at the bottom (middle) of its arc. Because total energy is equivalent to the sum of kinetic and potential energy, the kinetic energy at a given point is opposite of the potential energy. The kinetic energy is at its minimum at the ends of the arc, and at its maximum at the bottom of the arc. Recalling the equation for potential energy, $PE = mgh$, the potential energy is at half its maximum between the top and bottom of the pendulum's arc.

5. B: Remember that the force (F) required to stretch a spring a certain amount (d) is given by the equation $F = kd$. Therefore,

$$k = F/d = 10 \text{ N}/0.5 \text{ cm} = 20 \text{ N/cm}$$

Doubling the weight to 20 N gives the deflection:

$$d = \frac{F}{k} = \frac{20 \text{ N}}{20\frac{\text{N}}{\text{cm}}} = 1 \text{ cm}$$

All of the calculations can be bypassed by remembering that the relation between force and deflection is linear. This means that doubling the force doubles the deflection, as long as the spring isn't loaded past its elastic limit.

6. C: This question relies on Pascal's law, which states that a pressure change at any point in a confined incompressible fluid is transmitted throughout the fluid such that the same change occurs everywhere. This would mean that any pressure applied on piston A would equal the pressure put on piston B, making Choice C the correct answer. Choices A, B, and D are incorrect because they do not reflect Pascal's law. Pressure cannot decrease in a sealed hydraulic system and will be felt on all surfaces within, including piston B.

7. B: The amount of energy needed to power a certain device is expressed in kilowatt-hours. Therefore, Choices A and D are incorrect. The amount of energy needed is the product of the power in kilowatts multiplied by the time in hours. The air conditioner is 6000 watts or 6 kilowatts multiplied by 3 hours is 18 kilowatt-hours. Choice C did not properly convert the power from watts into kilowatts.

8. B: This is a simple calculation:

$$\frac{9.81 \text{ m}}{\text{s}^2} \times 150 \text{ kg} \times 1.5 \text{ m} = 3 \text{ m} \times F$$

Rearranging the equation to solve for the unknown force, F, yields:

$$F = \frac{9.81\frac{\text{m}}{\text{s}^2} \times 150 \text{ kg} \times 1.5\text{m}}{3 \text{ m}} = \frac{2207.25 \text{ N} \cdot \text{m}}{3 \text{ m}} = 735.75 \text{ N}$$

9. B: While meshed gears rotate in different directions, wheels linked by a belt turn in the same direction. This is true unless the belt is twisted, in which case they rotate in opposite directions. So, the twisted link between the upper two wheels causes the right-hand wheel to turn counterclockwise, and

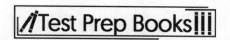

the bigger wheel at the bottom also rotates counterclockwise. Since it's twice as large as the upper wheel, it rotates with half the RPMs.

10. A: In accordance with Ohm's Law, $V = IR$, use the given variables:

$$3.0\,V = I \times 6.0\,\Omega$$

Solving for I:

$$I = 3.0\,V/6.0\,\Omega = 0.5\,A$$

Choice *B* incorporates a miscalculation in the equation by multiplying 3.0 V by 6.0 Ω, rather than dividing these values. Choice *C* is labeled with the wrong unit; Joules measure energy, not current.

11. B: In a parallel circuit, more charges will seek the path with the least resistance. Because of this, more current passes through circuit paths with lower resistance. If the resistance is the same in both paths, then the same amount of current passes through each resistor. An important feature of parallel circuits is that the voltage is the same across each resistor; it does not drop as it does in series circuits. In series circuits, voltage drops after each resistor, and current is constant, and in parallel circuits, voltage stays the same after each resistor, and current increases. The total current can be calculated as the sum of the electric current in each branch of the parallel circuit.

12. B: Current is measured in amperes, which indicate the number of electrons that pass a specific point per second. Volts are used to indicate the difference in potential between two separate points. Ohms are used when measuring the resistance. Watts are a measure of power or the rate at which electrical energy is used or converted into another type of energy.

13. D: The gears are in a 2:1 ratio because there are twice as many teeth in the large gear relative to the small one. Therefore, the smaller gear makes two revolutions for each complete revolution of the large gear:

$$8 \times 2 = 16$$

14. B: This question looks for understanding of basic energy principles. The mass of the box remains unchanged as it is lifted, and there is no rotational force bring applied. The only thing the box gains as its height off the ground increases is potential energy, making Choice *B* the correct answer. Choices *A* and *C* are incorrect because the box's weight and gravitational pull would remain unchanged, and Choice *D* is incorrect because the box does not experience torque in this example.

15. A: The physical structure of the atoms that compose matter lends itself to the production of electricity. The arrangement of the subatomic particles and the associated charges—mainly the negatively charged electrons in the cloud—are associated with the ability to create an electric current, which can be harnessed to do work.

16. C: This is the actual force recognized in a rotational situation. The reactive force acting opposite of the centripetal force is named the centrifugal force, but it is not an actual force on its own. A common mistake is to interchange the two terms. The real force acting in a rotational situation is pulling in toward the axis of rotation and is called the centripetal force. Gravity and friction technically act on all masses, so Choices *B* and *D* are not specific enough for the question.

17. B: The doppler effect is the perceived increase or decrease in frequency of a wave due to the relative velocity between the source and observer. If the source of a wave is moving towards the observer or vice versa, the waves arrive more quickly as well. This is identical to a higher frequency, even if the frequency at the source is unchanged. Conversely, if the source is moving away from the observer, the gaps between waves are larger, and thus the waves appear to be at a lower frequency. This effect can be commonly observed with the increase and decrease in pitch of an emergency vehicle's siren as it drives by.

18. C: Diodes function in electrical circuits much like valves do with fluid dynamics or in veins. They prevent current from flowing in the unintended direction and instead only permit flow in one direction. The symbol is:

The arrow points in the direction of permitted current flow. Choices *A* and *B* described potentiometers, and Choice *D* showed the symbol for the potentiometer.

19. B: Kinetic energy is energy an object has while moving. Potential energy is energy an object has based on its position or height. Solar energy is energy that comes from the sun. Heat energy is the energy produced from moving atoms, molecules, or ions, and can transfer between substances.

20. A: This question targets knowledge about the principles of work and incline planes/ramps. For an incline, the force (F) needed to push a weight (W) is $F = \left(\frac{H}{D}\right) \times W$, with H the vertical distance traveled and D the length of the ramp. In this case, the force needed is $F = \left(\frac{1 \text{ meter}}{5 \text{ meters}}\right) \times 500$ N, therefore $F = 100$ N, making Choice *A* the correct answer. Choices *B*, *C*, and *D* are incorrect because they describe excessive force relative to what is needed to push the box up the ramp.

21. D: Direct current circuits are circuits in which the current flows in a single direction and the voltage source is constant. This type of circuit is used in electronic devices such as televisions and cell phones. With an alternating current (AC), the voltage alternates over time, and AC/DC circuits have both types of current, making Choices *B* and *C* incorrect. Choice *A* is an incorrect wording of the term.

22. C: An inclined plane is a simple machine that can make it easier to raise or lower an object in height. Simple machines offer a mechanical advantage to performing tasks. While a screw, a level, and a pulley are also simple machines, they would be used to offer a mechanical advantage in other situations.

23. A: This question challenges one's ability to apply mathematical concepts to problems involving multiple variables. After 3 hours, the total water poured into the tank is:

$$\frac{4 \text{ gallons} \times 60 \text{ minutes}}{1 \text{ hour} \times 3 \text{ hours}} = 720 \text{ gallons}$$

The total water poured out of the tank is 50 gallons × 3 hours = 150 gallons. Remembering the 100 gallons already in the tank, the total becomes 720 + 100 − 150 = 670 gallons, making Choice *A* the correct answer. Choices *B*, *C*, and *D* are incorrect because they are insufficient amounts of water for the values given in the problem.

24. D: The difference in potential between two separate points is a measure of volts. Amperes indicate the number of electrons that pass a specific point per second. Ohms measure the resistance to flow

254

(essentially electrical friction). Watts are a measure of power or the rate at which electrical energy is used or converted into another type of energy. Watts are often converted to kilowatts or, when expressing power rates, kilowatt-hours.

25. C: Electric conductors tend to be metals, such as silver, copper, and aluminum. They "conduct" electricity, which means that they help the electric current flow easily. This is largely because metals have low resistance because the electrons are easily detached from these atoms, so they are then free to jump from atom to atom and create a current. In contrast, insulators (such as wood, plastic, or rubber) have high resistance but low conductivity. Conductivity and resistance are opposite properties; a given single material cannot be highly conductive and highly resistant at the same time.

26. C: The formula used in Ohm's Law demonstrates how the current of a circuit is proportional to the voltage and the resistance. The current is greater when the voltage goes up and the resistance goes down. As Choice *C* shows the correct formula, the other choices are incorrect.

27. D: Four times the force is needed to lift the box straight up as opposed to moving it up the ramp. The mechanical advantage of a ramp can be seen in the equation showing the mechanical advantage of a ramp:

$$MA = \frac{L}{h}$$

Where MA is the mechanical advantage, h is height, and L is the length of the ramp. In this case, the mechanical advantage would be a factor of 4:

$$MA = \frac{4}{1} = 4$$

Note that the work done is not reduced. The force applied is less at any given point but done over a greater distance.

28. B: Ice is not as dense as water, so a given mass of water has more volume in a solid state than in a liquid state. Thus, it floats. As the mass of ice in Basin A melts, its volume (as a liquid) is reduced. In the end, the water level doesn't change. The ice in Basin B isn't floating. It's perched on high ground in the center of the basin. When it melts, water is added to the basin and the water level rises.

29. C: Choice *A* is incorrect because $kg \times m/s^2$ is an expression of force, not power. Choice *B* is incorrect because N·m is an expression of work, not power. That leaves Choices *C* which is expressed in a unit of power: joules/second. Using an approximate calculation (as suggested):

$$1,000 \text{ kg} \times 10\frac{m}{s^2} \times 30 \text{ m} = 300,000 \text{ N} \cdot \text{m}$$

Dividing the total work done by 10 minutes, or 600 seconds, gives the approximate power expended:

$$\frac{300,000 \text{ N} \cdot \text{m}}{600 \text{ s}} = 500 \text{ watts} = 500 \text{ J/s}$$

30. A: The force of friction holding the box in place counteracts the force of gravity parallel to the slope. This is equivalent to sine of the angle times the mass of the box times gravity:

$$\sin(\theta) \times m \times 9.81 \frac{m}{s^2}$$

Aviation and Nautical Information

1. A: The nose of the helicopter always follows the direction the collective is moved. For example, if the collective is increased, the nose of the helicopter pitches up. It does the opposite when lowered. Also, when the collective is raised, it takes the left pedal to counteract the torque effect and the right pedal when the collective is reduced.

2. A: When raising the collective, more power will be needed to keep RPM up, which will require raising the throttle in sync. More power to the rotor will result in more torque, which will require using the anti-torque pedals to compensate. The cyclic, however, should not be needed during this maneuver, except perhaps to negate any drift caused by wind. Were the helicopter in forward flight, the cyclic would need to have slight rearwards pressure applied to account for the additional lift creating additional thrust.

3. D: With the cyclic pushed forward, additional lift is created by the rotor disk tipping forward, but this comes at the expense of lift. Thus, the collective will need to be raised to keep altitude up, which will require additional power from the throttle and additional counter torque from the anti-torque pedals.

4. C: Profile drag is fairly consistent at most speeds, and although profile drag does increase somewhat with airspeed, parasitic drag catches up to and then surpasses profile drag in magnitude.

5. B: Weathervaning occurs when the wind blows at the helicopter and strikes the tail, which usually sticks out significantly from the rest of the body. This effect makes attempting to turn the helicopter into the wind (and thus, turning the tail with it) require less power, while attempting to turn the helicopter with the wind (and the tail into it) requires more power. While this makes turning at all points trickier, the effect becomes particularly challenging when the helicopter reaches a heading directly with the wind. At this point, the wind will go from resisting the turn to assisting with the turn, which can result in the helicopter turning much faster than expected. The opposite happens when the heading is into the wind, at which point the wind goes from assisting the turn to opposing it. This will often stall the turn, giving the pilot plenty of time to adjust the controls to accommodate the problem.

6. A: While the throttle will need to be increased as the collective increases to maintain RPM, the throttle should never be used to increase the rotor's RPM beyond the normal range. Applying additional forward cyclic will actually decrease the rate of climb as the greater angle of attack results in greater thrust, but reduced lift. Therefore, decreasing the angle of attack by applying rearward pressure will result in less thrust being generated, but more lift, thus increasing the rate of climb.

7. A: Straight-and-level flight is actually the best place for a heavily encumbered helicopter as the angle of attack is usually lowest there, allowing for less thrust and more lift. Similarly, there is no reason to avoid a takeoff from hover, if the helicopter has sufficient power to do so. The main reason most heavily-laden helicopters use a takeoff from surface instead is that they are too heavy to hover properly; thus, they are unable to perform the maneuver. However, performing a steep banking turn can be very dangerous in a heavy helicopter as the load factor can get rather high and potentially damage the helicopter or reach a point where the helicopter cannot produce enough power to maintain altitude, resulting in an undesired descent.

8. D: Both weather and air density can affect the efficiency of the air rotor and, thus, the G load. However, while the helicopter's weight does have an effect on the actual effective load on the helicopter, the G load is a multiplicative factor applied to—rather than derived from—the weight of the helicopter to determine the helicopter's effective weight.

9. A: Even in ideal conditions, unless the helicopter is preparing to takeoff or is already in straight and level flight, there is no reason for the helicopter to move faster than a brisk walk.

10. D: The cyclic is an acceleration-controlled instrument, while both the collective and throttle are position-controlled. Only the anti-torque pedals are rate-controlled.

11. B: Faster flow of air over the wing than beneath it. The air moves over the curved surface of the wing at a higher rate of speed than the air moves under the lower flat surface, which creates lift due to the aircraft's forward airspeed and enables flight.

12. B: Longitudinal. The ailerons are mounted on the trailing edges of the wings, and they are used for controlling aircraft roll about the longitudinal axis.

13. A: Lateral. Elevators are mounted on the trailing edges of horizontal stabilizers and are used for controlling aircraft pitch about the lateral axis.

14. C: Vertical. The rudder is mounted on the trailing edge of the vertical fin and is used for controlling rotation (yaw) around the vertical axis.

15. C: Aileron. The aileron is a primary flight control.

16. D: Slats. Slats are part of the wing. The tail assembly of an aircraft is commonly referred to as the empennage. The empennage structure usually includes a tail cone, fixed stabilizers (horizontal and vertical), and moveable surfaces to assist in directional control. The moveable surfaces are the rudder, which is attached to the vertical stabilizer, and the elevators attached to the horizontal stabilizers.

17. B: Skate. Depending on what the aircraft is used for, it may have skis, skids, or floats, instead of tires, for landing on ice or water.

18. B: Semicoque. There are two types of fuselage structures: truss and monocoque. The truss fuselage is typically made of steel tubing welded together, which enables the structure to handle tension and compression loads. In lighter aircraft, an aluminum alloy may be used along with cross-bracing. A single-shell fuselage is referred to as monocoque, which uses a stronger skin to handle the tension and compression loads. There is also a semi-monocoque fuselage, which is basically a combination of the truss and monocoque fuselage and is the most commonly used. The semi-monocoque structure includes the use of frame assemblies, bulkheads, formers, longerons, and stringers.

19. A: The pilot. To ensure an aircraft is being operated properly, a pilot needs to be familiar with the aircraft's flight envelope before flying.

20. C: Stalling speed. The stalling speed is the minimum speed at which an aircraft can maintain level flight. As the aircraft gains altitude, the stall speed increases, since the aircraft's weight can be better supported through speed.

21. B: Torque is the correct answer because it is one of the forces subjected to a helicopter, but not an aircraft. Choice *A*, lift, is incorrect because it is an upward force on an airplane's wing. Choice *C*, weight,

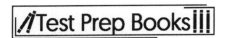

is incorrect because it is a force on any object created by gravitational pull towards earth. Therefore, weight is a force relevant to both airplanes and helicopters. Choice *D*, drag, is incorrect because it affects both airplanes and helicopters. Drag is a force that resists an object's movement through air.

22. D: Ground effect is the correct answer because it refers to increased lift and reduced drag when an aircraft is within close proximity to the ground. Choice *A*, center of gravity, is incorrect because it is the average location of the weight of an aircraft. Choice *B*, Coriolis effect, is incorrect because it is an inertial force that is perpendicular to the direction of motion in a rotating system. Choice *C*, effective translational lift, is incorrect because it is an improved efficiency in flight that results in directional flight.

23. D: Threshold lights is correct because they are green lights that show the start of a runway. Choice *A*, taxiway centerline lights, is incorrect because they are green lights that show the edges of a taxiway. Choice *B*, runway edge lights, is incorrect because they are white lights that indicate the borders of a runway. Choice *C*, approach lighting systems, is incorrect because it is a series of lights that lead towards a runway to allow a pilot to line up with the runway.

24. B: Ailerons is the correct answer because when they are positioned in opposite directions on an airplane, they initiate a roll. Choice *A*, stabilizers, is incorrect because their purpose is to maintain straight and steady flight of an airplane. Choice *C*, wing tips, is incorrect because their purpose is to reduce drag. Choice *D*, elevators, is incorrect because they control the pitch of an airplane.

25. D: Fuselage is the correct answer because an airfoil is a surface that controls an aircraft by manipulating the air around it. A fuselage is the main body of an aircraft and does not affect movement of the aircraft. Choice *A*, spoiler, is incorrect because a spoiler eliminates lift when landing. Choice *B*, elevator, is incorrect because they adjust the lift of an aircraft to control pitch. Choice *C*, aileron, is incorrect because it manipulates air to enable rotational movement.

26. C: "Air pressure below the wing increases" is the correct answer because for lift to occur, air pressure below the wing gets higher and air pressure above the wing decreases. Choice *A*, atmospheric pressure decreases, is incorrect because it is changed by variations in air density. Choice *B*, airplane temperature increases, is incorrect because the temperature of the aircraft is irrelevant to lift. Choice *D*, the airplane loses altitude, is incorrect because when lift increases, an airplane will increase in altitude.

27. A: 30° is the correct answer because a medium turn is defined as a turn between 20° and 45°. All other answer choices are incorrect because they do not fall within this range. Turns that are less than 20° are considered shallow, and turns that are greater than 45° are considered steep.

28. D: Yaw is the correct answer because the purpose of a vertical stabilizer is to control the yaw of a flying plane. Choices *A* and *C*, roll and pitch, are incorrect because various other stabilizers prevent unwanted changes in pitch and roll. Choice *B*, thrust, is incorrect because it is not a movement of an airplane.

29. D: Thrust is the correct answer because parasitic drag is a rearward slowing force caused by an aircraft's shape or material. Thrust is a force in the opposite direction of drag that causes acceleration. Choice *A*, lift, is incorrect because it is an upward force that is opposed by weight and gravity. Choices *B* and *C*, weight and gravity, are incorrect because they are downward forces that are opposed by lift.

30. D: Airspeed indicator is the correct answer because it works by utilizing the differential between static and ram pressure to measure the forward speed of an aircraft. Choice *A*, heading indicator, is incorrect because it gives the direction of an aircraft and works like a compass. Choice *B*, vertical speed

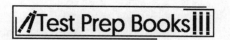

indicator, is incorrect because it measures changes in static pressure to measure the rate of change of altitude. Choice *C*, turn coordinator, is incorrect because it is a gyro-driven instrument that measures the rate of a turn.

Practice Test #3

To keep the size of this book manageable, save paper, and provide a digital test-taking experience, the 3rd practice test can be found online. Scan the QR code or go to this link to access it:

testprepbooks.com/bonus/astb

The first time you access the tests, you will need to register as a "new user" and verify your email address.

If you have any issues, please email support@testprepbooks.com

Dear ASTB Test Taker,

Thank you again for purchasing this study guide for your ASTB exam. We hope that we exceeded your expectations.

Our goal in creating this study guide was to cover all of the topics that you will see on the test. We also strove to make our practice questions as similar as possible to what you will encounter on test day. With that being said, if you found something that you feel was not up to your standards, please send us an email and let us know.

We would also like to let you know about other books in our catalog that may interest you.

AFOQT

amazon.com/dp/1637759037

ASVAB

amazon.com/dp/1637753241

OAR

amazon.com/dp/1637751087

SIFT

amazon.com/dp/1628458585

We have study guides in a wide variety of fields. If the one you are looking for isn't listed above, then try searching for it on Amazon or send us an email.

Thanks Again and Happy Testing!
Product Development Team
info@studyguideteam.com

FREE Test Taking Tips Video/DVD Offer

To better serve you, we created videos covering test taking tips that we want to give you for FREE. **These videos cover world-class tips that will help you succeed on your test.**

We just ask that you send us feedback about this product. Please let us know what you thought about it—whether good, bad, or indifferent.

To get your **FREE videos**, you can use the QR code below or email freevideos@studyguideteam.com with "Free Videos" in the subject line and the following information in the body of the email:

    a. The title of your product

    b. Your product rating on a scale of 1-5, with 5 being the highest

    c. Your feedback about the product

If you have any questions or concerns, please don't hesitate to contact us at info@studyguideteam.com.

Thank you!

Made in United States
Troutdale, OR
05/18/2024

19955368R00151